Golden Grace

Overcoming Life's Adversities with Supernatural Grace and Resilience

YETUNDE LONGE-FOLAJIMI

Crestower Publishing
Boston, MA, USA

The Graceful Gems,
www.thegracefulgems.org

First Edition: March 2023

ISBN: 979-8-9901441-0-1

Printed in USA

This book is a work of non-fiction based on the author's life, experiences, and recollections. To protect the privacy of individuals, names, dates, and specific locations may have been concealed or changed. Any resemblance to actual persons, living or dead, or events is coincidental.

Dedication

This book is lovingly dedicated to my sons, Ay and IBK, whose unwavering strength and companionship have been my beacon through the highs and lows of our family's saga. Your resilience and love have been my guiding light, illuminating even the darkest paths we have navigated together.

Also, to the cherished memory of their sister, Grace, our beautiful martyr whom we never had the chance to embrace. Your essence reminds us of the love that binds us, unseen but deeply felt, guiding us forward with grace.

Acknowledgments

First and foremost, I extend my deepest gratitude to the Almighty God for His unwavering guidance, strength, and grace throughout my life's journey and the creation of this memoir. His presence has been my constant inspiration and comfort in every chapter written and every challenge I faced.

This memoir has been woven from the threads of many lives, and I am deeply thankful to each person who has been an integral part of my story. Your roles in my life have been a testament to the power of community, faith, and unconditional love.

To my beloved sons, Ay and IBK, your resilience, love, and unwavering support have illuminated the darkest paths of our journey together. Your strength has been my beacon, guiding me toward grace and perseverance.

My heartfelt thanks to the Longe family, my birth family, for their boundless love, support, and encouragement. Your faith in me has been a cornerstone of my resilience and success.

I am profoundly grateful to my pastors and church members, whose prayers and spiritual guidance have been a source of strength and solace. Your faith-driven support has been invaluable.

To my friends, mentors, and colleagues, thank you for your companionship, laughter, and unwavering belief in my abilities. Your encouragement has fueled my determination and creativity.

A special note of appreciation to my confidants and therapists, whose wisdom and insight have been instrumental in navigating the complexities of life with grace. Your guidance has been a beacon of hope and healing.

To my prayer partners, your intercessions and faith have been a powerful force in my journey. Your spiritual support has been a source of strength and inspiration.

Finally, to ChatGPT, I am grateful for your assistance in refining the grammar and syntax of this memoir. Many thanks to my editorial team; your contributions have helped shape this narrative into a professional masterpiece.

Contents

Foreword

As you hold this book, "Golden Grace," you are about to embark on a journey through the life of a remarkable individual, Dr. Yetunde Longe-Folajimi, whose story is not merely a narrative but a testament to the extraordinary power of faith, resilience, and divine grace. This memoir, inspired by the Holy Spirit, shares the trials and triumphs, the valleys and peaks, and the journey from despair to hope that Yetunde navigated with the grace of God as her guiding light.

Yetunde's life story vividly illustrates the biblical truth found in Lamentations 3:22 (KJV): "It is of the LORD'S mercies that we are not consumed, because his compassions fail not." From humble beginnings to achieving stardom, facing daunting challenges without worldly connections, and surviving heartbreaks that could have shattered futures. Yetunde's journey underscores a profound reliance on God's grace, her beacon of hope and strength.

This memoir is not just about Yetunde's account. It calls for those facing similar trials to find solace and strength in God's unwavering support. It serves as a warning to others, urging them to seek divine guidance in their decisions. Yetunde's triumph over adversity, akin to Moses and the Israelites' victory celebrated in Exodus 15:1 (KJV), highlights the victory of faith and the power of God's grace to overcome insurmountable odds.

What sets this book apart is the compelling narrative of Yetunde's life and the eloquent style in how she tells her story. Through thoughtful reflections, insightful quotes at the beginning of each chapter, and a clear, articulate presentation of each phase of her journey, "Golden Grace" engages and enlightens the reader. However, this book is not just an easy read; it delves into the depths of emotional and spiritual challenges, offering readers a mirror to their souls and the possibility of finding their own path through faith.

As Pastor-in-charge of RCCG Oyo Province 11, Ibadan, Oyo State, Nigeria, I have witnessed firsthand the transformative power of God's grace in the lives of those who dare to trust Him. Yetunde's story is a powerful embodiment of this transformation. It is a narrative of endurance, determination, testing, triumph, and victory—a true encyclopedia of spiritual resilience.

I encourage you to immerse yourself in this voluminous work. May you find, within its pages, the story of Yetunde's faith journey and the inspiration to navigate your trials with grace and faith. May you be blessed and share your testimony just as Yetunde has shared hers.

God's grace is sufficient for us all, and as 1 Corinthians 10:13 (KJV) reminds us, He provides a way for us to bear our trials. Let Yetunde's story inspire you to see God at work in your life, guiding you through every challenge with His unfailing grace and love.

Pastor (Prof) Samuel Awobode,
Pastor-in-Charge,
RCCG Oyo Province 11, Ibadan, Nigeria.

Preface (For My Sons)

In the tapestry of life, every thread, every color, every knot is significant. Each contributes to the grand design that, only when stepped back and observed from a distance, reveals a picture more complex and beautiful than one could perceive up close. This memoir is one such tapestry woven from the threads of my life experiences—some bright with joy, others darkened by trials, but all saturated with the presence of God's grace.

So, as I stand on the brink of my 50th birthday, I look back at the journey that has led me to this moment—a journey I have chosen to share with you in this memoir—a celebration of resilience, a testimony to the power of faith, and a reflection on the bittersweet complexities of life.

My narrative will guide you through diverse terrains—from my humble origins in Africa, navigating the naivety and complexities of youth against a backdrop of academic rigor, to achieving professional success across continents. From the whispers of prayer in tranquil sanctuaries to confronting the spiritual dilemmas faced as a pastor's wife, navigating the trials of an abusive marriage, and emerging into the limelight of academic recognition in America, this memoir is a mosaic of life's contrasting experiences. It encapsulates the journey of holding onto faith amid life's tremors and mustering the courage to embark anew when all hopes are lost.

As you turn these pages, know that I have hidden the names of the people and places involved. While the heart of the story remains valid, their identities have been kept secret to respect the lives intertwined with mine.

This book is for you if you have ever felt alone in your struggles, if you have ever sought strength to face another day, or if you have ever wondered if there is grace after heartbreak. May you find companionship, courage, and comfort in my story. May it remind you that no matter how tough life gets, there is always hope, a way forward, and grace waiting to be discovered.

With a spirit of gratitude for the past and graceful anticipation for the future,

Yetunde Longe-Folajimi, Ph.D.

Unfolding Grace

ONE

My Roots

I am fundamentally an optimist. Whether that comes from nature or nurture, I cannot say. Part of being optimistic is keeping one's head pointed toward the sun, one's feet moving forward.

Nelson Mandela

My life story began beneath the expansive African sky, a starry canopy that had witnessed countless tales of hope, resilience, and dreams stretching into the horizon. In a humble community where almost everyone knew each other's name, I was born—destined, some would say, to be one of those shining stars.

My hometown was a symphony of contrasts: the lush green fields dancing to the tunes of the wind and the arid patches of land that stubbornly defied nature's generosity. In this environment, people had learned the art of coexisting with the elements, making the best out of what was given. It was a place where the community was your extended family, and every elder was a repository of wisdom.

My parents were simple yet ambitious individuals. My father, a stern and religious man with a heart of gold, believed in the transformative power of education. My mother, a midwife with a nurturing soul, was the emotional compass of our family. Together, they instilled in me the values of hard work, humility, and the pursuit of excellence. I was their pride, not just because I was their child, but because I showed an insatiable thirst for knowledge from an early age.

Just before my fourth birthday, a unique circumstance catapulted me into academia earlier than most, challenging the conventional entry requirements. The norm in my country was that children started school at age six, guided by a rather peculiar but widespread yardstick: they would be asked to stretch their right hand over their head and touch their left ear. Conventional wisdom dictated they would not be ready for school if they could not. I defied both measures. At just four years old, my right hand did not come close to reaching my left ear, nor did I meet the age requirement. However, destiny had other plans.

The unfolding of events that bypassed this rule was unanticipated. My mother was out of town and left me in the care of our relative, a primary school teacher. She took me to her school to keep an eye on me. In a classroom filled with children older than me, I found myself effortlessly answering math and English questions aimed at first graders—much to the surprise of everyone, including the teacher herself. At that moment, traditional rules were set aside, and swift recommendations were made for me to begin my formal education immediately.

The credit for this early display of academic aptitude must go to my father, a secondary school teacher whose soul I bless for instilling a love for learning from the earliest age. This unconventional start marked the beginning of a lifelong journey in education—a journey fueled by resilience and grace.

> “Beneath a sky that whispered tales of resilience, my thirst for knowledge was an echo of ancestral dreams, a star born in the cradle of hope and determination.

The school became my playground, where my mind felt free to explore, question, and absorb. Even as a young child navigating primary school, the thrill I felt when solving a complex math problem or writing a compelling essay was unparalleled. My teachers soon recognized my potential. I was not just another student in the class; I was the young girl who would stay back to ask questions, read beyond the prescribed materials, and volunteer for extracurricular activities that fueled my intellectual curiosity.

As I moved through the educational pipeline, my academic abilities continued to blossom. The early promise I had displayed was not a fluke but a genuine aptitude for learning that efficiently carried me through primary school. Recognizing my potential upon finishing primary school, my parents enrolled me as a boarding student in a Christian secondary school for girls in a neighboring town.

The boarding environment was a sanctuary that cultivated my intellectual and spiritual growth. Here, my days were regimented not just by rigorous academic schedules but also by times of communal prayer, Bible study, and worship. It was an education beyond textbooks and classrooms; it addressed the holistic development of character, ethics, and faith. In this nurturing atmosphere, I excelled, affirming my parents' decision and further fueling my aspirations. Each year, my name was a staple on the honors roll, often accompanied by numerous accolades and certificates that adorned the walls of our modest home. It was not the paper or the ink that made them special, but the pride in my parents' eyes—their unspoken words echoing the sentiment, "That is our girl." My father took it a step further. He began affectionately referring to me as "Doctor," as if prophesying the scholarly pursuits that would later define my career.

It was not merely a term of endearment but a declaration of faith in my potential. My father saw beyond the immediate accomplishments and looked at the possibilities ahead for me. His belief in me constantly reminded me that I was destined for more and that the boundaries of my achievements were yet to be defined. It was as if he was pouring into me the expectations of our family and generations past and future—a legacy of resilience, faith, and relentless pursuit of excellence.

To every parent reading this, never underestimate the power of speaking about your child's potential. Words can shape reality, build confidence, and plant seeds of possibilities in the fertile soil of young minds. Just as Proverbs 18:21 tells us, "Death and life are in the power of the tongue," so too is the ability to manifest dreams and aspirations. Your words can be the wind beneath their wings, giving them the courage to soar into unseen destinies.

Speak life, speak hope, and speak affirmations. Your words today could very well shape their world tomorrow.

Excellence came with its own set of challenges—the weight of expectations. Being the star pupil meant the spotlight was always on me, magnifying my achievements and my rare moments of vulnerability. Teachers expected the best from me, my parents dreamed of a future filled with accolades, and the community saw me as a beacon of hope, a testament to what could be achieved with dedication and a good education. While the pressure was immense, it never felt suffocating. Instead, it served as the wind beneath my wings, propelling me to soar higher, fueled by the collective hopes and dreams of those who believed in me.

Our family had a tradition of spending Easter Monday on the 'Plateau of Galilee,'[1] a verdant mountain nearby where local Christian families gathered in fellowship to commemorate the resurrection of Christ. This year was no different, and my heart was set on wearing my favorite dress for the occasion—a simple but cherished maxi dress. However, this joy was nearly thwarted by discovering a small tear—a rift in the fabric that felt like a rift in my plans. Upon discovering the tear, my initial dismay quickly turned into resolve. Remembering my mother's teachings about self-reliance, I decided to mend the dress myself, seeing it as a test of my resilience and independence.

At that moment, holding a piece of needle and thread and guarded by some lessons I had earlier received from my mother, I felt a connection transcending the mere act of sewing. As I sat there in the calm of that afternoon of Good Friday, the day's spiritual significance seemed to infuse my actions. Each stitch felt like a prayer, a symbolic act mirroring the themes of renewal and hope intrinsic to the Easter season. As I threaded the needle, I was unaware I was stitching a new chapter of my life. Each puncture of the fabric was a meditation, and with every pull of the thread, I was weaving my act of faith, reflecting the refreshing spirit of the season.

Although I was barely twelve and my stitches were far from perfect, I felt a profound sense of accomplishment as I tied the final knot. I had mended a

---

1

The Plateau of Galilee holds significance for Easter Monday as it is part of the region where Jesus ministered and appeared post-resurrection, which is a central theme in Easter celebrations.

dress, but in the process, I had also stumbled upon a new form of self-expression that deeply resonated with my spiritual beliefs and a pathway to impact others through fashion design. The concept of 'transformative learning,' explored by Mezirow (1991), resonates deeply with me. It is a process where simple actions lead to profound shifts in self-perception.[2]

For me, 'transformative learning' was a theoretical concept and a lived experience. My understanding of this concept began in an unexpected setting: my science class. I remember a particular biology lesson on ecosystems, where we learned how every organism, no matter how small, plays a crucial role in its environment. This concept struck a chord with me. Moreover, it became a manifestation of interconnectedness and individual impact. As I delved into the complexities of ecosystems, I began to see parallels in human society. This revelation from a science class transcended textbooks, instilling in me a sense of responsibility and a curiosity about my role in the larger scheme of things. It was a moment of cognitive shift, where science became a lens through which I viewed the natural world and my place within it.

Thus, Good Friday, the quiet act of sewing, enabled me to fix my dress and stitch a new pattern of self-awareness and confidence within me.

When Easter Monday arrived and we made our way to 'Galilee,' I wore that mended dress with a newfound grace and gratitude. So, as I reminisced over the horizon that Easter Monday, the 'Plateau of Galilee' became my liminal space, my sacred ground. Surrounded by family and community, I felt the embrace of divine love and the transformative power of simple acts guided by faith. I looked over the horizon and felt a deep sense of awe. It was as if the ordinary moment of mending my dress, under the lens of faith and God's grace, had become a turning point, directing me toward a deeper understanding of life's complexities and blessings.

This turning point, subtle in its arrival but seismic in its impact, would echo through the corridors of my life, a constant reminder that grace often arrives in the guise of ordinary things, transforming them and us into vessels of something far more significant. So, I returned to the boarding school the following week, realizing that hands can heal and that our small actions are

[2] Mezirow's theory emphasizes the power of dialogue, critical reflection, and self-awareness in transformative learning.

imbued with the power to change our narrative. Looking back, I can testify that grace often comes in the quietest moments, leaving an indelible mark on our journey.

One day, during a remarkably uneventful lecture at school, my mind began to wander. My fingers instinctively reached for a pencil, and before I knew it, I was sketching on the back of my school notebook. The design was simple—an A-line flair skirt resembling the skirt part of our school's evening uniform, which we fondly called the "green skirt." The drawing was far from revolutionary, yet it was distinctly mine, a tangible manifestation of an idea that was floating around my head during what was supposed to be a regular math class. The lines grew more confident as the concept crystallized in my mind. It was a basic design, but it represented many possibilities for me. That doodle was more than just a drawing; it was a blueprint, a tangible manifestation of my nascent aspirations in fashion.

> "Grace often arrives in the guise of ordinary things, transforming them and us into vessels of something far more significant.

Then came the incident that would be the actual test of my embryonic design ability. One fateful evening, as I prepared for evening activities, I realized that my green skirt, the school's official evening uniform, was missing! Panic set in as I rifled through my belongings, knowing that not wearing the designated evening attire would surely result in punishment. Then, my eyes landed on a green bed sheet my mother had given me as a spare sleeping sheet. It was a modest item, but it was full of potential, just like a canvas waiting for the brush, a piece of clay ready to be molded. The design I had sketched suddenly resurfaced in my memory. It looked like our green skirts. Could art imitate life quite literally? With these thoughts came a question: Could I transform this fabric into something more? An audacious and desperate idea popped into my head: I could transform that bed sheet into a skirt.

With no time to lose, I set to work with scissors, needle, and thread in hand. I echoed, "O Lord. Please help me." My hands shook as I made the first cut, but there was no turning back. As I sewed, I immersed myself in the process, each stitch bringing me closer to a solution; each step was a prayer, a dialogue with the Creator. Just as God had breathed life into the clay to form man,[3] I felt His presence guiding my hands as I breathed life into a mere piece of fabric, each seam fusing my burgeoning skills with immediate necessity.

At that moment, the room around me seemed to dissolve into a quiet nothingness, leaving just me, the whisper-soft fabric under my fingers, and the daunting challenge before me. It was a silent battle between me and my doubts, a test of my will against the complexities of the task. With each thread I wove, I stitched together the fabric and pieces of my resolve, threading my fears and hopes into the seams of creation. It was an intimate dance of determination, where every pull of the needle testified to my perseverance.

It was finally done after what seemed like an eternity, but it was just a couple of frantic hours meant to be our lunch and siesta time. I had transformed a simple bed sheet into a reasonable facsimile of our green skirt. It was far from perfect—uneven in parts, hastily sewn in others—but it was, without a doubt, a wrap-skirt. What emerged was a garment that testified to the ingenuity and the resilience of the human spirit. It was a wrap-skirt, imperfect yet imbued with a more profound perfection—the triumph of creativity over constraint. I put it on, looked into the mirror, and felt mixed emotions: relief, pride, and a newfound confidence in my ability to create under pressure.

As I stepped out of the dorm room, skirt in place and head held high, I realized this was much more than a clever workaround. It was a rite of passage, a moment where necessity had mothered invention, pushing me to apply my creative skills in a real-world scenario. I had not only evaded punishment but had also proven to myself that my designs had practical value and that my passion for fashion could solve tangible problems.

This incident became a cornerstone in my career journey, a clear signpost pointing toward my calling in fashion design. It was a practical manifestation of the biblical David's victory over Goliath—not by might or power, but by faith and the humblest of tools (1 Samuel 17). It taught me that God's

[3] According to the Bible, in Genesis 2:7, God breathed life into the clay that formed man, giving him a soul and a unique identity as a created being.

provision often comes packaged in our willingness to use what is at hand, to look beyond the ordinary, and to see the potential for the extraordinary.

It validated my belief in the transformative power of fashion, reinforcing my commitment to pursue this path with even greater zeal. It was a vivid reminder that sometimes, the most extraordinary opportunities come from the most ordinary moments, turning challenges into steppingstones on the path to success. It marked a pivotal moment in my passion for fashion design.

Thus, when you find yourself in the throes of the mundane or the grip of the uneventful, remember that these could be the moments God uses to sculpt your destiny. Each choice, each attempt, no matter how trivial it may seem, could be the very thing that sets you on the path to fulfilling your God-given purpose. In these moments, we are called to recognize the potential for divine grace to work through us, transforming our ordinary into His extraordinary.

As I stand here today, I look back at that young girl in a small African town with a sense of awe and gratitude. She laid the foundation for the woman I have become—a woman of intellect, resilience, and unwavering faith. Even though I am miles away from my homeland, I can almost feel the African sky above me winking in approval as I write down these memories. It is as if it is whispering, "You have always been one of us, a star destined to illuminate the world."

In the following chapters, you will journey with me through the labyrinth of life, love, and the pursuit of self-discovery. However, no matter where this journey takes us, remember that it all began under the African sky—a sky that holds within it the dreams of a young girl and the aspirations of a woman who dared to reach for the stars.

TWO

Unspoken Lessons

The best love is the kind that awakens the soul; that makes us reach for more, that plants the fire in our hearts and brings peace to our minds.

Nicholas Sparks

When I look back at my formative years, I cannot help but marvel at the dichotomy of my existence. I grew up in a devout Christian household where the pillars of faith were ever-present. We diligently followed biblical teachings and guidelines, attended church services, and engaged in communal prayers. My devout and God-fearing parents took immense pride in instilling a robust moral foundation in their children.

They raised us with prayers, hymns, and scriptural teachings, but a glaring omission existed—an unspoken taboo around intimate relationships. This silence left me navigating two distinct worlds. In one, I was engrossed in a world of academics and spirituality. However, on the other hand, I felt like a wanderer lost in the complex wilderness of intimate relationships, a landscape so unfamiliar that even my academic achievements could not serve as a guiding light. I often felt like a wanderer amidst unknown terrains, each step teaching me more about my emotional resilience and the complexities of human connections. This journey, though bewildering, became a cornerstone in my understanding of empathy and the nuances of the human heart.

Research on the intersection of cultural norms and emotional education by Grau and Dollahite (2004) explores how cultural factors within religious communities can influence family life, including attitudes toward discussing intimate relationships. Their study underscores the fact that in many Christian communities, especially in African settings, there is a prevalent cultural norm to avoid open discussions about romantic relationships, particularly with the youth. This approach, while intended to maintain moral integrity, often leaves young people unprepared for the realities of adult relationships.

This observation mirrors my journey, where a comprehensive educational experience on emotional and relational matters was notably absent, leaving a gap between academic and spiritual achievements and emotional preparedness. It reveals how deeply cultural and religious norms have shaped my understanding of relationships, realizing that my struggles were personal and part of a larger societal fabric.

The echoes of my first encounter with womanhood, the day I stepped into the complex realm of my menstrual cycle, still resonate in the corridors of my memory. It was a moment of profound biological metamorphosis entwined with a whirlwind of emotional tumult. The blend of excitement and apprehension was palpable as I navigated the unfamiliar territory of bodily transformations.

When I sought sanctuary in my mother's wisdom, she enveloped me in a bubble of love and concern. However, her counsel, though drenched in the deepest of maternal instincts, was shrouded in ambiguity. Her words, "Do not allow any man to touch you until you are ready," echoed an informative sentiment but lacked clarity in defining personal boundaries or understanding emotional maturity. This vagueness was not due to a shortfall in her parenting but rather a reflection of the cultural norms that shaped our society's approach to such conversations. In our culture, discussions about the nuances of adolescence and bodily changes were considered adult topics, reserved for later understanding.

Contrastingly, in many civilized societies, parents engage in "the talk" with their children. This conversation typically encompasses a comprehensive guide on navigating adolescence's physical, emotional, and social intricacies.

Such dialogues offer practical advice, emotional support, and clear boundary-setting, empowering young individuals with the knowledge and confidence to make informed decisions.

While my mother's intentions were rooted in safeguarding me, the cultural backdrop of our community meant that I had to explore and comprehend the complexities of this new phase of life independently. Thus, I was left to piece together this puzzle with fragments gathered from hushed conversations with friends, whispers laden with myths and half-truths. It was a voyage through the maze of adolescence guided by the flickering torch of trial and error.

This experience, though challenging, has given me a unique perspective on the importance of open and comprehensive communication between parents and children about the changes and challenges of adolescence. It underscores the value of guiding the young with caution and clarity, empowering them with knowledge and understanding to navigate life's transitions confidently and safely.

> " In the silent chambers of my upbringing, I learned the language of the heart, a dialect formed in the spaces between words, where true understanding blooms.

This silence around relationship guidance felt ironic, given the backdrop of my upbringing. Our family was deeply rooted in Christian values, a tradition of teachings celebrating love, companionship, and marital unity. The Bible itself narrates various love stories that offer wisdom about relationships, from the unity and temptation faced by Adam and Eve to the loyalty and divine providence exemplified by Ruth and Boaz. The Songs of Solomon even go so far as to glorify romantic love poetically. However, despite these rich biblical tales that could serve as conversation starters or educational frameworks, discussions about love and relationships were conspicuously absent in many homes.

The Bible makes it clear that "He who finds a wife finds a good thing" (Proverbs 18:22). Yet, despite this scriptural endorsement, the roadmap to finding this "good thing" was notably missing from my upbringing. It puzzled me. The Bible itself is far from silent on love; it celebrates it in various contexts. So why was my real-world Christian upbringing hesitant to address this critical aspect of human life?

The Bible also teaches us that "It is not good for man to be alone" (Genesis 2:18). Yet, the practical aspects of how not to be alone were left untouched. How does one form a meaningful relationship? What are the God-approved ways of finding and expressing love? What are the markers of an emotionally and spiritually fulfilling relationship? These questions loomed large in my mind, but any attempt to initiate such a dialogue was met with a change in topic or a generic "You will understand when you get older."

We can attribute a significant part of this silence to cultural norms. In many Christian communities, especially those in Africa, discussing intimate relationships with young people is often considered taboo or inappropriate. Though rooted in a desire to maintain moral integrity, this cultural stance often does a disservice to the young and impressionable minds it seeks to protect. Not addressing these crucial life lessons inadvertently sends young people into the world ill-equipped to handle the complexities of romantic relationships.

My secondary school[4] was a citadel of intellectual and spiritual maturation. However, when it came to the equally intricate and crucial topic of intimate relationships, a different, unspoken rule seemed to apply: "Do not speak, do not listen, do not engage." The subject appeared shrouded in a metaphorical veil, such as the Holy of Holies[5] in the Temple of Jerusalem—sacred, untouchable, and strictly off-limits.

I remember eavesdropping on hushed conversations among classmates about their romantic interests. These conversations, though muted, were filled with a yearning for understanding, a quest for a scriptural and societal balance that our educational system failed to provide.

This culture of silence was reinforced by the severe penalties that awaited anyone who dared to explore the realm of romantic relationships. One incident served as a vivid reminder to all of us. Some girls were caught sneaking out to visit their boyfriends at a neighboring boys-only school. The

---

[4] In the Nigerian school system, secondary school is equivalent to middle and high schools in the United States.

[5] "Holy of Holies" refers to the innermost and most sacred area of the ancient Temple of Jerusalem, accessible only to the High Priest. It is used metaphorically here to describe the subject of emotional relationships as sacred and forbidden territory.

consequence was immediate and severe: an immediate suspension from school. The atmosphere after the incident was one of collective fear and judgment, an unspoken story that solidified my resolve to abstain from romantic relationships throughout high school—a vow I kept diligently.

This self-imposed emotional abstinence had its merits. My academic and personal development were unhindered by the dramas and pitfalls often accompanying youthful relationships. I could focus on my studies and extracurricular activities, achieving discipline and self-improvement that aligned well with Proverbs 19:20: "Listen to advice and accept discipline, and at the end, you will be counted among the wise."

However, this emotional safeguarding came at a cost. While I excelled in academics and personal growth, I was left unprepared for the complexities of adult emotional relationships. The absence of romantic trials during those formative years meant a lack of romantic wisdom—an experience I would miss as I navigated the labyrinth of love and commitment later in life.

In many Christian circles, the dialogue surrounding relationships is often reduced to simplified binaries: Wait until marriage—date only Christians. Don't be unequally yoked. While these valid principles are grounded in scripture, they do not fully capture the emotional and psychological complexities of romantic involvement. There is an abundance of guidance on how to be a good Christian but a relative silence on how to be a good Christian partner.

In his letters to the Corinthians, Paul speaks deeply about love, urging us to love patiently and kindly, without envy or arrogance. However, how does one apply these lofty ideals in a real-world relationship fraught with human imperfections? How does one love kindly when faced with a partner's repeated shortcomings? How does one love without envy in a world that constantly compares one's relationship to the curated love stories on social media?

The Song of Solomon, often cited for its poetic portrayal of love, offers a more sensual perspective on the relationship between a man and a woman. However, while the book beautifully captures the passion and desire within a loving relationship, it does not address the darker issues of emotional manipulation, financial abuse, or marital infidelity that many couples struggle with, even within the church.

In academics, the metrics for success were clearly defined—exams, grades, and scholarships provided a structured path. However, the realm of relationships was far vaguer. What were the benchmarks for a successful relationship? Love, trust, and emotional compatibility are not easily measured, and there were no guides to help me navigate this complex emotional terrain.

In my formative years, particularly during my secondary school days, I was a devoted student, excelling academically and spiritually. However, my life's emotional and relational aspects were like uncharted territories, where even the most well-intentioned curricula fell short. This gap in my education became evident as I navigated the intricacies of relationships, feeling like a modern-day Solomon. While Solomon prayed for wisdom to govern a nation, my prayers were focused on gaining the discernment needed to navigate the mysterious terrain of love and relationships.

The church, my spiritual home, was a haven for my soul but less so for my emotional needs. Sermons and Bible studies often spoke about the importance of spiritual growth, urging us to wait for God's perfect timing for a spouse and to remain pure in our relationships. However, the spiritual guidance became less clear when God's plan involved heartache or waiting longer than expected. This left many in emotional uncertainty, with our spiritual compass offering little direction.

Nevertheless, my faith served as my anchor. In times of emotional turmoil, I turned to prayer and Scripture as both a guide and a reflection of my emotional state. In these divine texts, I found solace, particularly in the stories of biblical couples like Abraham and Sarah, Hosea and Gomer, and even Mary and Joseph. These stories offered hope, showing how God worked through flawed relationships to bring about redemption and love.

However, the journey of emotional growth is ongoing, and there is a compelling need for a more nuanced dialogue within the Christian community about the complexities of love and relationships. It is about loving God and learning how to love others, particularly those we invite into our lives. This learning curve is steep and demands divine grace and worldly wisdom.

Our society had norms, particularly for women, which were often more confounding than helpful. They did not guide me in understanding emotional exchange nuances or setting healthy boundaries. I yearned for a mentor who could offer the wisdom I desperately sought. This emotional wilderness seemed to intensify the challenges, leaving me and many of my peers ill-prepared for the complexities of adult relationships.

> " We are doing a disservice to our young people by sending them out into the world well-equipped, intellectually but emotionally vulnerable.

Faith-based educational institutions must evolve to meet the demands of a world that increasingly values emotional intelligence. They must provide a balanced education that includes academic and spiritual guidance and emotional and relational mentorship. This is not about promoting teenage romance but about preparing young people for the complexities of adult emotional relationships in a responsible and faith-compatible way. We are doing a disservice to our young people by sending them out into the world well-equipped, intellectually but emotionally vulnerable.

The Bible has timeless lessons that offer blueprints for emotional and relational living. If integrated into the educational system, these teachings could equip students with the emotional tools they need for a well-rounded life.

Reflecting on my journey, I can see that my emotional wilderness was a formative experience. However, it could have been much more enriching and less fraught with challenges had it been guided by open dialogue and scriptural wisdom. It is a lesson I have learned the hard way, but I hope it will inform a new approach to holistic education for future generations.

THREE

The Circuit of Change

I raise up my voice — not so I can shout, but so that those without a voice can be heard... we cannot succeed when half of us is held back.

Malala Yousafzai

From an early age, I learned the value of self-reliance and taking responsibility for my actions. These formative experiences shaped my character and set me on a path toward becoming the confident and capable person I am today. Growing up as the eldest daughter in a family with two older brothers and two younger sisters, I quickly learned that society had certain expectations of me. Traditionally, a daughter's education in the 'ways of womanhood' was a legacy passed down through generations, not just as life skills but cultural norms that often define the roles women are expected to play in family and society. However, in our household, this heirloom took on a different form.

My mother, a midwife dedicated to her nursing profession, often worked tirelessly into the night. Her efforts were not just for us, her five children, but also for her five orphaned siblings who sought refuge under the warm embrace of our home. This unique dynamic in our household altered the traditional fabric of mother-daughter bonding, often the channel through which life skills and domestic knowledge are passed down. Consequently, my childhood was not filled with learning the perfect recipes or mastering the delicate art of homemaking. Instead, I charted a course of independence and self-reliance, navigating the waters of life with a compass forged from necessity rather than tradition.

Financial constraints were a shadow that often loomed over our family. The reality of our situation was stark—school fees remained unpaid for extended periods, casting a cloud of uncertainty over our education. Meals were often modest, lacking the luxury of meat or fish, which in those days was akin to a garnish of affluence on a plate of humble carbohydrates.

I still vividly remember the heavy cloak of embarrassment and shame that enveloped me each time I, or one of my siblings, was sent home for the outstanding balance of our school fees. Those moments, filled with a profound sense of vulnerability, starkly contrast with my immense pride in my family's unwavering resilience and perseverance. The memories of those challenging days - the reluctant journey back to school with a heart weighed down by financial worries - have etched a permanent mark in my consciousness. However, these experiences have become a powerful driving force in my life. They have galvanized my resolve to achieve success and forge a future where financial stability is a given, not a luxury. This determination propels me forward, fueling my ambition to create a life where my family can thrive without the looming shadow of unpaid bills. This vision of a better future is a goal I am steadfastly working toward, a promise to myself and my loved ones that our past struggles will pave the way for a brighter, more secure tomorrow.

My mother, a beacon of vision and tenacity, seemed to glide through life's challenges with an inexhaustible energy, her spirit a relentless force for progress. In her unwavering determination, I saw the mirror of my emerging drive - a mutual hunger for hard work and the pursuit of betterment.

Confronted with the challenges, she seized a life-altering opportunity: to venture into a distant city in search of greener pastures. This decision, however, wielded the power of a double-edged sword - it was a gateway to new possibilities, yet it also invited the sting of societal scrutiny. In the watchful eyes of our community, she was a maverick, courageously crossing the invisible lines of traditional expectations for a mother and wife. Her audacious move, stepping out of the conventional mold, sparked a flurry of unsolicited advice and whispers of judgment.

"You should be here with your husband," they would say, their words wrapped in concern. "A woman's place is in with her husband," others would add, voicing the silent expectations of our community.

Ever watchful and brimming with opinions, the community often cast their words upon me like nets since I am my parents' first daughter, hoping to guide or reshape my path. "You are doing very well in your studies," they would say. "But remember, you must be a good wife and mother," echoes a time-worn narrative that equated a woman's success with her domestic prowess. Each piece of advice, though well-intentioned, was a mirror reflecting the deeply ingrained societal norms that prioritized domestic roles over personal aspirations.

Nevertheless, in the void left by my mother's absence, I found not a deficit but an opportunity. In this open field, I could sow the seeds of my dreams unhindered by the conventional expectations set for women in our community. It was a freedom to discover myself, to unearth my passions and abilities beyond the usual confines of domesticity.

This early life narrative is a testament to the power of circumstances in shaping a person. In the crucible of financial hardship and societal norms, I was forged into an individual of resilience and determination, traits that would become the bedrock of my journey through academia and beyond.

While societal judgments aimed to confine me to predetermined roles and expectations, my actions boldly told a different story—one filled with defiance, liberation, and unyielding creativity. Fashion design became my language of protest, a medium through which I challenged the outdated norms that tried to define me. I transformed every fabric I could find into a design, and each garment that emerged, though not worthy of any wall of fame, served to craft a statement, a piece of my identity boldly displayed. This sartorial expression intertwined with my academic pursuits, creating a unique personal narrative that challenged and reshaped the boundaries of my career expectations.

As if to add an exclamation point to my silent defiance, I excelled

Academically, securing straight A's, and consistently landing on the honor roll. This was not just in the expected science courses like Math and Physics, where societal norms could still find a way to rationalize my success; I also shone in courses like Yoruba Language and Fine Arts, areas that no one expected a science student like me to master. Each accolade refuted the notion that a woman's worth is confined to domestic roles.

Thus, while society insisted on viewing me through the narrow lens of gender expectations, I chose to see myself through the panoramic view of my capabilities and dreams. This dual narrative of judgment and liberation is a chapter in my past and the foundation for my future. It is why I can stand tall today, confident in my abilities and unapologetic about my ambitions. It proves that while society may attempt to write our story for us, we hold the pen and have the power to write our ending.

A pivotal moment came in an unexpected yet transformative act of youthful creativity. One day, during a holiday season, I tore apart my father's old 'agbada'—a traditional West African robe. From its fabric, I crafted small, stylish articles of clothing, some for myself and some for my dolls. Recognizing my budding potential, my mother introduced me to the family's underutilized sewing machine, which until then had been relegated to making simple 'iro and buba'—a traditional Yoruba outfit consisting of a wrapped piece of fabric and a matching blouse. This was a transformative moment, breathing new life into me and the sewing machine, which found a new purpose in my eager hands.

So, in a way, my story became one of seamless integration—of using my hands to create in the tactile world of fabric and design while also using my mind to explore the complex world of education and social interactions. These pursuits offered avenues for excellence, self-expression, and challenging the boundaries of what I could achieve.

As I progressed through the complexities of young adulthood, the pressures began to mount in more ways than one. The stakes became higher, the expectations more demanding, and life's balancing act increasingly precarious. However, amidst this swirling vortex of responsibilities, deadlines, and emotional intricacies, one constant remained: my sanctuary of fashion design.

On the surface, creating garments might seem mechanical, but it was deeply cathartic for me. Each stitch was a small victory, reclaiming control in a chaotic world. The fabric did not argue; it quietly complied, yielding to my envisioned shape and form. In this space, the equations of calculus and the theories of physics took a backseat, allowing a different kind of logic to reign—creative logic. Here, two plus two did not necessarily have to make four; it could make whatever I wanted—a dress, a blouse, or even an abstract textile art.

When the outside world became a tangled web of expectations and judgments, my sewing space remained a zone of unconditional acceptance. It was as if the walls whispered words of encouragement, telling me it was okay to make mistakes, undo stitches, and start over.

Thus, fashion remained my constant, my soft landing in a world filled with hard truths. It became the space where I could decompress, reassess, and gather the strength to face another day. It served as a tangible reminder that even when life's variables seem overwhelming, we all have constants that keep us grounded, give us purpose, and remind us of who we are.

> “In the fabric of my teenage years, every challenge stitched a pattern of resilience, weaving a garment of strength worn with pride and humility.

In my community, societal norms and traditional gender roles often demarcated the professional trajectories of young girls. Even my father, a pillar of encouragement, had cast me in the well-worn mold of a medical doctor—a role he believed would garner respect and align with the nurturing traits often ascribed to smartness. While medicine is a noble field, my heart leaned more toward engineering's problem-solving and hands-on work. However, my enthusiasm was often met with skepticism and sometimes even veiled mockery. The underlying tone was that a woman's place was not amidst wires and engines but within the safe confines of a home or perhaps a more 'feminine' profession.

The idea of a young girl contemplating a career among circuits, gears, and engines was met with disbelief and concern. "Those professions are for men," they warned, cautioning that a career so entrenched in technicalities would inevitably derail me from the divine mandate of womanhood and domesticity. The message could not have been more explicit: My technical inclinations were to be subordinated to traditional expectations that circumscribed my gender.

However, the tides turned when a young British African woman visited my school to discuss her computer science career. She was an anomaly in many ways—a young woman and a person of color thriving in a field predominantly associated with men.

Her British accent was so thick that the nuance of her speech was mostly lost on me. However, I did catch something far more profound than words: her aura of confidence, the charisma she spoke, and the air of authority she carried. She was in complete control, defying societal norms and breaking new ground in a rapidly evolving field. I remember sitting there, captivated not by the technical jargon that floated above my head but by the possibilities she represented. For the first time, I saw a version of what I could become—a woman of color in a field where few like me had ventured.

Her presence that day did something extraordinary for me; it shattered the glass ceilings I did not even know existed. Until then, the restrictive societal norms had subconsciously influenced my career aspirations. Medicine, as my father hoped, or perhaps some other 'respectable' profession that would dovetail nicely with traditional domestic roles, were the paths I thought I would eventually consider. However, this woman, this influential, confident African-British computer scientist, opened doors to an entirely new universe of opportunities.

Although my prior experience with computers was limited to the pixelated images flashing across my television screen, that encounter ignited a transformation. Computer science, a field I had been blissfully ignorant of until the spellbinding talk, metamorphosed into the blazing torch illuminating my path and the unquenchable fire that fueled my loftiest aspirations.

The inspiration derived from her talk was not about understanding the complexities of algorithms or programming languages but the potential for breaking barriers. If she, a young woman of African descent, could make her mark in British tech's challenging and competitive world, then why could not I? The seed was sown; a desire to explore the world of computer science took root. That day, I decided to be like her, a trailblazer who defied stereotypes, shattered ceilings, and carved a path for others to follow.

When I discovered my deep-rooted passion for computer science, the excitement was too overwhelming to keep to myself. I began sharing my aspirations with family, friends, and mentors, eager to let them in on my vision for my future. What I had not anticipated was the array of reactions I would receive—reactions that proved both enlightening and profoundly revealing.

A significant number of people, especially among the older generation, assumed that computer science was essentially typing. "Ah, a career in typing is a wise choice; it is not too demanding," they would say, nodding their heads in approval. Their responses were a double-edged sword. On the one hand, their endorsement reflected a glaring misunderstanding of what the field of computer science truly entails, reducing it to clerical work. On the other, it sheds light on long-standing gender stereotypes that have long dictated what roles are considered 'appropriate' for women.

In their worldview, a career in typing was a suitable choice for a young woman because it was perceived as 'easy' and 'less demanding,' allowing room for me to fulfill my domestic responsibilities. Little did they know that computer science is far from just typing. It is a realm that deepens into algorithms, data structures, artificial intelligence, and much more.

By stepping into a domain that was largely male-dominated and misunderstood, I was breaking free from a pre-written societal script. I was challenging the narrative imposed upon me by my gender, and in doing so, I was reclaiming my agency as an individual fueled by passion, curiosity, and intellectual rigor.

My ambitions were further fueled by the advice of my school counselor, who recognized my aptitude for mathematical and scientific subjects. These subjects, I was told, would be foundational to my success in a computer science program in higher education. I heeded this advice and excelled, creating a solid academic foundation for my future studies.

My academic journey was not without its share of challenges, but I persisted, buoyed by a profound sense of divine grace that I can only describe as golden. I completed secondary school with honors, and my name appeared on the rolls of distinction. The fruits of my labor were evident; offers of admission from four different universities lay before me like diverging paths in a forest.

My parents, grounded in their wisdom and bolstered by their faith, presented their counsel at this juncture. They strongly recommended I attend the state university close to home, allowing me to commute from the safe confines of our family residence. My teenage mind was torn; the allure of freedom and new experiences beckoned, but the weight of my parents' advice held me back.

With a mix of reluctance and respect, I acquiesced to their suggestion. It was a decision that seemed counterintuitive to my youthful desires but aligned with the Christian values of family and obedience that were deeply ingrained in me. Though it meant sacrificing some degree of personal freedom, it was a practical decision demonstrating fiscal responsibility. I took it as a leap of faith, entrusting my journey to God's larger plan, which was yet to unfold in its full glory.

Once ensconced in the state university, my academic prowess did not wane; if anything, the proximity to home provided a stable platform for my intellectual pursuits. It offered its unique challenges and blessings. On the one hand, the daily commute and the watchful eyes of my parents limited my social activities; on the other, they provided a moral and spiritual anchor that kept me grounded in my Christian values. It became a balancing act of honoring my parents, abiding by my faith, and navigating the complexities of young adulthood.

Thus, my story serves as an embodiment of the Christian teaching, "For I know the plans I have for you," declares the Lord, "plans for welfare and not for evil, to give you a future and a hope" (Jeremiah 29:11). Let this verse be a source of inspiration and resilience, empowering you to challenge the societal norms or any other barriers that seek to limit you. In doing so, you will redefine your story and contribute to a broader social transformation and equality narrative.

FOUR

The Gateway of Dreams

Education is the most powerful weapon which you can use to change the world.

Nelson Mandela

The first day of university was akin to hopes and dreams laced with youthful enthusiasm and the threads of academic aspiration. As I entered the sprawling campus, I felt a surge of emotions coursing through me—excitement, anticipation, and a tinge of nervousness. The university was a microcosm of life, a diverse community of minds and cultures. The air felt thick with the fragrance of old books, mingling with the fresh aroma of blooming flowers from the campus gardens. It was as if the very atmosphere was infused with knowledge and growth.

I vividly remember the first lecture, an introductory math session designed to ease us into the rigors of academic life. The professor stood at the podium and imparted the first pearls of wisdom. "Welcome to the beginning of the rest of your lives," he proclaimed, "This is where you will define who you are and what you will become. Make the most of it." Those words struck a chord deep within me, echoing the sentiments of my aspirations.

I looked around the lecture hall, taking in the faces of my peers. Each of us was a blank canvas, eager to be painted with the hues of experience and learning. Some looked nervous, clutching their notebooks as if they were lifelines. Others exuded confidence, their eyes gleaming with the prospect of future accomplishments. Moreover, there were those like me, a blend of eagerness and caution, our pens poised over paper, ready to jot down the lessons that would shape our destinies.

Reflecting, that day marked the beginning of a profound personal evolution. As the sun set, casting its golden glow across the campus, I stood in line waiting for the bus to take me back to town and eventually home. At that moment, I paused to grasp the day's significance. It was as if I were on the cusp of an entirely new world, my heart throbbing with the thrill of limitless possibilities. Filled with gratitude and offering up a prayer for divine guidance, I welcomed the uncertainties ahead. I knew I was at the starting point of a transformative journey—a pivotal new beginning that would set the stage for the unfolding story of my life.

My entry into university life was as smooth as it was refreshing. While many first-year students navigated through the initial phase with jitters and anxiety, I found myself in my natural habitat. Each lecture and lab assignment allowed me to deepen my understanding of the world, push the boundaries of my intellectual capabilities, and contribute meaningfully to academic discourse.

The campus library became my sanctuary, a quiet refuge where I could plunge into volumes of knowledge. However, alongside this academic crescendo was a softer, more discordant melody—a struggle with emotional connection.

While I could quickly dissect algorithms and analyze literary texts, the language of emotions remained a puzzle far more complex. This dichotomy became especially evident during my university.

One day, as I sat in the bustling cafeteria amidst the rhythmic clatter of cutlery and the constant hum of conversations, I felt like an observer on the fringes of a world I could not entirely penetrate. Around me, laughter erupted spontaneously, and groups huddled together, sharing stories and secrets. However, their laughter and chatter sounded like a foreign language I longed to decipher. Each smile, each shared glance among my peers, seemed to highlight the invisible barrier that separated me from them.

As I picked at my food, my thoughts drifted to the books and theories I had mastered in class. I found clarity and structure in those pages, but they sharply contrasted the elusive nuances of human emotions and connections I saw around me. I wondered, not for the first time if the pages of my textbooks could offer a formula to navigate the complexities of these social interactions. In these quiet moments, amidst the backdrop of others' laughter and conversations, I began to understand the paradox of my solitude: It was both a challenge to overcome and a quiet reminder of my unique path in the vast maze of life.

As the seasons at university transitioned from one to another, so did the rhythm of my life. The concept of true love, once a distant dream, now seemed essential. I yearned for romance and a partnership that resonated with the deepest parts of my being—a man who would stand beside me and grow with me for the rest of our lives.

However, the journey to find such a profound connection was far from the straightforward path I had envisioned. The values I cherished—unwavering commitment, mutual respect, and a spiritual bond that transcended the ordinary—were rare in the social landscape. This landscape was a mixture of modern love, where varying perspectives on dating and relationships spun around me, often clashing with my deep-seated convictions.

Adding to this complexity was the paradox my upbringing and religious background presented. Rooted in tradition, it had instilled in me the sanctity of marriage and the virtues of being a woman of substance and spirituality. However, it seemed silent on the preludes to matrimony—the emotional mazes and the intricate dances of courtship that are integral to modern relationships. No scripture or sermon had prepared me for the nuances of contemporary dating: the uncertainty that cloaked intentions, the labyrinth of mixed signals, or the sting of disappointments that seemed all too common in the quest for a soulmate.

As I navigated these unfamiliar terrains, I often reflected on and sought guidance from my faith and experiences. The search for love, I realized, was not just about finding someone who shared my beliefs but also about understanding and embracing the complexities of human connection. It was about learning to balance the ideals rooted in my soul with the realities of a world that often spun on a different axis.

Sitting on a weathered bench one beautiful afternoon, I watched a pair of butterflies dancing around each other, their movements harmonious yet fleeting. This dance reminded me of my interactions in the dating world - where ideals often clashed with reality. I recalled a recent evening spent with a group of friends. As we discussed love and relationships, I found myself in a silent struggle. Their views on casual dating and fleeting connections were so far removed from my search for a deeper, more spiritual bond. I felt a profound sense of isolation in these moments as if I were a solitary traveler on a path they could not understand.

The journey through this emotional maze was, at times, as confusing as it was enlightening. I pondered questions my textbooks had no answers to: What does it mean to love and be loved? How does one balance emotional vulnerability with spiritual strength? Moreover, how can a Christian navigate the complex world of romantic relationships while remaining true to their faith?

As the sun began to set, casting a golden hue over the garden, I contemplated the idea of a compromise. Could I find a middle ground where my faith and desire for companionship coexist? Or was I destined to walk a path defined by my beliefs, even if it meant walking alone?

That day, I realized this journey was about finding love and understanding myself. My faith was not just a set of rules; it reflected who I was and what I valued. Moreover, perhaps, by staying true to these values, I would eventually find someone who shared them and understood the language of my soul.

With this thought, I stood up, feeling a sense of peace. With their relaxed beauty, the fields had once again provided clarity. I stepped out, more resolved to embrace my journey, with all its complexities and uncertainties, knowing that my faith would be my guiding light.

In those first few weeks, the campus was alive with a vibrant energy, a palpable mix of excitement and anticipation. Everywhere I turned, there were new faces, sounds, and possibilities. It was against this backdrop of frenetic activity and buzzing social circles that our paths crossed. He stood out like a character from a novel – the seasoned student who moved through the campus with an ease and charm that seemed almost legendary.

There was an effortless grace in his manner, a confidence in his stride that caught the eye and held it. Amid throngs of students, he navigated the web of university life as if he had written the map himself. When his attention turned to me, it was like being touched by a ray of unexpected sunlight. For someone who had always found solace in the quiet company of books, this was an intoxicating new world of banter and laughter.

His interest in me was like a brush of color on a monochrome canvas, bringing excitement to my cheeks. I was unused to this kind of attention, and it sent a thrilling shiver down my spine. However, as the initial rush of exhilaration settled, a shadow of doubt began to creep in. His world was so different from mine; his ease in social situations contrasted with my reserved nature.

I soon began to see our budding relationship through the lens of my parents' counsel, a constant echo in the back of my mind: Beware of distractions, prioritize your education. This sentiment was deeply ingrained, a guiding principle that had led me to these moments. As days passed, I found myself torn between the allure of this new relationship and the steadfast commitment to my academics.

In the quiet of the night, I often reflected on our conversations, his plans that seemed to revolve around fleeting pleasures rather than long-term aspirations. It starkly contrasted my dreams, which were built on a foundation of hard work and academic success. This realization started to create a rift between us as an invisible barrier that grew with each passing day.

As the relationship began to wane, fate, or perhaps a mere coincidence, led me to cross paths with another – the more mature, seemingly grounded student. He appeared reflective, ambitious, and seemingly understanding of my academic focus. It felt like a breath of fresh air, a chance to connect with someone who shared my values of commitment and dedication.

However, as weeks turned into months, the veil of his maturity and guidance slowly lifted, revealing a more manipulative nature. His words, once encouraging, became directives, steering me in directions I had not intended to go. The realization that he was in love with someone else was the final unraveling of what I had once thought to be a promising connection. It left me questioning my judgment, wondering how the quest for a meaningful relationship had led me down such a convoluted path.

And then, the thought began to haunt me – perhaps true love was a mere illusion, a mirage in the desert of human connections. Maybe I should settle and embrace the practicality of companionship without the fire of passion I once yearned for. This was a time of inner turmoil, where dreams of 'happily ever after' were clouded by the sobering realities of life.

As my final undergraduate year unfolded—a time typically dominated by intense academic focus—my heart continued navigating the sea of doubt, wavering between dedication and disillusionment. However, life, in its uncanny rhythm, orchestrated an unexpected encounter. During this period of uncertainty, I crossed paths with someone who momentarily appeared as the embodiment of my unspoken desires, a potential architect of the 'happily ever after' I had long envisioned. He graduated from a famous university in another city, and with his advanced academic stage, I harbored hopes of maturity and understanding.

Unfortunately, this flicker of hope proved ephemeral. In a narrative that preceded the widespread use of 'Japa' in our societal vernacular, he was among the early wave of young Nigerians seeking refuge from our homeland's economic struggles. His eyes were set on the allure of the United States, a land perceived as a bastion of opportunity and prosperity. The phenomenon, colloquially known as 'Japa' in Nigeria, embodies the desire to leave one's country in search of better opportunities abroad, often with no intention of returning. Though prominently surfacing in the early 2020s, this phenomenon has roots stretching back years. This exodus, fueled by economic instability, lack of opportunities, and political unrest, raises critical questions about the future of Nigeria and other developing countries. It underscores the urgent need for systemic changes to curb the brain drain and foster an environment where citizens can thrive and prosper without feeling the need to flee.

His departure and silence marked the crumbling of my renewed hope in love. This revelation doused the flame of promise as swiftly as it had been kindled, leaving behind a trail of what-ifs and might-have-been. At that moment, I resolved to close the doors of my heart, to shutter the windows of my soul against the whims of romance. The pain of abandonment, compounded by the betrayal of trust, etched a deep scar. It seemed love was a luxury I could no longer afford in the economy of my emotions.

Thus, standing amidst the shadows of unfulfilled love and the realities of a nation grappling with its challenges, I soldiered on. Once a backdrop to my romantic aspirations, the university's corridors bore witness to a new resolve: to navigate life's journey alone, fortified by self-reliance and a guarded heart. I surrendered to the notion that perhaps love was not in my cards. The idea of 'happily ever after' faded into the background, replaced by a pragmatic acceptance of life's unpredictability.

As I continued to immerse myself in the pursuit of knowledge as a shield against the vulnerabilities of the heart, I occasionally ruminated on my past relationships. With every fractured relationship, I felt as if a part of my spirit was chipped away, leaving me disenchanted and increasingly skeptical about the institution of love. Each relationship was like a chapter in a book I had never read, filled with plot twists I could not foresee—reminding me that my understanding was flawed. Each breakup left me questioning my self-worth and the very nature of love itself.

However, today, my undergraduate love saga is history—a chapter from my past that has informed but not defined my present—a journey that, like my academic pursuits, has shaped me.

After these emotional rollercoasters, a troubling thought started to gnaw at me: "Maybe I am the problem." This self-doubt was like a persistent shadow, darkening my optimism and coloring my self-perception. Could it be that my approach to relationships was flawed or that my expectations were unreasonable? Maybe the root of these heartaches was not just incompatibility or misfortune but perhaps a more profound issue altogether.

> "True love is not just about the meeting of hearts, but the harmonious alignment of aspirations and values.

It occurred to me that many young people, including my younger self, often venture into relationships without the fear of God as their moral compass. In the whirlwind of youthful enthusiasm and societal pressure, the idea of a God-centered relationship can easily take a backseat.

The fear of God, in this context, is not about dread or terror but reverence, awe, and the desire to live in alignment with divine principles. Perhaps this absence of divine guidance led me, and many others, along a thorny path in our romantic quests.

After much soul-searching and wrestling with my faith, I made a pivotal decision: to preserve myself until marriage. This was not a retreat born out of fear or disillusionment but a step taken in faith and guided by my core beliefs. This choice was countercultural in a society that often prioritizes immediate gratification over long-term fulfillment. However, it was a conscious act of preserving my body and emotional and spiritual well-being. The Bible speaks about the body being a temple of the Holy Spirit (1 Corinthians 6:19)[6], and I felt a renewed commitment to honor this teaching.

With this decision came the expectation and hope that the right man would come along—one who would respect my choice, share my values, and be willing to wait. This would be a man whose heart was ruled by the fear of God, which is the beginning of wisdom, according to Proverbs 9:10.[7]

I was under no illusion that this would be an easy wait. The world is replete with temptations and shortcuts, each promising immediate happiness at the expense of long-term joy. However, I held onto the belief that a love rooted in mutual respect and shared values would be worth the wait.

If you find yourself at a similar crossroads, battling the demons of self-doubt and questioning the moral fabric of society, know that you are not alone. While it is easy to internalize the failures of past relationships, remember that they do not define you. Your worth is not determined by your relationship status but by who you are in Christ.

Choosing to wait for the right person is not an act of self-denial but one of self-respect and spiritual integrity. Do not rush the process; cherish the waiting period as a season of growth and self-discovery. Be confident that when the time is right, your path will intersect with someone who shares your values, respects your worth, and enriches your life in immeasurable ways.

Waiting is not just about finding the right person but also about becoming the right person. Use this time to draw closer to God, focus on personal development, and cultivate the virtues that will make you a better partner and individual. So, hold fast to your convictions, lean into your faith, and remember that the best things in life are often worth waiting for.

---

[6] "Do you not know that your bodies are temples of the Holy Spirit, who is in you, whom you have received from God? You are not your own." 1 Corinthians 6:19

[7] "The fear of the Lord is the beginning of wisdom, and knowledge of the Holy One is understanding." Proverbs 9:10.

FIVE

Designing Destiny

Fashion is not something that exists in dresses only. Fashion is in the sky, in the street, fashion has to do with ideas, the way we live, what is happening.

Coco Chanel

In the meantime, after all the love and heartbreak saga, I focused on building myself up academically, spiritually, and emotionally so that when the right person did come along, I would be ready—not just as a partner but also as an individual with a well-rounded life.

I also knew I had to channel my energies into something physically constructive. This is where my passion for fashion design came to full force. They say an idle mind is the devil's workshop, but my idle time was well invested in improving my fashion design and creativity skills. I found it therapeutic to sketch designs and create garments, a haven where I could escape the complexities of academic stress and societal expectations. The process was a form of self-expression, a way to articulate my identity in a material form.

Meanwhile, I started feeling a distinct social pressure to keep up with the latest fashion trends, but this challenge was compounded by my limited budget. Unlike some of my female peers, splurging on trendy clothes was not an option for me. However, this limitation became a canvas for my creativity and resourcefulness.

Determined to take control, I embarked on a journey of self-tailored fashion. Armed with fabric and inspired by the styles of my more fashion-forward friends, I set out to create my wardrobe. The early attempts were a far cry from perfection. My initial designs received mixed reactions. While some admired my endeavor and ingenuity, others could not help but comment on the uneven stitches and lopsided cuts that betrayed my novice status. However, instead of succumbing to discouragement, each critique catalyzed my development, spurring me on a path of continuous improvement in my tailoring skills.

This process paralleled the concept of "deliberate practice," as Ericsson et al. (1993) outlined. It emphasizes consciously and repeatedly performing a task to enhance one's abilities. In my case, each stitch, cut, and adjustment was a step toward mastering the art of tailoring, transforming each piece of fabric into not just an article of clothing but a testament to my resilience and adaptability in the face of constraints.

This process mirrored the concept of "deliberate practice," as put forth by Ericsson et al. (1993). It is the idea of engaging in a task consciously and repetitively to enhance one's abilities. Each criticism catalyzes growth, pushing me to meticulously refine my tailoring skills. Through this self-driven journey, I transformed each thread and needle stroke into a step toward mastering the art of fashion, sewing not just clothes but also a narrative of resilience and creativity.

One weekend, feeling the weight of academic pressures and the complexity of navigating social circles, I reached for a piece of navy blue silk. The fabric was smooth under my fingers, a sharp contrast to the turmoil in my mind. I decided to create something that was not just a garment but a piece of art that reflected my journey.

As I began to sketch, the design that emerged was a dress, simple yet elegant. It was a design inspired by fashion trends and my experiences. As the dress took shape, so did my thoughts. The needle and thread were my companions in solitude, helping me unravel the complexities of my emotions. The fitted and structured bodice of the dress symbolized the discipline and strength I had developed over my university years. I realized that this dress would be a manifestation of my resilience.

The day I finally wore the dress, I felt a sense of pride and accomplishment. Walking across the campus, the flair swirled around me and attracted many compliments. This was a tangible reminder of the journey I had undertaken. It symbolized my growth, a blend of my academic pursuits and evolution.

> “In the fabric of life, true strength lies in the intricate patterns of love, learning, and creativity.

As my designs gradually improved, my friends noticed my evolving skills and started requesting adjustments to their clothes, often in exchange for payment. While many initially hesitated to entrust me with brand-new items, my growing portfolio began to speak for itself.

I soon found an unexpected ally in one of my classmates. We built our friendship in the shared experience of being among the rare women in the computer science department. Our bond has only grown stronger with time, blossoming over the years into a cherished connection that endures to this day. It was she who first saw potential in my fledgling fashion endeavors. To me, she was the epitome of campus style, one of those fashion-forward icons whose every outfit I admired from afar. Imagine my astonishment when she approached me with words of encouragement and a request that filled me with excitement and nerves. She wanted me to design a dress for her, entrusting me with creating something worthy of her sophisticated taste.

With reverence and determination, I set about crafting the dress. I poured my heart into every stitch, carefully shaping the fabric to align with her vision. The day she wore the dress, her confession took me by surprise and filled me with a sense of accomplishment; she declared it one of the most beautiful pieces she had ever owned. Her feedback was a turning point, validating my skills and creativity.

In the following weeks and months, she became an ambassador of my work, spreading word of my fashion design skills like wildfire across the campus. She would often recount to me, her eyes sparkling with excitement, how people adored the designs I had crafted for her. Though I have chosen not to mention her name here, as I adhere to my practice of anonymizing characters for privacy, I know she will recognize herself in these lines. As she reads this, I imagine her nodding in agreement, a smile playing on her lips, reminiscing about our shared journey.

Our friendship has flourished over the years. It reminds us of the unexpected paths life can take us on and the surprising ways people around us can recognize and appreciate our talents.

By graduation, my abilities had reached a level where I could stand toe-to-toe with professional designers, very different from the hesitant stitches of my early days. My journey in fashion, parallel to my academic pursuits, is a story of growth, learning, and the blossoming of an unexpected talent, nurtured by the support and faith of friends and the relentless pursuit of excellence.

Today, I have received endless compliments on my outfits. Little do these admirers know that many of these clothes are my handmade creations. This journey through the world of fashion design has been a lesson in resilience, creativity, and the transformative power of self-belief.

To my dear readers, my advice to you is that you should never underestimate the power of resilience and continuous improvement. Whether it is fashion design or any other endeavor, each setback or piece of criticism can be a stepping stone to mastery if you approach it with the right mindset. Over time, the imperfect stitches will become seamless, and the asymmetrical cuts will find their balance. Moreover, who knows, the skills you develop may become a source of personal pride and open unexpected opportunities and pathways.

While my academic and emotional journeys were marked by their respective highs and lows, another significant aspect of my university experience was the friendships I forged. In a field notoriously dominated by men, being one of the few women in a Computer Science program was both a challenge and an opportunity. However, my experience differed remarkably from the stereotypical isolation or marginalization narrative.

Immersing in computer science, I found a sense of belonging within a group primarily composed of male peers. This setting, far from being daunting, felt surprisingly familiar and comfortable to me. My childhood experiences undoubtedly shaped my ease in this integration. Growing up as a middle child flanked by two elder brothers and two younger sisters, I learned to navigate both worlds effortlessly.

In their unassuming way, my elder brothers had been my early guides in understanding and interacting within male-dominated spaces. Their presence in my life had instilled confidence and adaptability in me, qualities that now made it seamless for me to engage and connect with my male classmates. They had, without realizing, prepared me for a world where I would often find myself in the minority. At the same time, my younger sisters kept me rooted in the feminine experience, balancing my perspectives and enriching my understanding of both genders. This unique position in my family, bridging brothers and sisters, had subtly equipped me with the skills to thrive in my academic and professional circle, making my journey in the tech field less about gender and more about shared passion and camaraderie.

Our group was united not by names, gender, or personal histories, which remained respectfully anonymous in this narrative but by a shared passion for unraveling the complexities of technology.

I remember a particularly challenging coding project where these bonds solidified. The assignment was daunting, a complex web of data structures and algorithms that tested even the brightest in the class. As we dove into the problem, a camaraderie emerged, different from any social circle I had known. No names or personal stories were exchanged, just mutual respect and a shared goal. Each of us brought our unique strengths to the table – I, with my keen eye for algorithm analysis, and they, with their robust understanding of data structure.

Hours we were ticked by as we dissected the problem. We debated, challenged each other, and sometimes even laughed at the absurdity of our errors. In these moments of intellectual exchange, I felt an unexpected sense of belonging. Our gender differences faded into the background, overshadowed by the thrill of collaborative problem-solving.

The moment we cracked the solution, a wave of exhilaration swept through us as we exchanged looks of triumph. It was a silent acknowledgment of our collective effort. That night, I realized these friendships were not formed from common pastimes or shared backgrounds but from the respect forged in the fires of intellectual challenge.

This experience was a defining moment in my university life. It taught me an invaluable lesson – in academia, and perhaps in life, it is not just about fitting in. It is about finding those unique spaces where your contributions are valued, where differences become insignificant in the face of shared passion and purpose. In that male-dominated field, I found more than just peers; I found a sense of community and an affirmation of my capabilities.

Of course, my social circle was not exclusively male. I also had female friends with whom I shared unique bonds. Our friendships often provided emotional support and a different kind of intellectual stimulation. It balanced out my experience, ensuring that I also had the invaluable perspective that female friendships offer. Their friendships, endowed with brilliant minds and generous spirits, profoundly influenced my academic voyage and contributed significantly to my personal development.

My university journey culminated in a series of final exams and a project defense, marking the pinnacle of my academic efforts. Beyond the grades, the enduring friendships and personal growth truly defined this chapter of my life. These relationships, fortified by social media, continue to enrich my life with support and intellectual engagement.

Thanks to the advent of social media, many of these friendships, including the bonds I formed during my secondary school years —both male and female—have stood the test of time. Platforms like Facebook, LinkedIn, and Instagram have served as virtual bridges, allowing us to celebrate each other's milestones, engage in intellectual discourse, and offer support during life's challenges.

If there is one lesson to glean from my experience, it is that friendships can transcend gender stereotypes, especially in spaces where one gender is notably underrepresented. Do not let societal norms limit your social interactions or intellectual partnerships. Seek friendships that will challenge, support, and inspire you to improve. Moreover, sustaining these friendships has never been easier in this digital age. Who knows? The person sitting next to you in class or collaborating with you on a project could become a lifelong friend, irrespective of gender.

To you, dear reader, let this chapter serve as a testament to the indomitable human spirit. The years can be full of highs and lows, but remember, during our lowest moments, we lay the foundation for our loftiest triumphs. Every struggle is a lesson, every challenge an opportunity for growth, and every setback a setup for a grand comeback.

> “The years can be full of highs and lows but remember; it is during our lowest moments that we lay the foundation for our loftiest triumphs.

Whatever your field of study or life journey, know you have a unique blend of talents, strengths, and a divine grace to navigate through it all. Remember that the essence of your journey is not solely captured by the accolades you receive or the hurdles you face. Instead, it lies in the resilience you demonstrate, the wisdom you acquire, and the friendships that enrich your soul.

Know that the same ‘Golden Grace’ that guided me is accessible. Hold fast to it, and let it illuminate your path as you write your compelling narrative. Whether at the peak of success or navigating the complexities of emotional relationships, this grace can be your guiding light, turning even your trials into triumphs.

So, as you turn the pages of your own life's chapters, may you do so with courage, resilience, and a heart full of hope. Your story is still being written, and the best chapters are yet to come.

SIX

Graceful Service

The best way to find yourself is to lose yourself in the service of others.

Mahatma Gandhi

Following graduation, I embarked on a pivotal chapter of my life with the National Youth Service Corps (NYSC), a rite of passage that proved transformative and enlightening. The NYSC is a mandatory one-year program to involve Nigerian graduates in nation-building and the country's development. During their service year, graduates are assigned to different states, often far from their region of origin, to promote national unity and cross-cultural integration. The program includes an initial orientation camp, community service, and professional placements, providing graduates with valuable life experiences and skills.

For my service year, the government posted me to Nigeria's culturally vibrant eastern region, a placement that presented various challenges and a wealth of opportunities for cultural immersion and personal growth.

Sstepping off the bus that brought me to the NYSC orientation camp, I felt a mix of exhilaration and trepidation. The air was thick with anticipation, and you could sense the collective curiosity emanating from hundreds of fresh-faced graduates. We were a sea of khaki-green and white—the signature colors of the NYSC uniform—each of us carrying our aspirations, fears, and questions into this new chapter of our lives.

During the two-week orientation phase of the NYSC program, I underwent a transformative experience marked by early morning drills and a journey toward self-reliance. Beginning at the crack of dawn, these drills were lessons in discipline and perseverance. They instilled a sense of structure and the importance of physical fitness, setting the tone for the day ahead.

After the two weeks of drills, I received my assignment: I was to serve as a youth corps member at a federal university, where I would serve for one year as a computer science faculty member under the mentorship of the head of the department. The university was conveniently located in a neighboring town. I secured modest one-room accommodation in the town to serve as my sanctuary for the coming year. Once settled, I focused on fulfilling another promise—a spiritual commitment I had made during my university days.

I prayed passionately and asked God to guide me through my service year and beyond. I also promised to dedicate myself more fully to Him. During that transformative period, I caught wind of a rapidly growing Pentecostal church that had garnered a reputation for its unyielding dedication to preaching God's pure, undiluted Word. Stories of miraculous signs and wonders that regularly unfolded within its sanctified walls had captivated my imagination.

> “In my dual life as a church usher and a computer science faculty member, I found the true essence of service – nourishing the soul while educating the mind.

Intrigued, I was attracted to the church's vibrant worship and transformative power in its congregants' lives. The allure was so potent that I had mentally resolved to transition from our family's traditional church to this spiritually electric atmosphere. However, there was one hitch: I was uncertain if this spiritual community had extended its branches to the eastern region where I was serving.

Then, as if ordained by some divine choreography, I discovered this church had a local assembly near the university where I was assigned. It felt like a spiritual rendezvous, predestined by the heavens. When I stepped into the Church, I felt an overwhelming sense of belonging, as though every prior spiritual experience had been a preamble leading to this sacred space.

The sermons spoke directly to my soul, often addressing the precise issues I grappled with. The community was warm and welcoming, embracing me as one of their own from day one. The miraculous signs and wonders I had heard of were not exaggerated; I witnessed transformations that defied logical explanation, further strengthening my faith and deepening my spiritual convictions. Joining this church became a significant milestone in my spiritual journey, and I sought to be a church worker in the ushering department.

Now that my spiritual home was secure, I focused on the academic frontier that awaited me. My first assignment was to teach first-year students an introductory computer science course. As fate would have it, the subject was right up my alley. However, because I started school much earlier than my peers, it turned out that I was logically older than many of my students by the time I embarked on the responsibility of educating and inspiring them. Given my cultural background, this scenario added a layer of complexity, where age is a significant factor in social hierarchies.

> "Your unique perspective, your skills, and, yes, even your challenges and limitations bring something unique to the table.

Nevertheless, instead of letting this age factor hinder me, I transformed it into an asset. I used my closeness in age to bridge the generational gap that often exists in academic settings. My relative youthfulness became a tool for better understanding their struggles, dreams, and aspirations. I related to them as a friend. I tried to instill in them a sense of purpose, a belief that they could surmount any obstacle, academic or otherwise, just as I had done in my life's journey.

So, dear reader, there may be times when you find yourself in roles that seem too big for your boots or that come with responsibilities and feel overwhelming. Remember, you are there for a reason. Your unique perspective, your skills, and, yes, even your challenges and limitations bring something unique to the table. Do not let cultural norms or societal expectations deter you from fulfilling your potential.

Your age, background, or experience level do not define your worth or ability to make a significant impact. What matters most is your willingness to embrace the role, learn, grow, and serve others in the best way you can. Your challenges can become your greatest assets, your stumbling blocks can become stepping stones, and your trials can become your triumphs. All it takes is a shift in perspective and the courage to take that first step. Trust in your journey, lean on your faith, and watch as doors open where there are only walls.

So, as the sun continued to dip below the horizon, casting its golden hues over the landscape, I found myself in two vastly different worlds. I stood in the sacred halls of our church as I welcomed worshippers with a smile every Sunday. During the weekdays, I had a different role— that of a Youth Corper, serving my nation with a one-year stint to give back to the community while laying the foundations for my career in the academic corridors of computer science. This duality of purpose enriched my life, yet something was amiss. I had ventured into one or two intimate relationships, hoping to find a connection that resonated with my soul. However, these attempts left me feeling used and unseen, leading to a profound realization: my true fulfillment did not lie in fleeting affections. Thus, I focused more intently on the church, nurturing a quiet hope that within this faith community, I might find the right man who shared my values and visions for the future.

As our National Youth Service Corps year ended, I faced a pivotal crossroads in my academic journey. I had boldly applied for a master's degree in the same department where I served the nation. This decision, while filled with hope, was not without its daunting challenges. I was all too aware of the harsh employment landscape in Nigeria, a reality starkly illustrated by the ongoing job search struggles of my two elder brothers years after their graduations.

In Nigeria, where the concept of student loans is virtually non-existent, pursuing a master's degree seemed akin to climbing a financial Everest without any ropes or safety nets. The uncertainty of securing a job after my NYSC year loomed large, and relying on my parents for such an endeavor was not a viable option. However, amidst these apprehensions, my faith stood as a beacon of hope. Nurtured through years of spiritual dedication and academic discipline, this faith was the cornerstone upon which I built my dreams. With every prayer and every step forward, I entrusted my future to the mighty hands of God, believing that the path I had chosen, though fraught with uncertainties, was guided by His divine hand.

When the admission letter for my master's program finally arrived, it was a moment of joy tinged with apprehension about how I would finance this next phase of my education. However, the journey thus far has taught me the power of perseverance and the strength of unwavering faith.

A revelation soon dawned upon me—my flair for fashion design was not just a hobby but a marketable skill, a talent that could be my financial lifeline. A survey of the town led me to a vacant store in a bustling area. As if fate had penned this chapter of my life, I also discovered a vacant bedroom for rent in the same building where the store was located—just as my current rent contract was nearing its expiration.

Armed with my mother's old sewing machine, I took the plunge. I rented the store and the bedroom. The bedroom was a charming space in a five-bedroom apartment offering panoramic city views. The kind-hearted landlord welcomed me into his home, and I quickly became a cherished friend of the family.

As Christmas approached, a miracle unfolded right before my eyes. Customers began to trickle in as if waiting for my store to open its doors. The sewing machine, though old, began to hum with the music of new beginnings as fabrics transformed into beautiful garments under my hands.

The first earnings from my shop confirmed that I was on the right path and became my financial cushion. I could pay my tuition for the master's program, defying the odds and the naysayers. It was as if the pieces of my life were falling into place, each guided by a divine hand.

At the same time, the year of our national service was ending, and the atmosphere was charged with a mixture of anticipation and nostalgia. We had come to form a community of sorts, bound by shared experiences and collective purpose.

While most of my peers were eager to round up the youth service year, receive their completion certificates, and return home before Christmas, I had a compelling reason to stay behind—my fledgling fashion business was thriving. A sea of orders awaited my attention.

During this busy period, a glimmer of opportunity arose that would potentially change the course of my career. Word reached me that there was an opening for a full-time faculty position at the university I had been serving. Given Nigeria's political landscape and societal intricacies, I knew the odds. In a country where connections often trump competence, securing such a position could be likened to a miracle. However, my life had been a series of miracles, each woven by the threads of grace and faith. I submitted the application with a prayer in my heart and confidence in my academic abilities. I then proceeded to the NYSC camp for the final ritual—receiving my national service completion certificate.

The program's climax was the passing-out parade, an event filled with pomp and pageantry befitting a gathering of Nigeria's future leaders. I felt a surge of pride as I was selected to be one of the flag-bearers during the parade. Carrying the flag in the company of other youth corps members, I felt the weight of the expectations and hopes of a nation on my shoulders. As we marched perfectly synchronously to the rhythmic beats of the drums, it was a moment frozen in time, capturing the essence of our youth, ambition, and patriotic zeal.

As the NYSC passing-out ceremony concluded, I felt a blend of emotions wash over me. The National Service Completion Certificate symbolized resilience, a diary of conquered challenges, and a summary of lessons learned. As I stood there, a certificate in hand, I felt like Daniel exiting the lion's den, and I knew that that was just the beginning of an unstoppable future. Though the road ahead was uncertain, especially concerning my aspiration to pursue my master's degree and potentially start a faculty career, my spirit was fortified.

Thus, as I stood there, I felt overwhelming gratitude. I was grateful for the spiritual nourishment that the church had provided, for the academic rigor that had honed my intellect, for the entrepreneurial leap that had kept my dreams afloat, and most importantly, for the Golden Grace that had guided me through it all.

I knew that each chapter of my life had prepared me for the next, and as I looked ahead, I was filled with a sense of hopeful anticipation. The road was long and undoubtedly filled with challenges, but I felt ready to embrace whatever lay ahead. With God's grace as my compass and a heart full of dreams, I was ready to step into the next chapter of my life. However, before venturing any further, I knew there were Christmas orders to fulfill.

SEVEN

Faith in Focus

The greatest achievement is not in never falling, but in rising again after you fall.

Vince Lombardi

"For I know the plans I have for you," declares the Lord, "plans for welfare and not for evil, to give you a future and a hope."

These words from Jeremiah 29:11 were my silent anthem as I diligently worked to meet my customers' Christmas requests. It was as if the air was imbued with a sense of divine purpose, a reminder that every stitch was a step closer to realizing God's plan for me.

When January rolled around, the season had been good—my fashion business had made substantial sales. With my heart full and my pockets not empty, I planned to travel west to visit my family. I wanted to present them with more than just seasonal greetings; I wanted to share tangible progress, a reason to extend my stay in the East.

On a brisk January morning, with the festive air now settling into a calm, I once again navigated the corridors of the computer science department. My purpose was twofold: a blend of business and uncertainty. Firstly, I was there to complete a straightforward transaction – delivering a dress I had crafted for a staff member and receiving my well-earned payment.

The second reason, however, was shrouded in doubt. I was there to check on the progress of my job application, specifically to see if it had even left the department head's desk. In truth, landing the job seemed like a distant dream, especially in a country where securing such positions often relied more on whom you knew and what you could offer rather than your qualifications or abilities.

Nevertheless, I was not overly consumed by the outcome of this job application. My focus was increasingly shifting toward the burgeoning success of my fashion design business. The past weeks, had been unexpectedly lucrative, with substantial earnings and an outpouring of praise from my clients. This surge of success bolstered my belief that my passion for fashion could flourish as a full-time career with continued hard work and dedication. It held the promise of sustaining my livelihood and funding my academic aspirations, easing the financial burdens of tuition and living expenses. This new year was unfolding with a clear agenda – to nurture and grow my entrepreneurial venture into something sustainable and fulfilling.

However, the atmosphere shifted dramatically when I entered the departmental secretary's office. It was as if I had walked into a room filled with angels singing "Glory to God in the Highest." Applause erupted, and congratulatory exclamations filled the air. To my utter disbelief, I had been offered a position as a Graduate Assistant[9] in the department. The Vice-Chancellor had approved my application without any strings attached—an unequivocal miracle.

"And my God will supply your every need according to his riches in glory in Christ Jesus." Philippians 4:19 [10]echoed in my mind. This was the divine providence I had always heard about but never fully grasped until that moment. It was as though God Himself had orchestrated these events,

---

[9] In Nigerian universities, a Graduate Assistant is usually a recent graduate pursuing postgraduate studies, who assists with teaching, research, and administrative tasks in their department. This position is an entry-level academic role that offers valuable experience for those aspiring to a career in academia.

[10] This verse from Philippians exemplifies the Christian belief in God's providence and care. It is often cited to encourage trust in God's provision in times of need.

aligning the stars, softening hearts, and opening doors that no man could shut. This is an affirmation that when God is the author of your story, not even sky-high obstacles can contain the unfolding plot. It solidified my belief that when you align your earthly pursuits with heavenly guidance, miracles are not just possible—they are inevitable.

To all those who walk in uncertainty, let my story be a beacon that lights your way. Know that no matter how insurmountable your challenges may seem, with faith as your shield and God as your guide, anything is possible.

> “When you align your earthly pursuits with heavenly guidance, miracles aren't just possible—they're inevitable.

So, my heart was aflutter as I accepted the offer and then proceeded on the planned journey to visit my family. Every mile under the bus's wheels felt like a stone lifted from years of uncertainty and struggle. I was not merely a traveler but a bearer of good news, a living testimony to the incredible ways God moves in our lives.

As I walked through the door of my family home, the atmosphere was charged with a palpable sense of anticipation. My father, bless his soul, wore an expression of fatherly curiosity, eager to understand what I had been doing in the East throughout the festive period. The air was thick with expectation as I shared the miraculous news.

“For everyone who asks receives; the one who seeks finds; and to the one who knocks, the door will be opened.” This Scripture from Matthew 7:8 reverberated as I unfolded the tale of my divine appointment as a Graduate Assistant in the computer science department. When the words finally left my lips, it was as if a dam had burst—filling the room with a torrent of cheers, laughter, and praises to God.

_“Train up a child in the way he should go; even when he is old, he will not depart from it.” - Proverbs 22:6 reverberated in my thoughts. My parents had done their part in instilling in me the values of hard work, faith, and integrity, and now it was my turn to honor their teachings by excelling in this new role.

So, dear reader, let this serve not just as a testament to what God has done in my life but as an assurance of what He can do in yours. In a world filled with uncertainties and closed doors, my story is a testament that with faith as your compass and God as your guide, you are bound for immeasurable blessings—beyond all you can ask or imagine.

After staying with my family for about a week, I returned to the East with a twist—I was coming back not out of failure but in triumph. That night, in the quiet of my room, overlooking the city that had become my field of dreams, I found a moment to pause. I reflected on the year that was—a tapestry of challenges, triumphs, and invaluable life lessons. I had come full circle, from ushering in church to serving my nation, from academic pursuits to entrepreneurial ventures. Each experience was a thread in the intricate fabric of my life; each challenges a knot that added strength to the weave.

As I stood on the threshold of new beginnings, my heart was filled with gratitude for the journey so far and a sense of eager anticipation for the chapters yet to be written. Moreover, above all, a quiet confidence that come what may, I was enfolded in a cloak of 'Golden Grace,' ready to embrace whatever lay ahead.

As I stepped onto the campus, the weight of my new role settled in. However, this was not a burden; it was a mantle I was ready to take up, knowing that the same God who had guided me thus far would not abandon me now.

"For we are His workmanship, created in Christ Jesus for good works, which God prepared beforehand, that we should walk in them." Ephesians 2:10 became my guiding scripture. I could now impact lives, shape young minds, and contribute to academia, even as I furthered my education. Balancing graduate studies with faculty responsibilities was a challenge, but every late-night grading session and every hour spent in research was a step toward fulfilling God's plan for me.

However, my fashion design business was not forgotten in all this hustle. It remained a passionate side pursuit, a creative outlet, and a financial buffer as I hired tailors and a manager to look after the business while I was away. However, more importantly, it stood as a constant reminder of God's faithfulness, a testimony that giving you a gift makes room for you.

Standing in front of the classroom, this time as a full-time faculty, I felt a sense of purpose and destiny wash over me. I looked into the eager eyes of my students, and I saw reflections of my younger self—hungry for knowledge, ripe for mentorship, and ready for challenges. At that moment, I understood this was not just a job or career. This was a calling.

By stepping into the role of a teacher, I found an opportunity to educate and fertile ground for my personal development. Teaching students my age or older was a humbling experience and a poignant reminder that leadership is not an age-dependent quality but a measure of one's ability and the sincerity of one's intentions.

In Nigeria, age is much more than a chronological measure of one's time on Earth. It is a social guideline for interpersonal interactions that dictates respect dynamics. In my culture, showing deference to someone older is not merely courteous; it is almost obligatory. Thus, teaching students who may be older requires a delicate balancing act. On the one hand, I had to establish my authority in the classroom; on the other, I had to navigate the intricate web of cultural norms concerning age and respect. It was a tightrope walk, but I managed with the grace and diplomacy I had honed over the years.

In those moments, I often thought of the grace that God bestows upon us—a grace that does not discriminate based on age, social standing, or any worldly measure. As you already know, dear reader, I term this "Golden Grace," a divine favor that equips us to navigate life's most complicated terrains. In the words of Bonhoeffer (1959), "Grace is free, but it is not cheap." It is a form of spiritual empowerment that requires us to rise above our human instincts and limitations, enabling us to act justly, love mercy, and walk humbly (Micah 6:8)[11].

The teachings of the Bible, particularly Matthew 20:26 - 'Whoever wants to become great among you must be your servant' - profoundly influenced my approach as an educator. This role was a spiritual journey, teaching me to wield authority with grace and to command respect through humility, academic rigor, and emotional intelligence. This approach, mirroring Christ's servant-leadership, enabled me to connect with students beyond age and cultural barriers, fostering respect not through demands but through earned trust.

This experience laid the foundation for relationships transcending

[11] Micah 6:8 (NIV): He has shown you, O mortal, what is good. And what does the Lord require of you? To act justly and to love mercy and to walk humbly[a] with your God.

traditional teacher-student dynamics, evolving into lasting friendships and collaborations. Such connections, fortified over time, proved the transformative power of divine grace in my life - turning potential conflicts into opportunities for mutual growth and understanding.

I learned that 'Golden Grace' is a universal principle available to anyone seeking to positively influence their environment, whether in academia, professional settings, or personal relationships. This grace, which I have embraced and witnessed in action, can transform challenges into opportunities for connection and growth. It is a principle that enriches lives, urging us to live by the wisdom of 1 Timothy 4:14 - 'Do not neglect the gift you have.' By embracing this grace, we overcome barriers and become agents of change in our lives and those around us.

EIGHT

Finding A Future

A marriage proposal is a question that influences the rest of your life, forever altering the future.

Nicholas Sparks

As a professor in the making, I became a harmonious blend of teaching, studying, and entrepreneurial ventures. Teaching was not just about imparting knowledge but also a learning experience for me. My life had a well-rounded rhythm: weekdays for academic and professional growth, late evenings and Saturdays for checking on my fashion design business, and Sundays dedicated to spiritual enrichment. During this period, I tried to make time for fun activities and explored intimate relationships, seeking a partner who shared my faith and values.

As I reached a juncture where my education and career began to blossom, an unexpected yet predictable shift occurred from my parents' perspective. Throughout my youth, discussions of romance and finding a life were barely explored and almost shrouded in a veil of unspoken taboo yet, as I stood on the threshold of what they deemed 'settling down age,' their interest in my romantic life suddenly sparked, igniting like a long-dormant flame.

It was as though, with my academic and professional milestones achieved, the next inevitable quest on life's journey was finding a soulmate. This newfound curiosity from my parents was laced with a mix of eagerness and subtle urgency, almost as if they were gently steering me toward a path they had hesitated to discuss before.

The irony of this situation was not lost on me. Here I was, equipped with degrees and accolades, prepared to navigate the complexities of the professional world, yet when it came to matters of the heart, I found myself on somewhat shaky ground. How could I expertly navigate the intricacies of romantic relationships when the topic had been a mere whisper in our household?

It seemed almost whimsical, the way my parents now envisioned a suitor – as if he would gracefully descend from the heavens, perfectly crafted to their expectations and ready to embark on a lifelong journey with me. This shift in their outlook was both amusing and bewildering.

However, despite this late bloom of interest in my romantic endeavors, I saw no pressure but a hope tinted with the colors of tradition and the hues of parental love. If anything, it highlighted the beautiful complexity of their affection and concern for me. They had always prioritized education and careers, viewing these as the pillars of a secure and prosperous future. As those pillars stood solid and unyielding, their focus gently shifted to the softer, more elusive aspect of life - love.

Their newfound interest in my romantic journey was a silent acknowledgment of a life stage unfolding, an unspoken admission that there was more to life than textbooks and boardrooms. It was, in essence, a testament to their desire to see me embrace the full spectrum of human experience - love, companionship, and the shared journey of finding a life partner.

In this, I found a delicate balance between amusement and appreciation. In their unique way, my parents were nudging me toward a future as rich in love and companionship as it was in knowledge and achievement. Their late-blooming interest in my romantic life, far from being an intrusion, became a gentle reminder of life's multifaceted beauty - a beauty that they, in their wisdom, hoped I would fully embrace.

This is a clarion call to all parents out there. Let this serve as a gentle reminder that your role in your children's lives extends beyond their academic and professional achievements. Do not shy away from guiding them through the intricate matters of the heart. Equip them with the wisdom and discernment they need to make godly choices. Please do not wait until it becomes a pressing issue or a subject of societal concern to start discussing it. Your timely counsel could be the anchor they need in a world where relationships are often rocky and transient.

In the grander scheme of things, I found peace in the idea that God is the author of my life story, including my romantic life. His timing is perfect, even when our patience wears thin. It is a virtue I hold dear as I navigate the complex intersection of faith, work, and personal life.

One Sunday, as I stood at the threshold of the church, hymns filling the air and sunlight streaming through the stained-glass windows, as I took my position by the entrance as an usher, ready to welcome the congregants, he walked in. He was a newcomer, his face unfamiliar but his presence unmistakable. Our eyes met, and there was a sense of recognition in that fleeting moment as if our souls had crossed paths in a past life.

"Good morning," I greeted, offering him a service program. "Welcome to our church."

"Thank you," he replied, his eyes meeting mine as he took the program. "I live in the neighborhood and was looking for a church close to my home."

He wasted no time integrating himself into the very fabric of our church community. Within mere weeks of his first visit, he enrolled in the Believers' Class, a foundational course aimed at deepening the understanding of new converts in the ways of Christ. His thirst for spiritual knowledge did not stop there; he went on to receive water baptism, a public declaration of his commitment to a new life in Christ.

However, his spiritual journey did not merely consist of rites and rituals; it was evident in his actions. He did the necessary training to become a worker in the church, a role that came with responsibilities far beyond attending Sunday services. Our church, you see, did not have the luxury of a permanent sanctuary. Instead, we gathered in a primary school classroom that transformed into a holy assembly every Sunday morning. This transformation required hard work, dedication, and an unwavering service commitment.

Likewise, serve, he did. He was often the first to arrive, sometimes as early as two hours before the service began. Armed with a broom in one hand and a heart full of devotion in the other, he took it upon himself to clean and rearrange the space, converting a humble classroom into a sanctuary where the Holy Spirit could dwell. His efforts were not lost on the congregation; they saw him as a man deeply committed to his faith, a blessing to the community, and a living example of servitude, and I could not help but be drawn to his seeming spiritual depth.

At first glance, his involvement in the church seemed like the natural enthusiasm of a devout Christian. He was always present, always active, and constantly engaged. However, as the weeks went by, a pattern began to emerge—a series of calculated moves designed to place him squarely in my orbit.

> "The church's sanctuary, in its true essence, should shield against manipulation, nurturing genuine spiritual growth.

In Sunday school, he was conspicuously vocal, raising his hand to ask probing questions or provide insightful answers. His contributions were often thought-provoking, eliciting nods of approval from the more seasoned congregation members. It was hard not to notice him, which was precisely the point.

After each service, he would linger around, ostensibly to offer support to the pastor or engage in deep theological conversations with church leaders. However, no matter how engrossed he was in these discussions, he never missed an opportunity to catch my eye, wave, or say hello. His presence was constant yet subtle—like a well-crafted melody, noticeable but not overwhelming.

Perhaps the most amusing of his swift moves was his decision to join the ushering unit. Under normal circumstances, ushering is a responsibility often left to those who have been long-standing church members because it requires arduous work. It was somewhat unconventional for a newcomer to express interest in this role. However, here he was, donning the usher's attire and standing alongside me, handing out programs and welcoming congregants.

The irony was not lost on me; we first met through the ushering department. His decision to join the unit seemed almost too convenient, but by this time, I was too captivated by his charm to question his motives. He would often use our time together in the ushering unit to engage me in conversation, asking about my week, family, and aspirations. Sometimes, we would find ourselves walking together after church activities, our steps in sync as we headed toward our respective homes.

Unbeknownst to me, each step he took was a piece of a giant puzzle that would take years to understand fully. I was drawn into his web, captivated by what appeared to be a shared spiritual journey but was, in reality, a carefully orchestrated plan. His calculated steps were a masterclass in persuasion, and I was his willing student, enchanted by his charisma and seemingly earnest spiritual commitment.

I was enamored by his attention and dedication, mistaking them as signs of a shared spiritual journey. His continual presence in my life, both within and outside the walls of our church, felt like a divine orchestration. A burgeoning relationship within the sanctity of a religious setting seemed almost predestined, an idea that was tacitly encouraged by the Christian literature and sermons that often extol the virtues of faith-based unions. After all, what could be more ideal than finding love in the very place where one also finds spiritual nourishment?

A few weeks after he joined the ushering unit, an opportunity presented itself for deeper dialogue. We found ourselves walking together from church, the sun casting golden hues over the horizon as if setting the stage for a momentous revelation. Then, he turned to me and broke the silence.

"I have something important to ask you," he said, his eyes locking onto mine, a slight nervous quiver in his voice.

"Go on," I replied, feeling a mix of anticipation and caution.

"I have been praying about this," he began, his voice tinged with a solemnity that immediately caught my attention. "I believe God is leading me, and I feel a deep conviction in my spirit. I am interested in marrying you."

The words lingered in the air, laden with tantalizing promises and complex undertones. For an instant, I was startled. Marriage is too weighty to be casually introduced, particularly soon after meeting someone—even within the sanctity of our faith-based journey. I suddenly realized that the proposal was everything I had been waiting for—a commitment, a sense of direction, and perhaps an end to the mounting pressure from my parents and society. Little did I know that his subsequent actions would soon unravel a web of illusions I was trapped in.

As I was lost in these ruminations, he broke the silence again. "Will you be my fiancée?" he asked, his eyes searching for an answer even before my lips could form one.

The earnest looks in his eyes and the invocation of divine guidance made it clear that his proposal was anything but casual. At that moment, I stood at a crossroads. On one side lay the possibility of a love story scripted in the heavens, reminiscent of the biblical love between Ruth and Boaz, where divine providence and human choice beautifully intersect (Ruth 4:13)12. On the other side stood the rational, cautious part of me, informed by scriptural wisdom, spiritual discernment, educational background, and life experiences.

As these thoughts swirled in my mind, I knew the decision before me should not be taken lightly. It was a matter of eternal consequence that required my emotional heart and rational mind to be in harmony. Therefore, my response had to be as thoughtful as the proposal itself.

As we continued walking, I responded with honesty and grace. "Your words are significant, and I appreciate your openness. However, this is a life-altering decision that requires prayerful discernment from both of us," I said, looking into his eyes. Thus, with that walk and that conversation, our relationship entered a new phase—one filled with the promise of love but also laden with the solemn responsibility of choice and discernment. It was a dramatic twist, setting the stage for a journey neither of us could have fully anticipated.

Fortunately for me, the church was preparing for our annual national convention in Lagos. I always looked forward to this because it allowed me to connect with God in a serene environment and seize the opportunity to visit my family back in the West. I asked if he would be coming with me to the convention so we could both pray about the proposal, but he gave what seemed to be a genuine excuse—the notice was too short. Disappointed but

---

[12] Ruth 4:13: "So Boaz took Ruth and she became his wife. When he made love to her, the Lord enabled her to conceive, and she gave birth to a son."

resolute, I decided to go alone, armed with one major prayer request—the proposal. I promised to give him an answer after returning from the convention.

With my heart brimming with questions and one major prayer request—the proposal—I embarked on the journey to the convention. Surrounded by the serenity of the environment and the unity of thousands of believers, I felt like I had entered the Biblical 'secret place' described in Psalm 91:1, 13a haven where I could hear God's voice directly.

Amid a profound spiritual worship session, I was enveloped in an overwhelming sense of tranquility, my hands lifted in a gesture of total surrender. Then, a poignant message resonated through the sanctuary, uttered by the minister at the altar. He said that someone was caught in the throes of indecision among the congregation, and he conveyed that the Lord had a message for this person: their waiting period had ended, and their time had arrived.

This message struck a chord, making me feel a sudden and strong conviction about the marriage proposal I had been contemplating. It felt as though the Divine had personally reached into the depths of my soul, affirming this union with a powerful echo.

As I joined the rest of our church members to embark on the return journey to the East, my spirit soared with joy and gratitude, buoyed by the certainty that God had responded to my heartfelt prayers.

Although I was imbued with newfound clarity, I believed it also called for earthly validation. So, my first order of business upon returning to the East was to consult with our pastor. So, as I sought his counsel, the pastor asked me a pivotal question: "Are you convinced you have heard from God?" My response was unhesitating: "Yes, I am." However, he cautioned me, "Tread carefully and continue in prayer." The pastor's advice echoed the Biblical imperative in 1 Thessalonians 5:21: "Test everything; hold fast to what is good." This was a sobering reminder that even within the confines of divine revelation, there remains a place for human caution and ongoing spiritual discernment.

---

[13] Psalm 91:1: "Whoever dwells in the shelter of the Most High will rest in the shadow of the Almighty."

In the long run, I was swept off my feet, finally captivated by the prospect of a life partner who shared my faith and passion for serving the community. I was confident I was on the right track and communicated my decision to him. I was also excited about sharing the good news with my family afterward.

Armed with divine assurance and pastoral counsel, I arranged to meet the man with whom I had hoped I would. Spend the rest of my life. When we met, the emotional atmosphere was almost palpable, yet it was as if the clarity of divine purpose had pierced it. I looked into his eyes—the very eyes that had once been the source of a thousand questions—and with a gentle and firm voice, I said, "Yes, I will marry you."

It was as though the heavens had orchestrated this moment like an angelic choir stamped our earthly union with a divine seal. However, I felt the need to introduce a note of caution. "But," I added, articulating each word carefully, "I believe we still need more time to know each other truly."

However, amidst the euphoria and the spiritual certitude, there was one glaring omission that I could not overlook: My soon-to-be husband had not sought the counsel of our pastor regarding this life-altering decision. This struck me as a red flag, an incongruity in what initially looked like a divinely orchestrated plan.

From a theological standpoint, Scripture places a high value on the authenticity and integrity of relationships. The Apostle Paul's letters are replete with exhortations to live in love, sincerity, and mutual respect. In a faith that considers Christ's selfless love its cornerstone, any form of manipulation for personal gain becomes especially troubling. Although the church setting is a natural environment for relationships to blossom, it should not be a place of personal manipulation.

In hindsight, what seemed like shared spiritual growth between my suitor and me was a series of well-planned actions to win my affection and trust. They were steps taken not in the spirit of mutual discovery and love but in pursuing a pre-defined outcome. Moreover, while the methods may have been effective, the cost—measured in ethical compromise and, later, in emotional pain—was high, as would be unfolded in this memoir.

NINE

The Red Flags

When you ignore the red flags because you want to see the good, the bad becomes your reality.

Germany Kent

Shortly after I joyfully accepted the marriage proposal, the atmosphere between us subtly yet noticeably shifted. The man who had once won me over with his eloquent expressions of faith and love gradually began to cross lines by making sexual advances.

Confusion clouded my mind as I grappled with this sudden change. "Wait, what is happening here?" I questioned internally, feeling a growing sense of unease. This was the same man who had just pledged a future with me and shared my values and beliefs. Why was he now hastily pushing past the boundaries our shared faith had always taught us to hold sacred?

I was voicing a reminder, hoping to steer us back onto the familiar, respectful ground. "As faithful believers, I think we should wait until marriage," I asserted, my voice laced with a firmness that masked my inner turmoil.

To my dismay, his response was dismissive, brushing off my concerns with a casualness that jolted me. He laughed lightly; a sound that once brought me joy now seemed tinged with impatience. "You are being too traditional," he chided gently. "We are in love; love like ours does not need to wait. It is a celebration of our future together."

I remember feeling a cold shock at his words, as if a bucket of ice water had been poured over me, drenching my skin and seeping into my bones. Time seemed to freeze; the air around us thickened with unsaid truths and shattered illusions. His words, once a source of warmth and comfort, now echoed in my ears like the distant, chilling howl of winter wind. My heart raced, pounding against my ribcage in a frantic plea for escape, while my mind reeled, trying to grasp the stark reality his words unveiled. It was a moment of profound betrayal, where the foundation of trust we had built seemed to crumble into dust, leaving me standing alone in the ruins of what I had believed to be an unbreakable bond.

This entire situation set off loud, clanging alarm bells in my head. It was a glaring red flag, gloomy and undeniable. The spiritual and emotional connection I thought we had was overshadowed by a physical expectation I was not ready to meet. His willingness to bypass our shared values and beliefs for immediate gratification was deeply concerning. It made me question not only his intentions but the very foundation of our relationship. The man from whom I had expected love and respect now seemed to prioritize his desires over the mutual understanding and commitment we had cultivated.

I found myself wrestling with a peculiar set of circumstances. I was at a stage where I felt overwhelmed by the scarcity of time. My professional commitments were demanding, and my personal life was equally challenging. The biological clock was not helping either. The failed relationships of my past weighed heavily on me, and the idea of starting anew was daunting. My parents, who had always been supportive, were becoming increasingly restless, eagerly awaiting the day they could see me walk down the aisle. It felt like I was carrying the hopes and expectations of myself and my entire family.

This intersection of personal, biological, and societal expectations created a powerful pressure cooker. I rationalized his behavior, thinking, "Well, a bird in the hand is worth ten in the bush." A pattern of self-blame and rationalization emerged, almost as if I was making excuses for him. After years of searching and failed relationships, here was a man who seemed to have a stable job and was willing to marry me. Shouldn't I be content with what I had? This emotional labor is involved in maintaining a facade of 'everything is fine,' it can be draining, as observed by Hochschild (1983).[14]

Navigating this predicament, I remained steadfast in my resolve, tactfully resisting his advances while emphasizing the importance of waiting until marriage. However, this brought another critical aspect to the forefront – our plans for marriage. Seeking clarity, I broached the subject, eager to understand his vision for our future together. His response, however, blindsided me completely.

He hesitated before revealing that he was not ready to tie the knot yet, citing financial responsibilities toward his immediate family as the primary reason. He elaborated, explaining that entering into marriage would be financially burdensome and that he could not contemplate starting his own family while still having significant obligations toward his birth family. This revelation, far from being a mere red flag, felt like a distress signal, a flare shot into the sky signaling an emergency.

The contradiction was apparent and unsettling. Here was a man who had pursued a romantic relationship with me, even pushing the boundaries of physical intimacy. He was now reluctant to move forward into the commitment he had initially seemed so eager to embrace. It raised fundamental questions about his priorities and the sincerity of his intentions in our relationship.

This juncture was a moment of profound realization for me. The man I had envisioned a future with, who I believed shared my values and life goals, was now presenting a reality entirely different from what I had anticipated. The situation demanded serious reflection and reevaluation of the relationship and its direction.

The situation presented a baffling paradox. A man well into his thirties, he held a respectable and stable position as senior personnel in state government service. Yet, his demeanor and reasoning felt oddly juvenile, more akin to a

[14] Emotional labor, a term coined by Arlie Russell Hochschild in "The Managed Heart," describes managing personal emotions to fulfill the emotional requirements of a job or relationship.

teenager's evasive tactics than that of a mature, responsible adult. This incongruity was striking and deeply disconcerting. Despite his age and solid professional standing, his reluctance to commit seriously contradicts the maturity and responsibility typically expected in adult relationships.

As a young faculty with a stable and promising career path, I could not help but feel even more perplexed by his stance. It was not just about emotional readiness; financially, we were both in positions that would comfortably allow us to not only start our family but also extend support to our respective birth families. His argument about financial constraints seemed flimsy, especially given our combined potential.

During this conversation, I could not help but mention our blessed circumstance, emphasizing that we could manage familial responsibilities while building our future together. Drawing on the biblical principle that "two are better than one" (Ecclesiastes 4:9-12) and the idea that "two shall chase thousands" (Deuteronomy 32:30), I highlighted how our union could amplify our strength and capacity to care for those dear to us.

He then dropped another startling revelation. He suggested we should plan toward starting a family, but we must postpone having children until after he has "settled his family." Despite my better judgment, I reluctantly agreed, swayed by the Biblical teaching that love endures all things. I told myself, "Marriage is a lifelong commitment; as long as we have love, the timing of children can be flexible." This concession, while seemingly minor then, would haunt me for years.

The complexity escalated when he suggested a trip to Lagos to introduce me to his family and demonstrate his seriousness about the relationship. At first, this seemed like a positive step, but the joy was short-lived. When we were about to board the bus for our journey, he claimed he did not have enough money to cover the trip. The financial responsibility, embarrassingly, fell on me.

"You have got to be kidding me!" My mind screamed. This was not just a financial burden; it was an emotional one. I was meeting my future in-laws for the first time, and here I was, shouldering the cost of our journey. It felt like a slap in the face.

At that moment, as I paid for our bus tickets and throughout the episodes, I constantly battled with my internal compass, which kept telling me that something was fundamentally wrong. Why had I ignored my better judgment and put his needs before mine? These questions loomed large, and the answers were deeply unsettling. I realized I had ignored several warning signs, entrapped by his promises and my self-imposed deadlines.

In hindsight, I should have consulted someone I trusted—my pastors, parents, a family friend, or even a relationship counselor. The Bible itself extols the virtues of seeking wise counsel (Proverbs 11:14).[15] I had chosen to navigate these treacherous waters alone, convinced that love would see us through. That decision would come at a considerable cost.

> " The most reliable promises are those we make to ourselves—to respect our boundaries and honor our self-worth.

As we embarked on the trip to Lagos, emotions engulfed me. A part of me was ecstatic at the thought of finally settling down, of building a future with a man I believed loved me. On the other hand, a nagging voice inside me kept questioning the recent developments, the financial imbalances, and the moral compromises.

The journey evolved into a financial saga that I had not anticipated; from covering the cost of our bus fares to paying for our meals and even purchasing the gifts we intended to present to our families, I shouldered more financial responsibilities than I had expected. However, these expenses paled in comparison to what came next.

He approached me with a proposal that required a substantial financial commitment from my end. He asked for a loan, an amount that almost totaled four months of my hard-earned salary, explaining that he needed it to finalize the payment for a plot of land in Lagos. "This will be our future home," he assured me, his words painting a picture of a shared life together in this new place. His voice had a convincing tone of certainty, a promise of a life we would build together.

Wanting to believe in the vision he laid out before me, my heart overruled my head. I saw this as more than a financial transaction; it was an investment in our future. So, I handed over a significant portion of my savings, entrusting him with my finances and the hopes and dreams accompanying

[15] "Where there is no guidance, a people falls', but in an abundance of counselors, there is safety." (Proverbs 11:14)

that sum.

This situation perfectly exemplified what Greer (2010)[16] termed "manipulative generosity," a tactic where one partner uses the promise of future benefits to gain present advantages. This kind of manipulation, coupled with financial imbalance, is a glaring indicator of a dysfunctional relationship. In my case, these were not just subtle hints but glaring red flags that should have prompted immediate caution.

I offer my readers this advice: Be vigilant and trust your instincts; if a relationship feels unbalanced or manipulative, it may be time to reassess and protect your well-being.

As I sat in a room shrouded in the dim twilight of my own making, I reflected on the path that led me to this point—a path paved with illusions, with the mirage of promises that evaporated before my very eyes. It was as if I had been walking through a desert, guided by what I believed to be an oasis of love, only to find mirages of affection that dissipated into the harsh winds of reality. A profound sense of betrayal washed over me—betrayal not just by my future husband but myself for disregarding the portents, the foreboding omens I had chosen to dismiss as mere imperfections.

The signs were there, as glaring as a crimson sunset over a barren landscape. The absence of a birthday gift, a seemingly small omission, spoke volumes. No gift ever materialized—neither for my birthday nor any other occasion. "Ah," I thought then, "It is just material. Love is more than gifts." However, he never failed to find a reason to avoid paying for our meals out, always lamenting his perennial brokenness and nudging me to cover the bill. "I will pay you back," he often said, but those promises vanished like mist in the morning sun.

I often reached into my purse, paying for dinners and fulfilling needs, all under the misguided belief that my financial stability could shield his fragile ego.

His indulgence was not limited to financial matters alone. I recall shared meals where he would voraciously devour the lion's share, leaving me with

[16] Greer's analysis delves into the intricacies of how promises of future gains can be strategically used to exploit and control in the present, creating a skewed power dynamic that can undermine the very foundation of a relationship.

mere crumbs. His appetite was ravenous, consuming not just food but also the core of our relationship—my contributions, sacrifices, and even my identity. I want to clarify that this observation is not meant to humiliate or tarnish his image. Instead, it is an honest account of our lived experience, an experience that people who know him can readily corroborate. The point here is not to focus on his eating habits per se but to highlight how such an essential aspect of life became a microcosm of the imbalance and selfishness that pervaded our relationship. This is to provide a genuine representation of my experiences to impart valuable lessons.

However, what lingers in my memory, casting a shadow over those days, is the collection of Christian literature on courtship I had brought back from our church convention. Full of optimism, I placed them on the table, imagining evenings spent together, growing spiritually as an aspiring couple. Each time I encouraged him to join me in exploring these readings, he evaded, giving excuses that, in my desire to be understanding, I accepted too readily.

> "Recognizing the red flags in a relationship is the first step towards steering your life's ship away from impending storms.

In a hopeful gesture, I once presented him with a specially chosen study guide for young bachelors preparing for marriage. I offered it to him alongside his favorite shortbread snacks, envisioning it as a gentle nudge toward our collective spiritual enrichment. However, the universe seemed to play a cruel joke on my aspirations. When I next opened my trash bin, a heart-sinking sight greeted me. There, amidst the crumpled wrappers of the snacks, lay the pages of the Christian literature, discarded and ignored. He had relished the treats but cast aside the essence of the wisdom they contained.

I tried to downplay this incident, labeling it as a minor oversight, insignificant in the larger canvas of our love. However, deep down, I knew this was no mere oversight. His act of discarding those pages was a profound rejection of our shared path in faith, a blasphemous act that belittled the spiritual essence of our intended union. It was a clear sign that our values and visions for the future were misaligned, a realization that I was perhaps too reluctant to acknowledge fully at the time.

My story is a haunting parable woven with ignored red flags, silenced intuition, and forsaken self-respect. Love is a powerful force in its purest form, but it is not a panacea for the glaring flaws and toxic behaviors that can poison a relationship. Love alone cannot bear the weight of disrespect, inequality, and emotional negligence. Here, we must invoke the wisdom of the Biblical King Solomon: "Above all else, guard your heart, for everything you do flows from it" (Proverbs 4:23).

If you find yourself trapped in a pattern of ignoring red flags, take a step back and reassess. Consult trusted advisors, spiritual leaders, friends, family, or professionals. Remember, boundaries are not just lines but fortifications for self-respect and well-being. Maintain your integrity, even when faced with the blinding allure of love or the weight of emotional or societal expectations. Your future self will thank you.

Now, as I turn the pages of this dolorous chapter in my life, I am not filled with regret but with a newfound appreciation for the lessons that have shaped me. This chapter of my life has taught me to be cautious, to listen to my instincts, and to never compromise on what truly matters. It was a painful chapter but also a chapter of enlightenment. A chapter that made me realize the most reliable promises are the ones we make to ourselves—to listen to our intuition, respect our boundaries, and never compromise our self-worth. Moreover, it is a lesson I hope you take to heart as you navigate your journey of love and life.

TEN

The Unplanned Union

In the arithmetic of love, one plus one equals everything, and two minus one equals nothing. But remember, it's not the speed at which the equation is solved, but the correctness of the solution that matters.

Mignon McLaughlin

A sense of relief washed over me as we returned from visiting our families. It was as though the endless conversations and pressures surrounding marriage were finally taking a tangible form. Sitting beside my fiancé, the bus rumbling beneath us, I felt a mix of emotions swirling within me. Relief was intertwined with a nagging sense of dilemma. Despite the red flags that fluttered in my mind, a part of me clung to the hope that perhaps I was steering our future in the right direction.

I whispered a prayer under my breath, almost inaudible amidst the hum of the tires on the road. "God, guide me," I murmured, seeking divine intervention. "Grant me clarity and wisdom."

As the landscape whisked by, my mind wandered to a realization that felt like a testament to divine intervention. Throughout my college years, my health had been in a state of constant battle against the vicious duo of malaria and typhoid fever. My life then was punctuated by frequent hospital visits, an exhausting routine that seemed to have no end. However, something shifted miraculously after the disillusionment from my previous relationship and my conscious decision to step back from sexual entanglements. My health began to improve, an improvement so dramatic it felt like a rebirth.

This correlation between my emotional state and physical well-being could not be mere coincidence. I pondered the biblical perspective that our body is the temple of the Holy Spirit (1 Corinthians 6:19-20),[17] and it dawned on me that perhaps, in preserving my emotional and spiritual purity, I had inadvertently nurtured my physical health. It was as if my body was responding to the sanctity of my decisions, aligning my physical well-being with my spiritual resolve.

However, returning to our familiar terrains, I was under increasing pressure from my partner, challenging my values and our trust. It was as if he knew exactly what to say, how, and when. He had calculated each word, each glance, each touch. Moreover, in that moment of vulnerability, I fell—like a pack of cards tumbling down. I compromised my sacred vow of abstinence.

"This has to end," I murmured as I tried to reassess the relationship and consider the difficult decision to end it. And then, I started plotting my exit strategy, strategizing each move and contemplating the best time to let him know it was over. However, something paralyzed me each time I braced myself to confront him. Was it fear? Shame? Or the crushing weight of expectations from our families and the society we lived in? The mere thought of the fallout stifled me.

Unfortunately, like a wretched dog returning to its vomit, after falling into the sin of fornication, my health deteriorated. First, it was malaria, an old foe that came to haunt me. Then typhoid fever joined the fray. As if that were not enough, an excruciating pain began to radiate through my backbone, so intense that it landed me in the hospital for days.

I had barely settled into my hospital room when my fiancé walked in. He looked genuinely concerned, his eyes filled with a warmth that I had almost forgotten was possible for him to express. He asked how I was feeling,

---

[17] "Do you not know that your bodies are temples of the Holy Spirit, who is in you, whom you have received from God? You are not your own; you were bought at a price. Therefore honor God with your bodies" (1 Corinthians 6:19-20).

inquired about my treatment, and even cracked a joke to lift my spirits. At that moment, I wondered, "Could I have been wrong about him?"

His compassion was so tender and genuine that it left me questioning my earlier judgments. Maybe I had been too harsh, too quick to jump to conclusions. His visits became more frequent, and with each visit, he seemed to metamorphose into the man I had initially fallen in love with. By the time I was discharged, I felt almost grateful for the hospitalization; it seemed to have brought a much-needed reset button to our relationship. Maybe we just needed more time to get to know each other. Oh, how I wish I were right.

Weeks passed, and something felt off. I started to feel nauseous frequently. My first instinct was to blame it on some residual effect from my hospitalization. However, then I realized—I had missed my period for about three weeks[18]. A heavy weight settled over me. I knew I had to confirm what I already suspected but was too afraid to admit it.

In those days, pregnancy tests were not as easily accessible as today. Summoning all the courage I could muster, I went to the lab. The tension in the air was palpable as I waited for the results. When the lab technician returned, the expression on her face said it all even before she handed me the positive result.

> “When faced with life's unexpected turns, the strength of our faith and character shines brightest.

"Oh God, what have I done?" There I was, caught in a web of my own making, wrestling with choices, consequences, and a future irrevocably altered. It was a moment of reckoning, a stark, unflinching mirror reflecting the life-altering cost of a single lapse in judgment.

And then, I informed him, but his manipulation took on a new dimension—a tighter grip that seemed to choke the air out of me.

As I broke the news, his face drained of color. There was no flicker of excitement, no joyous exclamation. Instead, his eyes were filled with a muddled mix of fear and anxiety. His reaction was eerily reminiscent of how teenage couples might respond to an unplanned pregnancy—entire of dread and a sense of impending doom. Such a situation might be understandably overwhelming for teenagers, but we were both adults, financially stable, and

[18] Missing a menstrual period is often the first sign of pregnancy, but it can also be influenced by other factors like stress, hormonal imbalances, or health issues.

ostensibly committed to a future together. What, then, was there to fear?

"What are your plans?" he inquired, his tone laced with caution, as though the life burgeoning within me was a burden I alone should bear. His words struck me, harsh and jarring, like an unexpected slap across the face. Instantly, my mind was catapulted back to a previous conversation, where he had cautiously articulated his desire to postpone having children, even after marriage, citing the financial implications of raising children. His words from that day—his caution about postponing children—reverberated in my ears, hauntingly clear.

Nevertheless, here I was, pregnant with his child, our wedding vows still unspoken. His question phrased singularly as 'my' plans, unsettled me deeply. Was he subtly shifting the responsibility, implying that the pregnancy and its consequences were mine to deal with alone? Was there an unspoken suggestion, a nudge toward an unthinkable solution like abortion lurking behind his words?

"God forbid," I thought.

Then, as if tuning into my thoughts, he broke my trance. "This baby changes everything," he said, trying to feign a sense of responsibility that was glaringly absent when it mattered. "We need to think about our future," he added as if the future was some distant land, not a life growing inside me.

"Our future?" I snapped back, my voice tinged with bitterness. "Or your future?"

It was a rhetorical question I did not need an answer to. I already knew. The manipulation had grown tighter, but I could not stop thinking about protecting my unborn child.

We subsequently agreed to revisit our families to announce the pregnancy, but this was a decision that weighed heavily on my heart and soul. While it is essential to seek the counsel and blessings of family members, especially in significant life changes, diving headlong into this without due self-examination can be a minefield. The Bible cautions against haste: "Desire without knowledge is not good—how much more will hasty feet miss the way!" (Proverbs 19:2, NIV).

We began by first visiting his parents to discuss our plans. They welcomed our news with an open mind, assuring us of their support regardless of my family's decision. Buoyed by their acceptance, we set out to inform my family, a journey that felt more daunting with each passing mile.

Arriving at my family home, we were seated in the living room, a familiar space now charged with an almost palpable tension. The room fell into a heavy silence following my announcement, each second stretching out interminably as I awaited my father's reaction. My heart raced, thumping audibly in my chest as the anticipation built.

The atmosphere in the room took on the gravity of a courtroom, with me in the uneasy role of the defendant. I felt every gaze upon me, every unspoken thought weighing heavily in the air. It was as if I was bracing for a judge's verdict, which held the power to alter the course of my life significantly.

You see, in my community, the societal disgrace and disdain for unwed mothers is very intense and can be unbearable, not just for the woman but for her entire family. So, you would understand that when I found out I was pregnant, it felt like my world had crumbled. I saw the life I had so meticulously built start to unravel.

Finally, my father spoke, "How many weeks is the pregnancy?"

"About four weeks," I stammered.

It was as if a weight had been lifted off his shoulders. And then, almost immediately, his mind began racing toward logistical concerns—how to plan a shotgun wedding.

"We need to start planning the wedding before the pregnancy becomes noticeable," he said, his words slicing through the thick air of the room.

This situation, as explored in a study by Geronimus (2003), highlights the psychosocial toll such rapid transitions to motherhood and marriage can have on an individual. The study underscores the immense stress and anxiety that often accompany these hurried life changes, mainly when they occur outside the socially accepted timelines. Moreover, the societal stigma associated with being an unwed mother, a sentiment still profoundly ingrained in conservative communities, adds a layer of emotional complexity.

Geronimus (2003) aptly points out that these personal milestones, when rushed, are further complicated by prevailing cultural norms and expectations. These societal pressures can heavily influence family advice, often pushing individuals toward decisions prioritizing social acceptance over personal well-being. The weight of these expectations can be overwhelming, especially when they conflict with one's readiness or mental and emotional health.

So, you can imagine the turmoil these factors were stirring within me. I was grappling with the sudden shift in my life's trajectory. I also had to navigate societal expectations and cultural norms that dictate handling such situations. It was a delicate balance between honoring my values and conforming to the expectations that surrounded me, a balance that was as challenging as necessary.

In southwestern Nigeria, where my roots lie, a wedding is a community event. Traditionally, Yoruba weddings unfold in three distinct phases. The first is the introduction, a modest gathering where the two families officially meet. This is followed by the traditional marriage ceremony, which often occurs back-to-back with the white, or religious, wedding. The whole event is a grand affair that usually takes months, if not years, of meticulous planning.

My father, eager to protect our family's reputation, arranged with his future in-laws to fix the wedding on the next available date on our local church's calendar. Easter Saturday it was.

We returned to the East with the weight of our decisions hanging over us like a dark cloud. A new life was growing inside me, but the looming dread of marrying a man filled with red flags I had already noticed was alongside this joy. Our families had fixed the introduction ceremony, and we had to miss it because we had to channel all our resources into planning this expedited wedding.

The next step was informing our church pastor. As we walked into his office, I took a deep breath, my stomach knotted with apprehension.

We were met with a compassionate yet disappointed response upon revealing the delicate circumstances to their pastor. The pastor informed us that, given the church's doctrine, he had no alternative but to suspend us from the church duties for a certain period.[19] Despite the weight of the

---

[19] This action of suspension by our church is consistent with the Christian doctrine that view premarital relationships as contradictory to biblical teachings (1 Corinthians 6:18-20).

decision, he assured us we would remain in his prayers. He reiterated, however, that we were required to come early to church and sit at the back, but we would not be allowed to serve in any capacity.

In those days, being a church worker was not just about showing up; it was about embodying the doctrine and principles of the church community. 'Obedience' was the watchword. I remember times when being late for a workers' meeting could result in extra chores or standing throughout the meeting. And now? Things have changed so much in this generation, but that is a story for another time.

So, there we were, relegated to the back rows of the church, stripped of our duties. We could not serve in any capacity, and it was humbling. However, this period also gave me something invaluable: time to reflect and seek God's face for mercy.

Now, let us talk about the wedding preparations. Ah, the hustle and bustle of making sure everything is perfect! However, here is the kicker: the burden of paying for the wedding fell squarely on my shoulders. My fiancé, who should have been my partner in all this, was nowhere to be found financially. His manipulation intensified, and I knew why. He knew I was vulnerable and had no choice; after all, I was already carrying his child, and both families had given us their blessings for the wedding.

Every time an expense came up, he had an excuse. "Oh, I cannot contribute to that right now," or "Something urgent came up." Even his wedding clothes, our wedding rings, and the traditional attire for our four parents became my responsibility.

Now, let us pause for a moment, dear reader. If you ever think you have no choice concerning your future, snap out of it. You always have a choice. In my case, I felt cornered, but was I indeed? No. I could have put my foot down and demanded financial transparency and contribution. However, the cultural and emotional factors made me feel like I had no voice.

So here I was, facing a complex emotional landscape. On one hand, I was experiencing the joy and anticipation of bringing a new life into the world. On the other hand, the emotional toll of a lopsided relationship and the societal judgments were draining. I grappled with complex decisions about my future, family, and identity. The church suspension, the judgmental glances from some community members who could spot a pregnancy right after it is conceived, the financial pressure—it was a lot to take.

However, it was also a period of intense spiritual growth. I found strength in those quiet moments at the back of the church. I realized that while I might be physically sitting in the back, I did not have to take a backseat in my own life. I decided then and there that no matter what the situation, I would take control, not just for my sake but for the sake of my unborn child, and I began to draw upon an inner reservoir of resilience I never knew I had.

Another pressing matter compounded the weight of these responsibilities: my master's thesis defense.

At this point, I had already completed my coursework and was in the final stages of preparing for the defense. However, the overwhelming demands of organizing a wedding and preparing for a baby—each a monumental project in its own right—made it virtually impossible to focus on my academic obligations. The result was a missed opportunity that carried significant repercussions.

In my academic institution, Master's thesis defenses were conducted annually and as a group. Missing the scheduled defense meant waiting an entire year for the next opportunity. So, there I was, cornered into delaying a pivotal moment in my academic career, all because life had thrown too many curveballs my way. The lesson is the importance of balancing and setting priorities, especially when juggling multiple life-altering projects. Sometimes, understanding your limits is the first step toward achieving your goals.

So, life will throw curveballs at you, but remember, you have a choice in how you respond. Do not allow societal pressures or manipulative partners to dictate your actions. Seek divine guidance, trust your instincts, and never underestimate your power to turn things around.

In hindsight, I now understand the importance of balancing cultural and familial expectations with personal, emotional, and psychological needs. While marriage and family are communal institutions, they are built on the individual well-being of the people involved. You cannot pour from an empty cup; you must prioritize your emotional health to contribute meaningfully to a partnership or community.

So, as you read this, understand that sometimes the most challenging decisions require balancing respect for tradition and community expectations against your well-being. It is okay to step back and reflect, even when faced with urgent decisions. Remember, life's most profound lessons often come in the garb of difficult choices.

Designs of Destiny

ELEVEN

The Wedding Bells

A successful marriage requires falling in love many times, always with the same person.

Mignon McLaughlin

Finally, the wedding day arrived, and the church bells echoed their joyful toll, marking the sanctity of the holy union that was about to take place. Guests dressed in their finest, and friends wielding cameras to capture the monumental moment—all were gathered to celebrate a promise of eternal love. The atmosphere was electric, blending anticipation, joy, and, perhaps, divine intervention.

However, beneath the grandeur of gowns, another sound was almost drowned by the jubilant atmosphere. It was the soft, almost imperceptible quivering of a heart. My heart.

While the world saw a bride walking down the aisle, radiant in her white gown, they did not see the storm of emotions churning inside me. A mix of hope, fear, and disquiet that refused to settle. It was as if the core of my being was sending out distress signals—a lighthouse warning of hidden rocks on a seemingly clear path. The bells tolled, but a silent alarm sounded within me, cautioning me that all might not be as it seemed. As I took each step down the aisle, it felt like I was walking a tightrope between two worlds. On one side was the promise of a life filled with love and companionship; on the other was an abyss of unknown challenges and potential heartbreak.

However, despite the internal turmoil, a glimmer of hope remained. Perhaps it was faith, perhaps it was desperation, or maybe it was just the innate human tendency to be optimistic even when the odds are stacked against us. I held onto that glimmer, believing against all logic that perhaps love would eventually blossom from this hastily formed union.

And then, as the moment for the exchange of rings drew near, a sudden realization washed over me—a gut-wrenching, heart-stopping realization. The rings were missing. Amid the anxiety that had clouded my morning, I had forgotten to put them in the box being carried by the ring bearer. Alas, I had left the rings at home! A brief panic gripped me, freezing me to the core. Then, instinctively, I whispered hurriedly to my chief bridesmaid, urging her to retrieve these vital symbols of eternal love.

Time, however, was not on our side. The pastor, sensing the delay in retrieving the rings yet unaware of its cause, made an executive decision that would later seem almost prophetic. In a creative and meaningful gesture, he replaced the traditional exchange of rings with the holding up of a Bible – the Holy Scripture. He solemnly pronounced us husband and wife with this sacred book in hand.

This unconventional twist, as unexpected as it was, brought me an unexpected sense of solace. The pastor's explanation further deepened this sentiment. He described how the Bible in our ceremony represented a more profound commitment than any symbolized by rings. By referencing Hebrews 4:12,[20] he talked about God's word's living and active nature, "sharper than any two-edged sword, piercing to the division of soul and spirit, of joints and marrow, and discerning the thoughts and intentions of the heart."

At that moment, something extraordinary happened. The atmosphere felt charged with human emotion and perhaps with divine intervention. The Bible—God's Word—had replaced the rings, and I could not help but

[20] Hebrews 4:12: "For the word of God is living and active, sharper than any two-edged sword, piercing to the division of soul and of spirit, of joints and of marrow, and discerning the thoughts and intentions of the heart."

wonder if this was a message from the Almighty Himself. Was it perhaps a sign, a divine caution, that our union needed more than just the material symbolism of rings? Was God signaling that the foundation of this marriage should be His Word and not just earthly vows? Well, you see, dear reader, while rings are a beautiful symbol, they are material objects—created by humans, subject to wear and tear and, eventually, erosion. The Bible, however, is eternal, a lasting testament to the promises and teachings that transcend our mortal lives.

> “ In every echo of a wedding bell, there lies a hidden lesson of love, resilience, and the courage to face the unknown.

So, as I took the final step to say "I do" to the man who would become my husband, I took a deep breath. In that breath were prayers for strength, wisdom, and the grace to navigate the jumble of the married life I was about to enter. The minister began to speak, and as we exchanged vows, I could not help but wonder which promises would stand the test of time and which would crumble under its weight. While I had missed the traditional moment where the ring is slid onto the finger for all to witness, this deviation from expectation was perhaps part of a larger divine design for our marriage.

Following this unconventional but significant ceremony, the wedding rings, which had been delayed, eventually arrived. In a quiet moment away from the eyes of the congregation, the pastor blessed these rings behind the scenes and handed them over to us.

At last, the final strains of the wedding reception music faded into the night, leaving behind a silence that weighed heavy with untold stories and unfulfilled expectations as we drove to my husband's hometown for the next phase of my wedding- welcoming the bride to her new family.

Most couples dream of exotic honeymoon destinations, envisioning romantic getaways to places where love blossoms under the golden sun or by moonlit seashores. Our reality, however, was different. The wedding had drained my savings, and my husband declared he could not bear the financial responsibility of a honeymoon trip. The compromise? A two-week trip to Lagos to spend the "honeymoon" at my husband's family home, an apartment bustling with family members. It was as humiliating as it sounds.

The beginning of a marriage is a critical phase where couples set the tone for their relationship, and a lack of privacy and autonomy, especially during the honeymoon, can stifle communication and growth, leading to long-term dissatisfaction and emotional detachment. So, I could not help but worry about how this critical step was compromised in our situation. Spending our honeymoon in a family home was far from ideal. It did not align with biblical teachings about establishing a new, independent life as a married couple, but what could I do? The deed had already been done, and my vision was already blurred.

Upon our return after two weeks, we were met with an unexpected turn of events. The new apartment we were supposed to move into, which was still under construction, was not ready for occupancy. The promise remained unfulfilled despite assurances from the landlord that it would be completed before our return. Given this predicament and considering my husband's living situation in a shared single room, we had no choice but to move into my single room, which, thankfully, I had to myself. While not ideal, this solution was the only practical option. My room was modest but decent, with basic facilities for a reasonable standard of living. It was not the dream home I had envisioned for the start of our marital life, but it was something. We finally settled into our new apartment after another two weeks.

Today, as I reflect on the early years of my marriage, I remind myself of a Yoruba proverb that my father often quoted. The proverb implies that when a lame man is asked why the load on his head is tilted, he responds that the imbalance begins at his very foundation. This adage resonated deeply with me as I pondered the skewed dynamics of my marital life. Like the lame man's tilted load, the imbalances in my relationship with my husband were not random or superficial; they were symptoms of deeper, foundational issues. These are issues that, unfortunately, I failed to address at the onset, leading to a marriage perpetually off-kilter.

> “ when a lame man is asked why the load on his head is tilted, he responds that the imbalance begins at his very foundation.

From a biblical perspective, Ephesians 5:25[21] tells husbands to love their

[21] Ephesians 5:25: “Husbands, love your wives, just as Christ loved the church and gave himself up for her.”

wives as Christ loved the church, sacrificing for her well-being. Love is not just a feeling but an action, and in a Christian marriage, this includes financial stewardship and shared responsibility. Remember, the beginning is just that—a start. It is never too late to make changes, demand fairness, and strive for a more balanced, fulfilling marriage. Both partners deserve respect and an equal stake in shaping their shared future.

TWELVE

A Dream Deferred

The only thing worse than being blind is having sight but no vision.

Helen Keller

As life resumed its usual rhythm, I found myself confronted once again by an all-too-familiar adversary – the persistent ache of back pain that had troubled me in the past slowly insinuated itself back into my daily experience. At first, I attempted to dismiss this discomfort as a minor inconvenience. Each day, following my standard work routine, I steadfastly devoted myself to my fashion design business. My resolve was fueled by a determination not to let my husband's neglect impact our financial security, especially given the mounting expenses of my graduate studies tuition and the increasing demands of maintaining our household. I was steadfast in my commitment not to allow this physical discomfort to hinder our family's financial well-being. Nevertheless, as time passed, the backache intensified, transforming from a minor annoyance into relentless pain. This was particularly concerning as I was nurturing a new life within me. With the well-being of my unborn child in mind, I made the difficult but necessary decision to pause my business operations.

However, life, as we know, does not pause for anyone. Bills continued to pile up, and the rent on the store was a looming presence. So, after several sleepless nights pondering our financial future, an idea emerged. I suggested we keep the store but change to a less physically demanding business. The year was the early 2000s. In my country, business centers were booming, offering computer typing, printing services, and even mobile phone calls. Few could afford mobile phones, and many relied on business centers like the one I envisioned to stay connected.

A plan formed in my mind. "We could shift gears and start a computer business center," I suggested to my husband. Since my expertise lay in computer science, the transition felt natural. My husband seemed to agree, and for a fleeting moment, a spark of shared responsibility ignited between us. We could both see the potential. We could hire staff to work there during the daytime. I would supervise the computing business aspect, leveraging my expertise in computer science, and he would manage the mobile phone calls after closing at his workplace. It seemed like the perfect partnership, a balance that would harness our strengths.

> " In the tapestry of life, every thread of challenge weaves a pattern of resilience; adapting our dreams doesn't mean surrendering them.

Pooling the remaining resources from my now-defunct fashion business, we made our first investment—a Nokia 3310. In those days, owning a mobile phone was a luxury, and paid calls at business centers like ours became a lifeline for many. With a wistful glance at my sewing machine, now collecting dust, we transformed the shop. We hired a daytime employee to keep the business running while we fulfilled our day jobs.

Each evening, after my faculty duties, I would stop by the shop, my heart swelling with pride and relief. I was proud because I saw the business thrive under our shared vision. Equally, there was a sense of relief seeing my husband actively engaging and taking ownership, which signaled his growing commitment to our joint financial endeavors.

My husband would arrive after work, managing the phone call side of the business until late into the evening. Watching him serve customers and tally earnings, I felt a burgeoning sense of hope. "Maybe this is it," I thought.

"Maybe this is the turning point where he becomes the responsible partner I have yearned for." This change gave me hope that his frequent complaints about financial constraints would soon cease, and he would become more transparent about his earnings.

However, as the days passed, a pattern emerged that was all too familiar. Though he was physically present in the shop, his financial contributions remained noticeably absent. It was as if he were a ghost, haunting the place but never truly inhabiting it. The experience was a painful lesson in reality: not all changes are transformations, and not all participation is a contribution. Thus, as the printer hummed and the phone rang in that little shop, I came to a sobering realization. The dream of a balanced marriage remained just that—a dream flickering on the horizon but never indeed reached.

> " Not all changes are transformations, and not all participation is a contribution.

As the weeks passed in our new business venture, the air grew thick with dissatisfaction. My husband began to express his discontent with the business's sluggish pace, often lamenting how he felt his time was wasted sitting idly at the store with minimal business turnover. His words were increasingly laced with bitterness.

I attempted to quell his frustrations with encouraging words, reminding him that all great endeavors require time and patience. However, my reassurances made little impact, falling on deaf ears.

Amidst this growing tension, my health took a turn for the worse, leading to frequent hospital visits. One evening, upon returning from the hospital, I was surprised to find our shop had closed prematurely. Expecting a bustling store and my husband's active presence, I was shocked to discover him at home, relaxing nonchalantly.

I inquired about his absence from the store, my voice tinged with disbelief and concern. His response was blunt and decisive – he had chosen to abandon the business, claiming it was no longer worth his effort. The room seemed to spin. However, what came next was even more shocking.

Then came a moment of unimaginable betrayal, a double-edged deceit that left me reeling. He had sold the phone – our Nokia 3310, the linchpin of our joint business venture. It was not just the handset; he had also Parted with its SIM card. The buyer, shockingly someone well known to us, had already paid half the price and taken the phone.

My husband tried to explain away his decision, a move he had made without my consent. He pointed to the pressing need to cover the upcoming rent for our store and the mounting expenses for our yet-to-be-born child. Despite his reasoning, the sense of betrayal from his unilateral action was profound and undeniable.

My heart did not just sink; it plummeted into an abyss of disbelief. His actions were a betrayal on multiple levels: a betrayal of our business partnership, of our marital vows, and perhaps most painfully, of my trust. He had made a unilateral decision, executed without a shred of dialogue between us and with zero regard for our shared investments and the uncertain financial landscape we were navigating. I was already physically weakened by my pregnancy, and now, his actions felt like a gut punch to an already bruised spirit. Was this an unspoken manifestation of his initial reluctance to start a family? Now, with a baby on the horizon, could he not find within himself a shred of responsibility instead of projecting his frustrations onto an innocent life yet to see the world?

Here was the deeper sting: that phone was more than a business asset; it had also become emotional and social. It was our link to the outside world, our families and friends who were geographically distant but emotionally close. By selling it without my consent, he had severed a business lifeline and a personal one.

That night, as I lay in bed, questions flooded my mind. What would become of our business? How would we handle the financial strain, especially with a baby on the way? Moreover, most disturbing, if we could not manage a business together, what would that say about our ability to manage a life together? If a simple business decision could cause such a rift, what would happen if more serious challenges inevitably come our way? It was a harrowing thought I had neither the energy nor the heart to confront fully. Thus, I braced for the arduous journey ahead in that quiet room. A journey that now seemed more uncertain than ever.

On a more positive note, the period of our suspension from church duties came to an end, allowing us to re-engage in the church's assignments. The following Sunday was particularly significant as my husband took to the podium, addressing the congregation with a heartfelt speech. He expressed sincere repentance for our actions leading to pregnancy outside of marriage and offered an apology for the embarrassment we had brought upon our church community. His words were met with appreciation from our pastor and warm applause from the congregation, acknowledging our perseverance and grace in facing the situation.

Despite the apparent reconciliation showcased to our congregation, a lingering sense of unrest unsettled me internally. Deep within, I understood that our relationship's intricate complexities and hurdles were far too profound to be mended simply by public speeches. A part of me held onto the hope that this public act of humility might mark the beginning of a true transformation in my husband. Maybe, just maybe, this moment of self-reflection and accountability before the church was the turning point for a genuine change in him. More than anything, I yearned that this promise of change would transcend the church walls and manifest in the privacy of our home life, bringing about a true and lasting transformation in our relationship dynamics.

However, as time unfolded, it became increasingly clear that the promise of change remained confined to the Church domain. Despite my hopes for a genuine transformation, there was no discernible improvement in his actions, particularly in the privacy of our home.

As the pregnancy progressed, my health continued to get worse. I suspect this was not only because of the physical demands of pregnancy but also due to the emotional and psychological stress I was under. My advice to you, dear reader, is that if you find yourself in a similar situation, it is crucial to prioritize your well-being and that of your unborn child. Emotional stress during pregnancy can lead to complications that could affect both the mother and the baby. If your partner is unwilling or unable to support you emotionally, seek support from other trusted sources—family, friends, or healthcare providers. God calls us to care for our bodies, which are temples of the Holy Spirit (1 Corinthians 6:19-20).

At that moment, I realized I needed to shift my focus. It was not about him anymore; it was about me and our unborn child. I could not afford to let his emotional unavailability destabilize me. I made a promise to myself: to be strong for the baby. After the baby arrived, there would be time enough to confront the issues in our marriage.

THIRTEEN

The Hidden Struggle

We are only as sick as our secrets.

Sigmund Freud

As our married life progressed, its initial luster faded, like a once-gleaming golden ring slowly tarnishing under the relentless assault of harsh realities. My husband, who was aspiring to reach the pulpit's moral heights, remained ensnared by a world steeped in pornography, masturbation, and different forms of sexual immorality.

Each discovery of hidden pornographic material was a jolt to my sense of reality, a bitter pill that challenged my understanding of integrity and faith.

Standing at the pulpit each Sunday, his voice resonated with the teachings of love, faith, and righteousness. His words soared through the church, touching the congregation's hearts and moving them to nods of agreement and murmurs of amen. However, those words felt hollow, echoing the emptiness of unfulfilled promises and neglected duties in my mind.

The more he was revered in the church, the more his moral compass seemed to malfunction within the walls of our home. His pornography addiction, a vice he publicly denounced, was a cancer-eating away at the sanctity of our marriage. Psychological research on this kind of addiction explains how it alters the brain's wiring, distorts the perception of intimacy, and creates unrealistic expectations.

The scripture is clear about the perils of such a double life, especially if we are to hold spiritual authority. In Matthew 23:27, Jesus condemns the Pharisees, saying, "Woe to you, teachers of the law and Pharisees, you hypocrites! You are like whitewashed tombs, which look beautiful on the outside but on the inside are full of the bones of the dead and everything unclean."

The conflict between the two opposing sides of his life finally escalated to a point where I could no longer bear it. I found myself compelled to confront him, earnestly appealing for him to bring his conduct into harmony with the values of our shared faith and the spiritual integrity we both professed. A somber tone marked his response; he acknowledged the need for change and vowed to make amends. However, this promise came with a condition - he implored me to keep the nature of his transgressions a secret, insisting that no one else should ever learn of his dishonorable actions.

Though seemingly sincere, his words lacked the conviction and resolve necessary for genuine transformation. So, as time would reveal, his commitment to change was nothing more than a hollow promise, an empty assurance that would crumble under the test of time. The main problem was that he remained blind to the underlying issue, denying the need for therapy or counseling. In his eyes, there was no problem to confront and no addiction to acknowledge.

This stance was not uncommon in the circles of African men, where a man's struggle, especially one of a moral or sexual nature, is rarely discussed openly, let alone addressed through counseling or therapy. Such matters are often cloaked in silence, buried under the guise of normalcy.

In the African landscape, the admission of such a struggle, or seeking help, is frequently seen as a weakness, an affront to the stoic, unyielding image of masculinity that society upholds. This attitude creates a barrier to addressing such deep-seated issues. It perpetuates a cycle where men, trapped in their struggles, continue to wear a façade of normalcy while their personal and familial lives suffer silently.

The 1988 study by Zillmann and Bryant on "Pornography's Impact on Sexual Satisfaction" provides insightful findings on how pornography consumption can significantly affect marital relationships. Their research brings to light how pornography can lead to a weakening of the bonds of trust and emotional intimacy that are fundamental to a healthy family dynamic. The study is a wake-up call for reevaluating how we address mental and emotional health, particularly in the context of African societies. It is essential to create an environment where seeking help for issues stemming from pornography consumption and other forms of sexual immorality is not seen as a sign of weakness but as an essential step toward recovery and strengthening personal and familial relationships.

Research within addiction psychology strongly emphasizes the importance of identifying and tackling the foundational factors that drive addictive behaviors. This approach is particularly critical in the context of sexual addiction, where the addiction often represents deeper underlying emotional or psychological issues. Schneider and Weiss (2001) emphasized that addressing these core issues is crucial for genuine healing and recovery.

Participation in counseling is an essential step in this journey, especially for individuals and couples dealing with the fallout of sexual addiction. Counseling provides a safe space to examine the profound effects of addiction on both personal and interpersonal levels. It enables an in-depth exploration of these ramifications and assists in devising strategies to rebuild trust, intimacy, and a sense of connection within relationships.

IIf you are in a similar situation, remember you are not alone. Seek professional and spiritual guidance. Addiction, especially of a sexual nature, is often a symptom of deeper emotional or psychological issues that may require specialized treatment. While prayer and faith are powerful, they are most effective when combined with actionable steps, like counseling and accountability. Above all, protect your emotional and spiritual well-being. In the words of Proverbs 4:23, "Above all else, guard your heart, for everything you do flows from it."

The covert nature of sexual immorality is a silent destroyer of relationships. It creates an invisible barrier, a wall that separates hearts and souls. It operates in the shadows, masking its destructive force behind a veil of normalcy and secrecy. The journey starts with a seemingly harmless step but ends in isolation and despair.

The path to redemption is not easy. It requires confession, repentance, and a steadfast commitment to change. It demands a turning away from sin and a turning toward God, seeking His strength and guidance to overcome the chains of addiction. There is hope in the power of Christ's redemption. Seek help, lean on your faith, and remember that through Christ, all chains can be broken. "Therefore, if the Son makes you free, you shall be free indeed" (John 8:36).

As we navigate together through this chapter, I want to assure you that my intention is not to bring shame or dishonor to my spouse or to air our private struggles for the world to see. Instead, this narrative of healing and hope is shared with the utmost respect and sensitivity. It is a story told to comfort and guide those walking a similar path. I hope that this chapter will shed light on the arduous path of overcoming addiction—a path characterized by its share of setbacks and victories, tears, and moments of triumph.

Embarking on a journey to overcome addiction is akin to traversing a terrain filled with both challenges and milestones, tears, and moments of triumph. More importantly, it is a journey illuminated by the light of hope. This hope is rooted in the belief that with faith, understanding, and unwavering commitment, the bonds of addiction can be unshackled, and the sacredness of marriage can be renewed and revitalized.

Whether you are grappling with addiction yourself or bearing the scars from its impact on a loved one, remember that the path to recovery, though steep, is not impossible to climb. My journey has been learning to forgive, holding onto hope even in the darkest times, and discovering strength in moments of vulnerability.

As you continue to explore the pages of my story, my heartfelt prayer is that you, too, will find comfort in the promise of healing and the strength of divine grace that surpasses our human weaknesses. May this book serve as a beacon of light, guiding you toward a horizon where forgiveness and redemption await.

FOURTEEN

A Crucible of Life and Death

Strength does not come from physical capacity. It comes from an indomitable will.

Mahatma Gandhi

I had always considered myself a resilient woman, fortified by faith and molded by adversity. However, nothing could have prepared me for the harrowing ordeal that awaited me—a crucible that would test not just my faith but my very will to live. This chapter of my life has remained sealed for years; it has been too painful to revisit and too raw to articulate. However, healing comes in layers. I thank God for mending my spirit enough to share this story now, hoping it serves as a cautionary tale for others going through similar situations.

The air was thick with dark premonition a week before my due date. I felt an unease I could not shake off. Soon, I was diagnosed with acute malaria, a cruel parasite that courses through the bloodstream like a malevolent spirit. Coupled with soaring high blood pressure, I was a ticking time bomb[22]. I was immediately hospitalized, but instead of being a sanctuary of healing, the

[22] High blood pressure and acute infections like malaria can pose serious risks during pregnancy, often leading to complications that require emergency intervention (Duley, 2009; Nosten et al., 2004).

hospital became a theater of despair. The walls of the hospital felt like they were closing in on me as I lay in my sterile bed, tormented by the uncertainty of my condition and the life I was carrying inside me. My body was betraying me when I needed it the most; I was growing weaker by the day, drained by the double onslaught of illness and imminent labor.

> "In the darkest moments of despair, the flicker of inner strength illuminates the path to survival.

Then, the contractions started—painful reminders that my baby was ready to come into the world. Nevertheless, something was wrong. The baby was not engaged and not positioned correctly for a natural birth. The doctor looked at my husband and me, his eyes veiled with concern, and delivered the news: an emergency operation was needed to save both the baby and me.

"But we need a blood donor," he added, "or you must pay for the blood."

"In my country, money is the key to well-being," I thought bitterly. The cruel policy of "pay before service" has claimed countless innocent lives, a grim testament to the systemic inequality that persists.[23] This was not just a medical emergency; it was a financial one. The hospital, instead of being a temple of healing, felt like a marketplace where life itself was on auction to the highest bidder. I looked into my husband's eyes, searching for a glimmer of hope, a sign that he would rise to the occasion. However, all I saw was a reflection of my despair.

At that moment, as I lay on the hospital bed, I could not help but think of the countless stories in the Bible where faith triumphed over the most insurmountable odds. "The Lord is my shepherd; I shall not want" (Psalm 23:1), I whispered, praying for a miracle. As the clock ticked away, each second felt like an eternity. My life and that of my unborn child hung in the balance, hostages to a system that prioritized money over human life. Would we become just another statistic, another grim tale of what could have been?

The atmosphere in the dimly lit hospital room continued to be thick with tension, a cauldron of unspoken sentiments and silent recriminations.

[23] According to a study by the World Health Organization, healthcare inequality is a pervasive issue in many developing countries. Financial barriers often prevent patients from receiving timely and adequate medical treatment, leading to avoidable morbidity and mortality (WHO, 2010).

Fluorescent lights flickered overhead, casting eerie shadows that seemed to dance on the walls, accentuating the somber mood. Like clockwork, my husband would walk through the door each morning, his face a jumble of evasion and avoidance. With every arrival, he brought not the much-needed blood for my transfusion but a litany of feeble excuses. "We have not found a matching donor," he would murmur. "They said we can get compatible blood from a big lab in our neighboring city," he would offer the next day. His eyes rarely met mine, skirting around the room as if seeking escape routes.

At that moment, with the weight of my declining health bearing down on me, I gathered what little strength I had left. "Call my mother," I rasped, my voice barely a whisper but with an urgency that was impossible to ignore. My mother, a seasoned midwife whose life testified to resilience and care, was my last hope.

> " Even when the world's systems fail us, the unwavering spirit of love and resilience prevails against all odd.

My husband hesitated, his eyes finally meeting mine. It was as if he realized the gravity of the situation and understood at last that he was failing me, himself, and our unborn child. With a reluctant nod, he left the room to make the call.

My mother, true to her nature, wasted not a second. Abandoning sleep and comfort, she boarded an overnight bus, embarking on a journey guided by a mother's instinct and years of medical expertise.

When she strode into the hospital room the following morning, I barely recognized her. Her face, usually a portrait of composure and warmth, was etched with lines of concern and fatigue, each wrinkle a testament to the miles she had covered and the sleep she had sacrificed. My vision was blurry, my consciousness waning; the moment she entered, the room seemed to brighten as if her presence could ward off the looming darkness.

My mother quickly scanned the room with her eyes, taking in my ashen face and the inadequate medical setup. And then, as if spurred by an internal battle cry, she sprang into action. Orders were barked at nurses, medical charts were scrutinized, and equipment was audited—all within minutes. She was a whirlwind of efficiency, her every move calculated and deliberate, each step dancing in a war against time and negligence.

A flood of emotions washed over me as I lay there watching her. Relief and love, but also a bittersweet realization: my mother, once again, was doing what someone else should have done. She was filling gaps, fixing errors, and, most importantly, saving a life—my life. Moreover, as she moved around the room, I knew I had a fighting chance with her by my side. A warrior had arrived, and the battle for my life had just turned hopeful.

Her eyes, those deep wells of wisdom and experience, narrowed as she leaned over me, her stethoscope moving in a practiced dance over my abdomen. The air in the room seemed to freeze, crystallizing in a moment of unspeakable heartbreak. Her face, a canvas of life's trials and triumphs, registered the devastating truth: our baby was no longer with us. The soul-crushing news weighed heavy on her lips, but she bit them shut, choosing to carry the burden alone.

My mother knew, perhaps better than anyone that revealing this news to me would be akin to throwing a lit match into a reservoir of emotional gasoline. I was already teetering on the edge of despair, my spirit as fragile as glass. To shatter me with this revelation would not only break her daughter but likely jeopardize my already precarious medical state. Her maternal instincts roared into action, fortifying her with a grim determination that etched its way into every line and wrinkle of her weary face.

Turning away from me, she surveyed the hospital room with a critical eye that missed nothing. The peeling paint on the walls, the outdated equipment that looked like relics from another era, and the air of neglect that seemed to cling to the walls all screamed an appalling lack of care. Her eyes met those of the medical staff who shuffled about, their faces masks of indifference. She sensed their unspoken prioritization of financial gain over human life, and her disappointment was as palpable as the heavy air in the room.

"How could they put financial gain over life?" she muttered, her voice tinged with disbelief and sorrow. However, her seasoned gaze saw beyond the immediate scene before her. She knew this was not just a failure of one hospital or a handful of medical professionals. This was a malignant symptom of a far more significant, systemic problem plaguing our country's healthcare system—a disease without an easy cure.

As she stood there, locked in her thoughts, a haunting realization swept over me, as sudden and chilling as a gust of winter wind. My husband, who stood at a distance, his eyes averted, had never wanted this baby. Not only had he literarily told me about his unreadiness to bear children, but the signs had also always been there, lurking in his hesitations, excuses, and silences. However, now, in this dire crisis, the truth was as clear as daylight—his absence of urgency and his reluctance to act culminated in an inescapable, agonizing reality.

Thus, we were three souls bound by blood and tragedy yet divided by unspoken truths and untold secrets. We are locked in our private battle yet irrevocably entangled in a shared destiny that none could escape. It was a moment that would forever be etched in the annals of our family's history.

My mother's face was a mask of determination as she took charge, her eyes locking onto my husband's, cutting through his hesitation like a hot knife through butter. "We are moving her to a better hospital in Lagos," she declared, her voice tinged with authority and unyielding resolve.

For a fleeting moment, my husband's complexion drained to a ghostly pallor, his eyes flickering away in silent contemplation of our financial predicament, clearly pondering how we could afford the journey ahead. In an almost divinely timed intervention, his very close friend, akin to a guardian angel clad in everyday attire, energetically entered the room. He extended a generous wad of bills with a benevolent gesture that seemed heaven-sent, thrusting them into my husband's astonished hands. "Go charter a vehicle. Now," he instructed with a decisive kindness, cutting through the moment's tension like a beacon of unexpected hope.

At this juncture, you might wonder: "Why a chartered vehicle? Why not an ambulance?" Well, dear readers, let me enlighten you. In Western countries, the wail of an ambulance siren is a symbol of immediate medical attention, a promise of aid rushing to the scene. However, the reality is far grimmer in my home country and many developing countries worldwide. Here, ambulances are often a luxury reserved for the dead, the dying, or the exceedingly affluent who can afford the exorbitant fees. A private or commercial vehicle is often the only alternative for the rest of us, a desperate grasp on life when the system has failed us.

With the weight of this harsh truth pressing down on us, we had no time to lose. My husband dashed out of the room, his friend's generosity fueling his newfound urgency. As my husband went to secure our ride, my mother took a deep breath, her chest expanding as if gathering the very air that contained the strength she would need for the trials ahead. She turned her attention to the medical equipment surrounding me, her eyes scanning each item with the meticulous care of a seasoned nurse—because that is precisely what she was.

She disconnected the infusion bag that had been hanging limply by my side as if its previous placement symbolized the failing hope in this ill-equipped hospital. She gathered syringes, additional IV fluids, antiseptics, and bandages, tucking them into a bag she slung over her shoulder. The infusion bag, now securely in her grip, was no longer a mere object in the room; it was transformed into a symbol of her unwavering resolve to keep me alive. This was a road fraught with uncertainties, where even the vehicle we would use was a compromise, a cruel testament to the inadequacies of our healthcare system. Nevertheless, if love could be distilled into medicine, if determination could be translated into a cure, then that bag she held was the most potent elixir.

So, there we were, a pregnant daughter barely clinging to life and a mother refusing to let go. The atmosphere was tinged with urgency as we scrambled to leave. Within what felt like mere moments, we found ourselves huddled in the back of a battered Peugeot 504, its body worn and dented as if echoing our bruised spirits. The car's engine growled to life, a mechanical beast carrying precious cargo as it lurched onto the chaotic roads.

Inside the vehicle, my mother positioned me carefully, my head resting in her lap, a sanctuary in this whirlpool of uncertainty. Her eyes were twin beacons of hope and desperation, locked onto the road ahead but ever-conscious of the daughter lying broken in her arms. Her hands would wield the tools of her trade, monitoring my weakening heartbeat, every squeeze of the infusion bag a pulse of hope, a heartbeat in a race against time. At the same time, my husband took a comfortable position in the passenger's seat.

As my mother clutched an infusion bag in one hand, she wielded a stethoscope in the other hand. Like a vigilant sentinel, she listened intently to my heartbeat, its rhythm syncopating with the potholes that jolted the car.

Outside, the car maneuvered through the roads, honking horns and shouting voices, creating a cacophonous symphony that seemed to mock our plight. Every bump, every swerve, sent ripples of agony through me, but my mother's lap remained a constant, a stabilizing force amidst the chaos.

Thus, as we navigated the streets leading to Lagos, a city renowned for its medical prowess, my mother whispered prayers under her breath, her words a sacred incantation. Each uttered syllable carried the weight of her love and desperation, imbued with the power of a mother's indomitable will.

FIFTEEN

Whispers of Grace

What we have once enjoyed deeply we can never lose. All that we love deeply becomes a part of us.

Helen Keller

Finally, the city lights of Lagos began to shimmer in the distance, beacons in the dark sea of night. They promised hope, healing, and a battle yet to be won. However, as we drew nearer, my heartbeat weakening with each passing mile, it was not the city lights that held my gaze. It was the unwavering eyes of my mother, each pulse of her love a lifeline pulling me back from the abyss.

As we approached the unassuming but reputable private hospital, I knew that my contractions had stopped, an ominous sign that the baby was no longer with us. However, I fought for life, compelled by a delusion, perhaps a desperate hope, that I was still fighting for two.

My mother, her face etched with lines of worry and exhaustion, led the way as the hospital staff wheeled me into the building. She was a woman on a mission, bypassing pleasantries and small talk. We navigated the sterile, antiseptic-scented hallways until we arrived at a door marked 'Consultation Room.'

Inside, the doctor sat behind a sprawling desk, his face a canvas of calculated professionalism. He was one of Lagos' top gynecologists, a man whose skilled hands had brought countless lives into the world. He was also a man my mother had worked with while she was in government service, a man she trusted.

"Doctor, I would not be here if there were any other options," my mother began, her voice tinged with desperation. "We need your help. My daughter is on the edge, and I fear we may lose her."

The atmosphere in the room turned tense with a palpable sense of urgency. The doctor, recognizing the seriousness of the situation, quickly initiated a flurry of actions. I found myself on the hospital bed, enveloped by an array of tubes and wires that entwined around me, reminiscent of serpents in their complexity. The doctor's gaze was intense and deeply concentrated as he meticulously examined the results of the comprehensive tests.

The readings from the EKGs[24] and ultrasounds,[25] along with the blood test results, all converged on a grave diagnosis: Peripartum Cardiomyopathy (PPCM), an often overlooked but severe heart condition that can manifest late in pregnancy or the postpartum period.

At this critical moment, it becomes essential to illuminate PPCM, the medical condition that had suddenly claimed the stage in my life. For those unacquainted, PPCM is far more than a cruel twist in an otherwise jubilant chapter of life—pregnancy and postpartum. It is a nefarious form of heart failure that can ambush a woman without a preamble, turning a time of expected joy into a life-or-death emergency.

This insidious disease cripples the heart's fundamental function—to efficiently circulate blood—putting not only the mother at grave risk but also the unborn child (Elkayam, 2011). According to a seminal study published in

---

[24] EKG (Electrocardiogram) is a test that records the electrical activity of the heart and helps in diagnosing heart conditions by detecting irregularities in heart rhythm and structure.

[25] A cardiac ultrasound (or echocardiogram) uses sound waves to produce images of the heart, allowing doctors to see how the heart is beating and pumping blood.

the Journal of the American College of Cardiology, the mortality rate for PPCM oscillates between a harrowing 4% and 11% (Haghikia et al., 2015). These statistics underscore the urgent need for swift and specialized medical care, a need made more urgent given PPCM's relative obscurity in public health discourse.

As grim as PPCM is, its metamorphosis into full-blown heart failure adds another layer of complexity and danger to an already dire situation.

The doctor's eyes met my mother's, thickening the air with unspoken dread. The gravity of PPCM and my rapidly declining state were the twin elephants in the room, each magnifying the enormity of the other. It was not just a case of PPCM; it had escalated into heart failure, necessitating immediate life-saving interventions. The room felt like a pressure cooker, each beep of the monitor amplifying the gravity of the condition that had ensnared me.

"Your daughter's condition is critical," The doctor began, his voice carrying a heavy burden. Her heart is significantly weakened, and the PPCM complicates any surgical interventions we might consider."

The doctor sighed a heavy, loaded exhalation. "You know we have come a long way together, but her condition is grave. Admitting her into my private facility poses significant risks, and you would have to move her to a public hospital." The coldness of his clinical logic hung in the air like a guillotine blade.

My mother's face went ashen. Realizing that even a top-notch medical facility was ready to turn her daughter away, she felt the weight of despair settle on her shoulders.[26] However, her eyes, those reservoirs of endless love and resolve, filled with tears.

"Doctor, I implore you. I am not asking you to take a medical risk. I am asking you to take a leap of faith". Still sensing the reluctance on the doctor's side, my mother continued, "She needs a miracle, Doctor, and I know that miracles can happen here, under your care." She paused, her voice thick with

26 High-risk pregnancies, such as those complicated by conditions like Peripartum Cardiomyopathy (PPCM), often require specialized medical care and monitoring to ensure the safety of both mother and child. Such cases can pose significant challenges for healthcare providers.

emotion. "I will bring in pastors, Men and women of faith, who will stand around this hospital and intercede in prayer. We will call upon a power greater than any of us. Divine intervention is the only thing that can save her now."

A palpable silence filled the room. The doctor, trained to trust empirical evidence, was at a crossroads. He glanced at me, lying there on the stretcher, teetering on the brink of existence. And then he looked back at my mother, her eyes pleading, her spirit unbreakable. Whatever he saw there—the fierce maternal love or the unwavering faith—moved him."

"All right," he finally said, his voice tinged with a newfound resolve. "Your faith moves me. We will admit her. I cannot promise a miracle, but I will do everything medically possible. The rest is in God's hands."

As I was transferred into the operating room, my consciousness ebbing away, I felt a newfound strength surge within me. Whether it was the result of medical expertise or divine intervention—or perhaps a miraculous fusion of both—I could not say. Nevertheless, at that moment, I knew I was enveloped by an extraordinary tapestry of love, science, and faith, each thread woven tightly by those fighting for me. Thus, with a room full of earthly and heavenly witnesses, I fought on.

The operating room was a sterile reserve of scientific precision, where scalpels and sutures took precedence over prayers and prophecies. However, a different intervention occurred in the waiting room beyond its sealed doors. Pastors and prophets sat huddled together, their voices rising and falling in a rhythmic cadence of prayer and intercession. Their petitions for divine intervention permeated the walls as if attempting to breach the boundaries of the physical world to touch the divine.

Inside the operating room, I was enveloped in a foggy haze, teetering on the edge of consciousness. The bright surgical lights above me blurred into an ethereal glow like I was floating between reality and an otherworldly realm. My thoughts wandered, swirling in a cocktail of confusion and hallucination. Was I nearing the end? Was this the final threshold?

Just then, in a moment as inexplicable as it is miraculous, something primal within me stirred. With a newfound clarity that shattered the semi-conscious mist I was lost in, I cried out, "Doctor! Come and save me!"

The room erupted into immediate action. The surgeon and nurses, momentarily stunned by my sudden cry, locked their eyes in a shared instant of disbelief and urgency. Medical instruments clanged against metal trays as they scrambled to assess the situation. Alas! The baby was making her tragic exit. Grasping the forceps with skilled hands, the doctor navigated the delicate terrain of life and loss, delivering our baby girl and averting the looming threat of surgery.

Outside, the prayer warriors felt a palpable shift in the room's energy. They opened their eyes, sharing glances of wonder and relief when they heard the news. Was it a coincidence or divine orchestration that their prayers seemed to concur with this situation? Back in my hospital room, my mother's face was full of emotion—relief, sorrow, and indescribable love—as she tenderly cared for me. She chose the most delicate words to convey the heartbreaking news of our loss, her nurse's training merging with her motherly instincts in a profound act of love and compassion.

Thus, life's most complex emotions converged in that sacred space of miracles and losses. The hospital walls seemed to reverberate with echoes of prayers and medical jargon, each in its way a plea for the miracle of life. Amidst the dichotomy of science and faith, I was cradled at the intersection, a living testament to the fragile balance of life and death and the mysterious, earthly, and divine forces that can tip the scales.

Let me be clear: The purpose of recounting this harrowing journey is not to cast blame on the flawed medical system, my husband's shortcomings, or the myriad societal issues that framed my experience. Nor is it to instill a sense of dread in those who dare to venture into the beautiful world of motherhood. Instead, this tale serves as a cathartic release, a way to lift the weight of a story that has long laid like a millstone around my heart. This is my odyssey—riddled with miraculous and heartbreaking moments, a poignant testament to the enigmatic tapestry of life, love, and unbearable loss.

The memory of my child—my beautiful, stillborn daughter—is not whole but fragmented. Those fragments are shards of glass, each piercing into the very fabric of my soul. They are snippets, mere moments where she was being pulled away from me in a desperate act to save my life. Each fragment is a haunting melody, a lullaby left unsung, a story untold. It is a future that will never unfold. Nevertheless, in its paradoxical way, it is also miraculous. In those final moments, when the veil between this world and the next was whisper-thin, I felt her presence as never before. It is as if she knew her short journey was a sacrifice, a final act of love from a daughter to her mother.

Therefore, I posthumously give her a name in ink and paper. A name that encapsulates both her ephemeral existence and her everlasting impact on my life. I named her Grace.

Grace was a beacon that guided me through my darkest night, an emblem of the divine intervention that saved my life when all earthly hopes had vanished. This book is her legacy. Through these pages, she lives on—not as a whisper, but as a shout; not as an absence, but as a presence; not as a question, but as an answer.

> “From loss blooms a legacy of love; in our deepest sorrow, we find an undying hope.

So, as the final words of this chapter settle on the page, I dedicate it to Grace, my beautiful daughter, who became a beacon of light in my darkest moments. Her brief journey, though fleeting, has left an indelible mark on my soul, teaching me about the profound strength of maternity, the resilience of the human spirit, and the mysterious ways in which life unfolds. Through these words, her spirit resonates, a testament to the fact that even in our deepest despair, an undercurrent of grace sustains and uplifts us. Grace Folajimi, your name is etched not just in this chapter but in the fabric of my being, a reminder that out of loss can emerge an enduring legacy of love and hope.

May this chapter serve as a reminder that even in the depths of despair, grace can be found; that even when the chords of life strike a dissonant note, a sacred melody still plays on; that even when the book of Life seems to end in a tragic cliffhanger, there is an Author who writes us into a broader, eternal narrative.

Grace Folajimi, this chapter is a tribute to your ephemeral yet eternal presence in my life.

In the Quiet Whispers of Grace: A Poetic Tribute

In the silent rhythm of the night,
Where stars whisper tales of light,
There danced a star, intense, pure, and bright,
A fleeting presence, soft as lace,
In the quiet whispers of Grace.

A journey brief yet vast in-depth,
In every heartbeat, in my breath,
Her essence lingers, a silent guest,
In dreams, I chase, in love's embrace,
In the quiet whispers of Grace.

Not in the clamor of my days,
But in silent moments, she finds her way,
A gentle nudge when skies are gray,
A touch of calm in my fast pace,
In the quiet whispers of Grace.

A melody unsung, a story untold,
In her, the universe did boldly mold,
A tale of love, both brave and bold,
In every tear that trails my face,
In the quiet whispers of Grace.

In every ripple on the water's surface,
In every prayer, in every solace,
She lives beyond time and space,
A celestial child in eternal grace,
In the quiet whispers of Grace.

A name unspoken yet forever known,
In the garden of my heart, she is grown,
Her legacy, a light that's shown,
Guiding me to a higher place,
In the quiet whispers of Grace.

So, I hear her in the rustling leaves,
In whispered wind, in sighing trees,
In every moment that love weaves,
In my complex, wondrous maze,
In the quiet whispers of Grace.

SIXTEEN

Echoes of Pain

Turn your wounds into wisdom.

Oprah Winfrey

The week that followed was a time of gradual restoration. My mother, ever the vigilant nurse, orchestrated my recovery with the precision of a maestro. Doctors and nurses came and went, but her unwavering presence was the constant backdrop to my healing. Finally, the doctor declared I was stable enough to be discharged, but not without a pivotal recommendation: "I believe it is time to move you to your mother's nursing home," he said, his eyes meeting mine. "Under her expert supervision, you will receive exceptional postpartum care there." The convalescent nursing home was an inpatient rehabilitation facility in the bustling city of Lagos. As a testament to her lifelong commitment to healing and nurturing lives, my mother founded it as a sanctuary of healing and love, pouring her years of expertise and compassion into every corner after leaving public service. The proposed transition warmed my soul.

As preparations were underway to move me, the doctor summoned my husband and me to his office. His face was stern, etched with the gravity of the message he was about to deliver. "Listen carefully," he began, locking eyes with both of us. "Your survival is nothing short of a miracle. If you value this gift of life—and I believe you do—you should avoid future pregnancies, or at the very least, space them out significantly under medical supervision."

I knew this was medical advice and a spiritual mandate—a call to respect the delicate nature of life and death woven by hands greater than ours. I looked over at my husband, then the doctor, and nodded. The room was thick with the scent of antiseptics, yet somehow, it smelled like a new beginning.

I took a deep, introspective breath. To everyone else, it was an ordinary inhalation, but it carried a universe of thought for me. My husband was quiet, his face unreadable. I wondered if he grasped the enormity of the situation. It is said that "the heart is deceitful above all things and beyond cure" (Jeremiah 17:9).

I could not stop thinking about my husband, who had revealed surprising and alarming sexual addictions just weeks into our marriage. In the depths of my heart, I harbored a glimmer of hope that the life-threatening events we had just navigated were for a purpose. The agony, I wondered, could it have occurred for a purpose? Could this harrowing experience change the trajectory of our relationship, instilling a sense of gravity and responsibility in him? I was convinced that occurrence would inspire a sense of sobriety, self-control, and marital decency in him. Oh, how I wish I were right!

The journey to my mother's nursing home was like crossing the threshold into a new world. As we arrived, I felt enveloped by an aura of peace and love. I felt a strange sense of pride and gratitude; proud of the woman who had given me life and had now saved it and grateful for the haven she had built a place like this for people like me. My mother and her nurses provided me with unparalleled postpartum care in the following days.

As I lay on the bed in the small nursing room that my mother had transformed into a temporary bedroom for my husband and me, I looked at my husband's narrow face. I was grasping at the hope that the trauma had sculpted us into better versions of ourselves, that it had instilled in us a newfound respect for the sanctity and fragility of life. Oh, how wrong I was. What you discover next will send a chill down your spine, making you question the foundations upon which you understand love, commitment, and personal growth.

The room my mother chose for me was a modest outpatient room remarkably close to her office. The walls exuded an aura of comfort, painted in hues that evoked peace and tranquility. Photos of angels adorned the walls, and the soft glow of a crystal lamp illuminated the words of Psalm 91:4, which was displayed on a beautiful frame on the wall: "He will cover you with his feathers, and under his wings, you will find refuge." My mother, sensing the need for her constant vigilance, moved her office desk just a stone's throw from my door. It was a symbolic act, just like the Biblical shepherd who leaves the ninety-nine sheep to find the lost one (Luke 15:4). She declared to me and the world that I was her priority, her child who needed her most.

Nevertheless, even in this sacred space, a serpent entered Eden.

My husband began making intimate advancements, oblivious to the doctor's stern warnings and my fragile state. I looked at him, astonished. Could he not see the agony in my eyes, the phantom cries of our dead child echoing in the room? My body was a battleground of conflicting sensations: the acute pain from severe tears I sustained during the ordeal of forceps delivery to save my life, the painful lactation with no child to nurse, the emotional wreckage of a lost baby with no time to grieve. However, here he was, looking for carnal satisfaction.

My heart sank into an abyss. It was as if Job's lament had come to life: "Does a wild donkey bray when it has grass, or an ox bellow when it has fodder?" (Job 6:5). Was he so blind to human suffering, so disconnected from the reality of the moment? He had built walls around his empathy, turning himself into a fortress impenetrable to reason or compassion.

> “In the refiner's fire of betrayal and pain, our truest strength is forged, unyielding and pure.

The tension in that room became palpable each time my husband attempted his advances. Despite my physical and emotional fragility, I summoned the willpower to rebuff him repeatedly. It was like a game of emotional chess, where I had to calculate each move for the immediate outcome and its future implications.

I resisted him for as long as I could, summoning all the emotional and spiritual strength within me. Nevertheless, eventually, he had his way. The details are too raw to delve into, but the experience shattered me, leaving me in disbelief. How could this be happening? How could a space consecrated for healing become a theater of pain?

This experience, horrific as it was, forged in me an unbreakable spirit and taught me about the boundaries of human decency. I felt like Hagar in the wilderness, forsaken and desolate. However, even in that nadir of despair, I found a flicker of strength, a tiny ember of dignity that could not be extinguished. The Apostle Paul's words in 2 Corinthians 12:9 resonated deeply: "My grace is sufficient for you, for my power is made perfect in weakness."

Curiously, throughout this ordeal, I chose not to confide in my mother or my two sisters, who had been so present in my life, especially during my periods of illness. Perhaps it was a desire to shield them from further worry, or maybe my inability to process and articulate the turmoil I was experiencing fully. In hindsight, this silence was not my best decision. Keeping them in the dark meant walking a solitary path in a situation where their support could have been my fortress.

This silence reflected a more significant issue prevalent in many African marriages. It is a cultural predicament, especially within the Christian community—a lack of education on setting boundaries and the potential harm of silence.

> “Amidst the broken shards of trust and commitment, the will to heal and rise remains unbroken.

All through my ordeal, my husband's words continued to echo in my mind like a haunting refrain: "Whatever goes on within our marriage should stay within our marriage." Somehow, I may have believed that by not opening up to my mother, I was 'protecting' my marriage. However, in that silence, I was also imprisoning my voice, shackling my pain in the chains of secrecy. So, even under acute stress and betrayal, I remained silent. I harbored the storms, believing I was shielding my marriage.

In hindsight, I realize this silence was not protection but a self-imposed exile from the support and understanding I desperately needed. The African proverb, "It takes a village to raise a child," holds profound wisdom, yet when it comes to marriage, the lines are often blurred, leaving many in a solitary struggle.

For readers who might find themselves in similar situations, I offer this piece of advice: Do not underestimate the power of sharing your struggles with trusted loved ones. While it may seem like a burden, the support and understanding of family can be a source of immense strength and healing. Remember, enduring pain in silence may sometimes seem like the easiest path, but allowing others to help can lead you toward quicker healing and renewed strength.

The room became a prism through which I saw the myriad facets of human existence: love and betrayal, joy and sorrow, life and death. It was a visceral, painful education that no classroom or sermon could provide. Moreover, in that brutal, unforgiving school of life, I graduated with the highest honors: the wisdom to discern, the strength to endure, and the grace to forgive.

My mother found moments to mourn together with me. She was all I needed during those gruesome times that I needed to mourn, not just the loss of my baby but also the loss of trust, the loss of what could have been a supportive partnership with my husband. In that room, I found physical recovery and experienced a spiritual renewal.

I hoped that one day, my husband would understand this truth: that the trials we face are not merely hurdles to survive but opportunities for profound personal growth and transformation. They are, in essence, divine crucibles. Within these intense moments of life, we are confronted with our most authentic selves, greatest strengths, and profound weaknesses. In these crucibles, we are presented with a critical choice – to emerge as refined gold, stronger and more resilient, or to crumble into dust, succumbing to our circumstances. This realization, born from the most painful experiences, was a lesson in resilience and the enduring capacity for renewal within us all.

> “ in that brutal, unforgiving school of life, I graduated with the highest honors: the wisdom to discern, the strength to endure, and the grace to forgive.

As my health gradually returned, like a sun timidly peeking through a stormy sky, the day came for me to leave the nurturing embrace of my mother's nursing home. I stood on the threshold, gazing at the road ahead. This metaphorical journey beckoned me to my physical dwelling and toward a profound awakening of my worth and identity.

Throughout the tumultuous journey of my marriage, especially in the wake of losing our child, one might question why I continued to stay bound to my husband. Why didn't I cut the ties of our relationship, particularly after such a profound tragedy? These queries haunt me, echoing in my mind like spectral whispers in a desolate hall. A deep-seated belief, ingrained by church teachings, held me in place—that God disfavors divorce, as suggested by scriptures like Malachi 2:16, and that a wife's body is a sanctuary for her husband, as implied in 1 Corinthians 7:4.

While these teachings are revered in religious and societal contexts, they inadvertently became a dark glass through which I viewed my marriage. This perspective blurred the lines between sacred commitment and dangerous self-sacrifice. Contemporary theologians such as Elisabeth Schüssler Fiorenza (Fiorenza, 2001) and Phyllis Trible (Tribl have critiqued this rigid interpretation of biblical passages. They emphasize the importance of a balanced and context-sensitive understanding of the scriptures. These scholars advocate for interpretations that prioritize compassion and the holistic well-being of individuals, challenging traditional views that may inadvertently perpetuate suffering and injustice, Trible, 1984).

I wish the church had armed its flock with more than just verses and hymns; I wish the congregation had been equipped with the intellectual and emotional tools to navigate the complicated corridors of irretrievable divorce in marriage. The invaluable work of clinical psychologist John Gottman, particularly his research into the complexities of marital relationships and the factors leading to divorce (Gottman, 1994),[27] would have been a significant resource in this regard.

How does one continue to respect and honor a partner who blatantly disregards the sanctity of your union? What steps does one take when the fundamental cornerstone of trust has been irreparably damaged? The question becomes even more complex when the union threatens one's well-being, pushing the boundaries of what can be endured or forgiven.

In such cases, the usual tenets of marital commitment and the vows to uphold respect and honor may need to be reevaluated in light of personal

---

[27] Gottman's studies provide profound insights into the emotional and communicative aspects that are crucial for sustaining a healthy marriage and understanding the signs of potential breakdowns.

safety and mental health. When the cornerstone of trust is shattered, especially in a manner that endangers one's safety, it may become necessary to prioritize self-preservation and well-being over the preservation of the marriage.

The decision to step away from a life-threatening situation is not an abandonment of marital vows but rather an affirmation of one's right to safety and respect. It involves recognizing that preserving one's life and dignity should precede a relationship that has devolved into harm. In these instances, seeking support from loved ones, counselors, or legal and safety professionals becomes crucial. It is about finding the strength to make difficult choices that may involve leaving the marriage to protect oneself from further harm.

Reflecting on my journey, I realize that my choice to remain silent and endure the challenges alone led to significant emotional and, potentially, physical harm. By withholding my feelings, I unintentionally strengthened the barriers of misunderstanding and deepened the pain. This decision, though made with the best intentions, could have had more disastrous consequences if not for the sustaining grace of God. This realization highlights the importance of open communication and emotional honesty in addressing marital challenges, which Gottman's work emphasizes as essential for relationship health and longevity (Gottman, 1994).

My experience underscores the importance of speaking out and seeking support when faced with marital strife, especially of a severe nature. Remaining silent in the face of marital discord, especially when it escalates to a dangerous level, is not a sustainable or safe strategy. It is essential to acknowledge and address issues in a relationship early on and not let silence or fear dictate your actions. Seek support from trusted friends, family, or professional counselors. The path to healing and resolution requires the courage to confront the issues and the wisdom to take appropriate action for one's safety and well-being.

Ultimately, the decision in such dire circumstances is deeply personal and often heart-wrenching. It requires careful consideration, support, and sometimes the courage to choose a path that leads away from danger and toward healing and safety.

SEVENTEEN

Against All Odds

The human capacity for burden is like bamboo – far more flexible than you'd ever believe at first glance.

Jodi Picoult

Life seemed to return to its regular rhythm as we settled back into our routines in the East. The church's doors welcomed us, and work beckoned with its familiar demands. The memory of my ordeal began to recede, like a painful dream fading at daybreak. Little did I know that the next chapter of my life would be as dramatic.

December arrived, and with it, my scheduled postpartum appointment in Lagos. I remember having some odd sensations, inklings of something amiss, that I planned to discuss with the doctor. The day of the follow-up appointment arrived, and with it, an unforeseen revelation would shake the foundations of my world.

As I sat in the waiting room, flipping through the pages of a worn-out magazine, I rehearsed what I would say to the doctor. However, nothing, absolutely nothing, could have prepared me for what was to come.

The doctor's eyes widened as he reviewed the results. He looked at me, then back at the papers, as if trying to reconcile the two. The words that followed were as dramatic as they were unexpected.

"Against all odds, you are pregnant again," the doctor announced, his voice a mix of astonishment and concern. "Six weeks along."

The room fell into a stunned silence. My mother, a pillar of strength throughout my ordeal, looked as if she had seen a ghost. Her face, usually composed, was a canvas of shock and disbelief. The medical staff, who had witnessed my previous complications, exchanged glances of disbelief. The echoes of the doctor's warning about avoiding pregnancy reverberated in my mind, amplifying the shock of the moment.

> " Life's unexpected storms reveal the uncharted strength of our spirit, guiding us to shores of unforeseen triumphs.

Hadn't the doctor warned me? Hadn't he made it clear that another pregnancy could be life-threatening? The whispers and murmurs filled the room, a discord of disbelief and worry.

Abortion was not an option for me. Even if it was, the doctor warned that it also carries a considerable risk, given my medical history. So, I resolved to turn to divine intervention, to place my fate and the life growing inside me in God's hands.

As it happened, it was the week of our church's annual global gathering at the Church's campground. Hence, instead of returning home, I headed there, drawn as if by a divine magnet.

Before the program began that afternoon, I was alone at the altar. I lay down, stomach flat against the cold floor, and poured my heart out to God. Tears streamed down my face as I cried for salvation, for protection, for a miracle.

"Lord, You are the giver of life. You know the depths of my despair and the height of my hope. Save me, save this child," I cried, my voice echoing in the empty sanctuary.

It is worth noting that my path was marked by contradictions throughout the nine months of my second pregnancy. While I felt alone in many aspects of this journey, there were fleeting moments when my husband's care surfaced, albeit often tied to the fulfillment of his sexual desires, and these moments, rare as they were, brought a complex mixture of emotions.

Despite the intense physical and emotional demands of pregnancy, I still strove to fulfill my marital duties and meet the economic needs of our home, often without expecting much in return. My husband's support, I realized, was a vanishing hope, constantly thwarted by excuses and evasions. However, in this journey of near solitude, God proved to be my steadfast companion, providing abundant strength and resilience.

The concept of resilience in adverse circumstances has been widely studied from a scholarly viewpoint. Resilience is the ability to bounce back from hardships and to adapt positively in the face of adversity. It is a trait often forged in the crucible of challenges, much like my journey. My reliance was not on the man I had married but on the divine strength that God provided. It was a walk of faith, a testament to the belief that one with God is a majority.

As my final trimester dawned, a sense of foreboding grew within me, hinting at potential complications on the horizon. Perhaps intuitively aware of the situation's severity, my husband journeyed with me to Lagos. However, he left me in my mother's hands once we arrived and returned to the East.

The climactic day finally arrived, marking the end of nine months filled with steadfast faith, fervent prayers, and unwavering resilience. Our son was born against all odds, triumphing in a world where miracles are often sought but rarely witnessed. Despite the challenges of cesarean birth, his arrival was a moment of unadulterated joy and celebration, a vivid demonstration of the wonders that faith and strength can yield.

This part of my story almost defies belief, resembling a tale of mythic proportions. After the birth of Grace, my stillborn daughter, medical advice cautioned against another pregnancy, or at the very least, recommended a significant gap before attempting to conceive again. When I became pregnant mere weeks following Grace's delivery, the doctors were nearly resigned to despair. Yet, it was by the grace and glory of God that I navigated through the pregnancy.

Now, let me draw you into the dramatic tapestry of time. Grace was born in October, and astonishingly, just nine months and two weeks later, our next child was born in the warm embrace of the following July. This birth was a living, breathing testament to the miraculous. Each breath he took was a testament to the relentless power of hope and the enduring strength of a mother's love, underscored by divine grace. My story, unbelievable as it may sound, is a living testimony that sometimes, life's most significant challenges are followed by its most profound blessings.

As I held our newborn son for the first time, I was overwhelmed by awe and gratitude. This child was a living testament to the power of faith, a reminder that even in the darkest moments, there is light. He was a gift, a miracle, a testament to the unyielding grace that had carried me through.

My husband arrived in Lagos the day after the miraculous delivery of our son. His return, though expected, brought a swirl of emotions and silent contemplations. As he entered the room, I studied his face intently, searching for signs of the change I so deeply yearned for. A tumult of thoughts and hopes churned in the quiet of my mind.

Cradling our newborn son, I glanced from the tiny, innocent face of our child to the familiar features of my husband. At that moment, a silent prayer began to take shape within me. I prayed fervently, my heart whispering words of hope and desperation that the profound responsibility of fatherhood would awaken something new in him. I yearned for this beautiful and vulnerable life we had created together to be the catalyst, turning my husband into a father in name, spirit, and action.

With every gentle breath our son took, I wished for my husband to see in our son's eyes a reflection of the man he could be – a better version of himself, someone who embodied strength, kindness, and responsibility. I prayed that this tiny being, so pure and unmarked by the world's complexities, would instill in him a desire to set the best example – to be a man his son could look up to, learn from, and eventually emulate. Nevertheless, the reality was starkly different.

A few weeks post-delivery, we returned to the Eastern part of the country, a homecoming tinged with hope and apprehension. However, as days unfurled into months, it became clear that the birth of our child did little to quell the torrents of my husband's sexual addiction, addiction to pornography, or aversion to financial responsibilities. The burden of rent, feeding, and the kaleidoscope of needs that came with our growing boy lay heavily upon my shoulders. His world remained an enclave of self-absorption, where the tentacles of addiction seemed to tighten rather than loosen their grip.

Undeterred by the relentless cycle of neglect, I fortified my resolve, turning my gaze toward the horizon of my career aspirations. My master's degree was essential to the ultimate goal—a Ph.D. in Computer Science. It was a pursuit that promised empowerment for me and the family I was single-handedly nurturing.

Embracing my role as a mother and dedicating myself to academia required sacrificing a part of my identity. However, in this sacrifice, I found a different kind of fulfillment and purpose, a testament to the resilience and adaptability of my spirit amidst life's unpredictable tides. I was no longer the naïve bride of yesteryears but a seasoned warrior armed with the wisdom of experience. I navigated the treacherous waters of our marriage with a navigator's precision, ensuring that the gaps between our children were deliberate, a shield against the unpredictability of our union.

Three years wove themselves into our lives before the blessing of another baby graced our family. His arrival, like his brother's, was through the incisions of a cesarean section—a procedure that now seemed a metaphor for the precise control I sought over my life. The shadows of past surgeries and the specter of my husband's neglect loomed large. However, in the theater of the operating room, as the cries of our newborn baby pierced the sterile silence, I felt an overwhelming sense of divine intervention. It was as if God Himself was orchestrating the symphony of life, assuring me that His omnipotent hand was at work no matter the human frailty around me.

> "In the dance of life, each step of hardship is matched by a stride of resilience, leading us to the rhythm of hope.

After our second son's birth, life settled into a rhythm. My husband's occasional forays into a semblance of care were like the sporadic flickers of a faulty light—unreliable and fleeting. However, my focus remained unwavering. I poured my energy into nurturing our children and the relentless pursuit of academic excellence. It was a dual path fraught with challenges, but I walked with the indomitable spirit of a woman who had weathered storms and emerged unbroken and unyielding.

This chapter of my life is a dramatic narrative that serves as a voice to the countless women who find the strength to rise above their circumstances and forge a path of success, underscored by a faith that does not waver and a determination that does not tire.

So, in the face of adversity, my journey continued, a lone but determined trek guided by a blend of scholarly ambition and maternal devotion—a journey of a woman who, amid life's disharmony, found her symphony in the whispers of divine grace and the echoes of her steadfast resolve.

EIGHTEEN

Behind the Masks

We all wear masks, and the time comes when we cannot remove them without removing some of our own skin.

André Berthiaume

The masquerade of our marriage was a carefully choreographed dance, with masks so firmly in place that sometimes we forgot who we were beneath them. I, the ever-smiling wife, donned the facade of happiness like a second skin, parading the illusion of marital bliss before friends and family. I extolled my spouse as the epitome of husbandly virtue, spinning tales of our 'perfect life' to anyone who would listen.

This deception was a script I had learned to recite with the precision of an actor on the stage of life, hiding the truth behind a guise of contentment. It was a mistake that too many people make, often with the noblest intentions but always with the most corrosive consequences. Many people fall into the trap of narrating the perfect marriage due to a snare set by societal expectations and the fear of judgment. In our quest to embody the ideal, we lose sight of reality, of authenticity. We become prisoners of the illusion, captives of the facade. We smile for the cameras, post the highlights, and carefully curate the image of perfection that we think the world wants to see.

Nevertheless, behind closed doors, the makeup comes off, and the cracks in the foundation show. The danger in this performance is not just in the lie itself but in the isolation; it creates a disconnect between who we are and who we pretend to be.

My husband also wore his mask, that of the devout churchgoer, the pillar of the community. His devotion to church activities was exemplary, and his involvement appeared to be deeply committed. To the growing congregation, he was a tireless worker in the Lord's vineyard.

> "In seeking to embody the ideal, we become prisoners of the illusion, losing ourselves in a facade we meticulously craft for the world.

However, this facade concealed his spiritual life and his abdication of duty at home. While immersed in every church group and activity, he abandoned the people who needed him most—his family. The discrepancy between his public persona and private failings was stark, yet I helped maintain this duality, praising him publicly and reinforcing the image of the model husband and father.

And then, as if by some divine script, the day came when he returned home with news that seemed as surreal as it was unsettling. He informed me with an air of irrefutable conviction that the church leaders, in their spiritual discernment, had seen fit to entrust us with pastoring a new parish. A responsibility that was both an honor and an anchor—a symbol of faith and yet a weight of expectation that threatened to pull us into uncharted depths.

As he talked of his intention to accept the position as the will of God, I remember staring into his eyes, searching for any sign of hesitation or humility, but found none. Instead, there was an intensity, a fervor I had seldom seen. This was no reluctance; he was resolute and determined and even mentioned that he had heard from God. However, a storm was brewing within me, a tempest of apprehension and conflict.

My response was a whisper against the tide of his enthusiasm. In the marrow of my bones, I knew that the path he was determined to embark upon was fraught with hypocrisy and peril. How could I stand beside him, a pillar of faith, when our foundation was riddled with deep, dark cracks? However, to voice these doubts was to court the wrath of a man slowly consumed by the shadow of anger at home.

For months, I stood as a lone figure of resistance amidst mounting expectations from the church. My litany of reasons – my career, my children, and my academic goals – were a mosaic of excuses. While valid, I knew they were not the true barricades to my acceptance. The natural barrier was the concealed turmoil of my marriage, an agonizing reality I could not voice, especially with my husband, a man of contradictions, sitting beside me, cloaked in an air of righteousness.

Our senior pastor addresses these concerns by preaching about the virtue found in our inadequacies and the divine power inherent in human frailty. His words were soft, urging me toward a path they believed God had chosen for me. This argument struck a chord with my fundamental spiritual beliefs – the conviction that God equips those He calls rather than solely calling the already equipped.

The pastor's words made me wonder if this was the answer to my prayers, the divine intervention needed to transform our fractured relationship into a testament to His work. This notion offered a sense of solace to my burdened soul, a hint of divine intervention in our imperfect journey.

Amid this, I noticed a transformation in my husband. The man who had been a stranger to self-restraint seemed to have turned a new leaf. His demeanor toward me and the children softened, and a cautious hope sprouted within me. I thought that this was probably the turning point I had been praying for—a calling that would redeem him and restore us.

So, with a heart laden with trepidation and a mind swirling with what-ifs, I conceded. We stood before the congregation, hands united, as the pastor commissioned us to shepherd the new flock. As the applause thundered around us and the title of 'Pastor's Wife' settled upon my shoulders like a mantle, I felt a complex tapestry of emotions—fear, hope, and a silent plea that this new chapter would be the catalyst for a true transformation.

The irony was not lost on me; the woman who had been playing the role of a content wife and mother was now donning a new role, this time with a title that carried the weight of spiritual authority. It was a role I had never auditioned for, and yet, I was stepping onto the pulpit into a spotlight that illuminated not just my face but the depths of my soul.

This unexpected turn of events was like the plot twist in a novel you cannot put down—the kind that keeps you reading into the early hours of the morning, desperate to see how the story unfolds. Moreover, unfold it in ways that were both extraordinary and, at times, excruciating. As I navigated my new duties, I found myself playing not just the part of a pastor's wife but also the architect of my destiny, building bridges where there were once barriers and finding strength in places I did not know existed. There was no turning back; the die had been cast, the stage was set, and the story of the pastor's wife was underway.

Thus, I embarked upon this new chapter with a delicate blend of faith and fear. Would this sacred duty be the crucible that purified our marriage? Or would it be the stage upon which the final act of our private tragedy would be played? Alternatively, perhaps it was merely the beginning of a deeper descent into a charade I had never wished to play. The answer was a whisper in the wind, an enigma waiting to be unraveled in the fullness of time. Only time would reveal the truth hidden beneath the robes of service and clergy collars.

NINETEEN

The Unspoken Side

The deepest pain I ever felt was denying my own feelings to make everyone else comfortable.

Nicole Lyons

The mantle of a pastor is often viewed as a sacred cloak woven with threads of grace and the expectations of an entire congregation. It is a role replete with respect, admiration, and the silent whispers of responsibility that echo through the church. Nevertheless, beneath the surface of reverence and perceived spiritual tranquility, there can lie tumultuous seas of personal struggles and the shackles of societal expectations.

As a woman of faith, the weight of my marital vows hung heavily upon me. It was a yoke fashioned not only by the promises I had made before God and man but also by the unspoken societal expectations of a pastor's wife. I was to be a beacon of unwavering faith, a pillar of support for my husband's ministry. However, behind the veneer of this sacred duty, I grappled with a gnawing emptiness, a longing for a genuine connection with the man I had vowed to stand beside.

In this chapter, I will unravel the complexity of my life as a pastor's wife, shedding light on the shadows that often go unseen behind the pulpit. It is a tale of trials and tribulations, unyielding faith, and undying hope that dawn is a prayer away, even on the darkest nights.

> Beneath my cloak as a pastor's wife lies a tumultuous sea of personal struggle, unseen but deeply felt.

I had envisioned that my husband's elevation to a pastor would herald a new chapter of piety and shared spiritual growth. I believed that the sanctity of his role would seep into our home life, cleansing it of the vices that had so firmly rooted themselves within the confines of our marriage. However, the reality that unfolded was in contrast to my husband's secret life of addiction to pornography, masturbation, and all forms of sexual immorality.

In addition, I experienced firsthand the harsh reality of financial abuse, a phenomenon I had previously only encountered in articles. The responsibility for our financial obligations weighed heavily upon me, reminiscent of the biblical burden of the cross at Golgotha.[28] Despite having a substantial income, I was caught in a relentless cycle of debt and loans, frequently finding myself reaching out to my siblings for financial assistance.

The concept of financial abuse in intimate relationships, as explored by Johnson in his 1995 study, became a tangible part of my life. This study sheds light on the prevalence and profound impact of financial abuse, illustrating how it often intertwines with other forms of abuse. It paints a picture of a complex web of control and dominance, where financial abuse serves as both a tool and a symbol of the abuser's power (Johnson, 1995). Living through this experience, I realized how financial abuse could be as crippling as any physical or emotional abuse. It is a silent predator, lurking in the shadows of a relationship, and can go unrecognized until the damage is profound. Understanding and acknowledging this form of abuse is crucial in both preventing it and supporting those who find themselves caught in its grasp.

The burden of managing our household finances – from paying the rent and providing meals to covering the children's school fees and other domestic necessities, increasingly rested on my shoulders alone. This responsibility became more challenging daily, as my husband persistently

---

[28] "Biblical cross of Golgotha" refers to the Christian narrative of Jesus Christ carrying his cross to Golgotha, the site of his crucifixion, symbolizing a heavy and burdensome load (John 19:17).

cited external demands as his primary excuse for his inability to contribute to our family's upkeep.

Whenever we encountered a financial need, he consistently expressed concerns about insufficient funds, and he never actively took any initiative until I stepped up to resolve the issue. This pattern aligns with the concept of 'financial infidelity,' a term used by psychologists to describe scenarios where one partner is either dishonest or secretive about financial matters. This behavior typically leaves the other partner grappling with ongoing uncertainty and stress. Atwood and Schwartz (2002) have examined financial infidelity in depth, discussing the psychological underpinnings of such behaviors and their impact on the dynamics of a relationship. This dynamic, they suggest, can cause significant emotional and psychological strain, affecting not only the financial health of the couple but also their emotional and relational well-being.

As I grappled with this disparity, I often pondered what complex financial webs I had become entangled in. Our combined income should have been more than sufficient. My husband was a full-time senior staff working for the state government. However, the opacity of his financial contributions at home remained a perplexing mystery. His excuses, revolving around his responsibilities toward his extended family, often felt more like a convenient scapegoat than a genuine explanation.

This situation presented a stark irony. Outside, I was perceived as a successful woman who had broken professional barriers and achieved commendable career heights. However, within the walls of my own home, I grappled with the heavy load of financial pressures exacerbated by my husband's apparent disregard. It was also evident that the financial abuse was intertwined with a broader pattern of control and neglect, a reality far removed from the professional successes and accolades that defined my public persona.

Academic studies in family dynamics suggest that such behavior may stem from deep-seated control and power imbalance issues. It reflects a desire to maintain dominance by withholding support, be it financial, physical, or emotional. This creates a toxic environment where one partner is overburdened with the practicalities of managing a household and the emotional toll of feeling undervalued and ignored.

I vividly recall an incident with our faulty refrigerator. As the appliance lay in disrepair, my husband showed no inclination to address the issue. Ultimately, I took the initiative to purchase a new fridge. His indifference was palpable that day as he sat engrossed in his favorite show, not lifting a finger to assist as the taxi driver and I struggled to maneuver the new appliance into our home. This incident was emblematic of the man I had married.

This paradox of public success and private struggle became a crucible for my faith. I wrestled with the meaning of true success – was it the accolades and achievements or the unseen battles fought with grace? This period of my life was a canvas of contrasts, painting a picture of a God present in both the light of victory and the shadows of hardship. It reshaped my understanding of God's blessings, teaching me that they are not always wrapped in comfort but often come dressed in challenges that refine our spirit.

Amidst this tumult, I clung to my academic aspirations as a lifeline, enrolling in a Ph.D. program I knew would be the keystone to my professional ascension. Concurrently, I persuaded my husband to pursue his master's degree, partly to bridge the educational gap between us—a chasm that, in the African context, could swallow a marriage whole.

> “ In marriages, particularly where cultural norms weigh heavily, balance in education can be as crucial as the scales of justice.

The delicate dance of respect and obedience becomes intricate when a wife's academic laurels overshadow her husband's. Thus, I took great care to maintain a demeanor of humility and submission, not allowing my scholarly achievements to cast a shadow upon him. I navigated a cultural muddle with the dexterity of a seasoned acrobat, balancing faith, respect, obedience, and ambition with the finesse that my multiple roles demanded.

My husband eventually agreed to begin his master's program, albeit not until I provided the finance to cover the burden of his tuition. Nevertheless, as the days turned into months, his emotional detachment from me and our children deepened, and his pleasure derived solely from the dark corners of his addiction. My efforts to fulfill the role of a supportive wife were met with cold indifference. I walked on eggshells, careful not to disturb the precarious peace, cautious not to demand the support that should have been my due. It was a silent struggle, one I bore alone to maintain the facade of an exemplary couple within our church.

Meanwhile, I had vowed to be an impervious fortress for my children, to shield them from the tempest of confusion and the whirlwinds of uncertainty that now threatened to engulf our home. My resolve was steel; not even the seductive whispers of temptation could lure me into the desire for another child, and certainly not while my husband's understanding of family planning remained as distant as the horizon where the earth kissed the heavens.

Unfortunately, my body had suddenly become a sacrificial offering on the altar of family planning methods—each one leaving its unique scar on my well-being. The hormonal tumult within me was a relentless storm that raged with each pill, injection, or device I tried. However, amidst this turmoil, my husband stood firm in his traditional beliefs, a belief system as old as the hills that cradled our town—a belief that family planning was the woman's burden.

He was a man carved from the very bedrock of tradition, where the concept of a man involving himself in family planning was as alien as rain in the desert. He wore his traditions like a mantle, demonstrating a culture that stretched back through generations of African men who viewed contraception as an exclusively feminine concern. This was the unspoken creed etched into the psyche of many African husbands: the woman worries about family planning; the man does not.

While culturally ingrained, this perspective screams for enlightenment—a dialogue where scholarly insights and biblical wisdom converge to challenge archaic norms. The World Health Organization underscores the importance of shared responsibility in family planning, advocating for male involvement as a cornerstone for reproductive health. Nevertheless, the resistance persists, an invisible yet impenetrable barrier wrought from threads of tradition and gender roles long outdated.

The church, a bastion of spiritual solace, fervently upholds the sanctity of marriage. It echoes the teachings of Apostle Paul to the Corinthians, emphasizing that a wife's body does not belong solely to her but also to her husband (1 Corinthians 7:4). Yet, this raises a critical question: When does this divine scripture transform into a yoke too burdensome to be shouldered? Distinguished Christian authors like Gary Thomas encourage us to reevaluate our understanding of marital dynamics. They advocate that a marriage devoid of mutual respect and love falls short of embodying God's true vision for this sacred union. Thomas (2015) contends that marriage is not just an earthly contract but a spiritual covenant that should reflect the essence of divine love and respect.

Amidst our family life, I found myself navigating the challenging waters of family planning, a journey my body seemed to resist at every turn. Each method I tried – be it pills, injections, or devices – left its mark, stirring a hormonal tempest that refused to calm. Yet, in this struggle, my husband remained anchored in his deep-seated traditional beliefs, a stance that viewed family planning solely as a woman's responsibility.

It was during this complex period that I discovered I was pregnant again, my fourth. There I was, still nursing our eight-month-old son and grappling with the physical and emotional toll of a deteriorating marriage. This pregnancy, unexpected and daunting, struck me with a wave of fear. The challenge was not only about weaning our young son but also about the precarious nature of my previous pregnancies and the potential risk of complications in the future. The pregnancy, arriving amidst such a delicate health scenario and a lack of emotional support from my husband, deepened my apprehension and sense of vulnerability.

Entangled in the complexities of a community that strictly upholds the principle of 'What happens within a marriage stays within the marriage,' I was caught in a web of private suffering. This philosophy, intended to safeguard marital privacy, ironically became a suffocating vine, stifling my desperate cries for help and muting my attempts to seek guidance. In marital discord, the silence imposed by this maxim can be more harmful than protective.

Dr. David Hawkins, renowned for his expertise in counseling couples, cautions against the peril of isolation in marriage. He advocates for a more community-centric approach to addressing marital challenges (Hawkins, 2017). This perspective resonates with the scriptural wisdom found in Proverbs 11:14, which states, "Where there is no guidance, a people fall, but in an abundance of counselors there is safety." This underscores the importance of seeking external support and counsel in navigating marital difficulties, emphasizing that the health of a marriage often depends on the strength of the community support system surrounding it.

Thus, in the throes of this new, unwelcome reality, I turned to the only source of strength I knew could never fail me—prayer. In the solitude of prayer, I found solace. This peace surpasses all understanding, as promised in Philippians 4:7. I weaned my son, trusting in God's providence, believing this fourth pregnancy would unfold under His watchful eyes and loving hands. It was a testament to the resilience of faith, a dance with the Divine where each step of surrender led to a deeper trust in the Almighty's grand choreography of my life.

The next storm approached far sooner than I could have ever envisaged. Three months into my fourth pregnancy, an ominous sign appeared on a Sunday morning when I planned to attend church service. I awoke to find blood stains on my clothes—a sight no expectant mother ever wishes to see, especially not at such a delicate stage. The fear was instant and all-consuming; the implications were clear and dire.

I alerted my husband immediately. While wrapped in a guise of concern, his response suggested I rest while he fulfilled his pastoral duties. So, I remained at home as he left, my anxiety mounting with each tick of the clock.

Upon his return, the bleeding had not subsided, prompting a decisive journey to the teaching hospital where I used to have my antenatal care. This journey was tinged with déjà vu, taking us back to where we had once celebrated life's arrival. Now, the stakes were higher, with life itself hanging in the balance.

This journey was unique as it was our first long trip to our newly acquired Mitsubishi Gallant. This car purchased mainly with my husband's financial contribution, quickly became his pride and joy. To him, it was more than just a vehicle; it symbolized success, a tangible result of his hard work, and a source of immense pride. His attachment to it was palpable, almost like the car was a living, breathing extension of himself.

The wisdom of scholars often echoes that true character is laid bare in moments of crisis. As we embarked on this challenging journey, my husband's actions spoke volumes about his priorities. His focus was primarily on the car's well-being, his treasured possession, rather than my increasingly precarious state. Each jolt and jostle along the uneven road seemed to elicit from him a reaction not of concern for me but of apprehension for the car. This stark display of his priorities was a revelation to me, a real-life illustration of the Biblical adage, "For where your treasure is, there your heart will also be" (Matthew 6:21). His affection for this inanimate object, his car, overshadowed his concern for my well-being.

In his misplaced attention, my husband made an unbelievable decision that further illuminated the dynamics of our relationship. As we encountered rough patches on our journey, he suggested, with a concern more for the car than me, that I should get out and walk. His rationale was that the car, with its precious underside, might suffer damage under the additional weight.

Navigating those rugged patches on foot, laboring to catch up with him on the relatively smoother sections of our route, the stark reality of my situation became overwhelmingly apparent. There I was, vulnerable and on the brink of a threatened abortion, yet compelled to walk alone. This heart-wrenching experience brought me face to face with the harrowing truth about the man I had married – a callous man who was devoid of compassion.

His decision, perhaps logical in his eyes, resonated with a cold and disconcerting truth. That he placed the car's condition above my well-being was a wake-up call. This moment would prompt any rational person to reevaluate their relationship. Yet, in those moments of painful realization, I remained silent, choosing not to voice my distress and doubts.

To those reading this and finding echoes of their own experiences in my story, I offer advice: Prioritize your well-being and do not silence your voice in situations that compromise your safety and dignity. A relationship should be a sanctuary of care and mutual respect, not a place where material concerns overshadow essential human compassion. Open communication and mutual understanding are critical; if these are lacking, it may be time to reevaluate the partnership dynamics. Remember, your safety and well-being are paramount, and no relationship should require you to compromise on these fundamental principles.

Ultimately, we arrived at the hospital only for my fears to be realized. The baby had to be evacuated to save my life. Thus, amidst the sterile white of the hospital room, in my most broken state, I wept—a deluge of sorrow and supplication to the Almighty. My promises to God were fervent and unwavering. I vowed to safeguard His temple—my body—from further harm. I pledged that, should He guide me through this maelstrom, my allegiance to His divine plan would stand paramount over my marital vows and that self-care would become my sacred mantra.

TWENTY

Pathways of Providence

Sometimes when you're in a dark place you think you've been buried, but you've actually been planted.

Christine Caine

As you already know, I found myself navigating through tempestuous waters, both in my personal life and my professional sphere, in the wake of embracing my new role as a pastor's wife. The responsibility was immense, and the expectations were high—from the congregation and within me.

However, unfortunately for me, the struggles at home soon mirrored those at my workplace. A once harmonious relationship with my then Head of Department (HOD),[29] a figure I had held in high esteem, began to sour. The details of the discord need not be disclosed, for they are but a shadow of a more significant battle—a battle that transcended the physical realm and waged war upon my spirit. However, I will provide some insights to benefit those navigating a similar situation.

Gradually, the harmony of my work environment at the university began to unravel like a garment whose threads were being pulled by an unseen

[29] Equivalent to the department chair in America.

force. The HOD, whom I had revered and who had reciprocated with mentorship and support, began to display a sharp turn in demeanor.

> "In marriages, particularly where cultural norms weigh heavily, balance in education can be as crucial as the scales of justice.

This shift seemed ignited by an incident at the core of my values. I was presented with an assignment that blatantly contradicted my moral compass. Standing at this crossroads, my decision was clear—though fraught with repercussions. I chose integrity over compliance, a stand that, unbeknownst to me then, would spark a series of confrontations and a cascade of isolation.

The department became a battleground, with lines drawn and allegiances tested. Colleagues whom I had considered confidants now averted their gazes, aligning themselves with the newfound favoritism of our leader. It was as if an invisible hierarchy had been established, where the currency was not scholarly contribution but the appeasement of authority.

Amidst this brewing storm, my shock was compounded when the person I relied on most, my husband, suggested that I accept the HOD's demands. His words struck me like a tempest, bewildering my spirit as he advised me to compromise my stand, an echo that reverberated within the hollows of my resolve.

I was aghast. This was not the counsel I expected from a man of God, a pastor, or my partner. It appears the pressures of our public life were infiltrating our private sanctum, urging compromise where there should have been support and unity. Amidst this crucible of adversity, my resolve did not waver. While I knew it was the right thing to honor my husband, I found solace in the scripture, in the enduring words of James 1:12, which promised that those who stood firm under trial would be blessed, receiving the crown of life the Lord had promised to those who love Him. So, I stood firm in my resolve not to succumb to the HOD's wish.

Subsequently, I encountered a challenging phase where the HOD seemingly conspired with some colleagues to remove me from my position. They set traps, hoping to see me falter and fail. However, their plans did not come to fruition. The specifics of these incidents are unnecessary, for the crucial takeaway is that I emerged as an overcomer.

Despite these victories, these experiences inevitably altered my perception of my workplace. What was once a professional growth and collaboration space had transformed into an environment marked by hostility and uncertainty. Yet, amid this adversity, I began to perceive my circumstances through a different lens. I chose to view these trials not as punishments but as opportunities for personal and spiritual growth. In this divine classroom, each challenge was a lesson in resilience, faith, and perseverance. It underscored the truth that adversity, while challenging, can also be a profound teacher. I survived and grew stronger, wiser, and more attuned to the world's complexities.

Once foyers of enlightenment, the university corridors now felt like a labyrinth designed to test my mettle. However, I leaned into my faith with a renewed vigor, finding strength in the timeless wisdom of Proverbs 3:5-6: "Trust in the Lord with all your heart and lean not on your understanding; in all your ways submit to Him, and He will make your paths straight."

> “In the divine classroom of life, every hardship is a lesson, every challenge, an opportunity for growth.

This chapter of my life, marked by the stark contrast between my public and private challenges, was one of the most transformative. I navigated those battles for myself and everyone who has ever stood at the crossroads of conviction and compromise. It illuminates a path of courage, faith, and an unwavering dedication to righteousness and hopes for others, braving their tempests.

The then HOD, bless his soul, is no longer with us, but his role in my narrative remains significant. His legacy and those of others who crossed my path form an integral part of the tapestry of my life's story. I hope those who played a part in this chapter of my life, though their names remain unspoken, will one day read this book and find a reflection that sparks understanding and learning. I write not with bitterness but with the hope that my experiences might offer them insights into their journeys.

In sharing these experiences, my aim is not just to recount the past but to offer guidance and wisdom to those who may find themselves in similar situations. If my words can light even a single step on someone else's path, my journey and the battles I have fought will serve a greater purpose.

Meanwhile, with my children's future etched in my mind, I embarked on a journey to scale the academic heights: Pursuing my Ph.D. at a University some 200 miles away. The decision was not without its sacrifices. It meant traveling vast distances, often before the first light of dawn broke the horizon and returning when the night was steeped in silence. It meant hiring a domestic aide to tend to my children's laughter and tears, ensuring my absence was a brief interlude in their daily lives.

However, my maternal chord refused to remain distant even with this support. My heart was always with my children, and the miles I traveled were measured not in distance but in the longing to return to them. My return, often under the shroud of night, was my silent vow that nothing, not even the pursuit of knowledge, would keep me from the sacred duty of motherhood.

During this delicate balancing of roles, I attended a seminar on campus by a fellow Ph.D. student. What followed was an unexpected exchange that went beyond academic discourse. Exiting the seminar room, I walked down the hallway and chanced upon another Ph.D. Student colleague grappling with a malfunctioning ATM. He was in a bind, needing cash to refuel his car for his journey back to the West, but the uncooperative technology was proving to be a hindrance.

> “ A simple act of giving could be an investment in the unseen currency of providence.

Instinctively, I offered to help, providing him with the necessary funds to ensure his safe journey home. His expression of gratitude was heartfelt, and he promised to return the favor through a bank transfer.

Our conversation flowed naturally, and it was then that he revealed his affiliation with one of the most prestigious universities in Nigeria, located in the country's western region—my place of origin, my dream destination. My heart skipped a beat when he mentioned an opening in the Department of Computer Science; it was the university that had long been etched in my aspirations. True to his word, he later sent me the information about the job posting. This was the spark I needed, a divine nudge steering me toward my prophesied destiny.

When I shared the news with my husband, expecting some concern, his excitement was a surprise that rippled through our conversation. Despite my reservations about the strains of a long-distance relationship, he encouraged me to soar, to at least cast my lot into the ring of consideration. His encouragement was a rare alignment in our disjointed symphony.

So, I took a breath that tasted of hope and submitted my application. The following days were a blend of prayer and anticipation, a mixture that became my daily bread. And then, the call came—an invitation for an interview, a door swinging wide to a future bright with promise.

As I sat before the interview panel, I felt the weight of my journey, the silent strength of my faith, and the quiet yet fervent prayers that had carried me there. When the word came that I had succeeded, that I was to become a part of this venerable institution, the framework of my life shimmered with new lines of gold.

One major lesson from here, dear readers, is that God often weaves our paths through small acts of kindness, creating intersections where obeying His prompting can lead to significant breakthroughs. It is easy to overlook the small, seemingly insignificant moments—those acts of kindness, those instances of divine alignment that may appear inconsequential in the grand scheme. However, as my journey vividly illustrates, these moments often serve as the cornerstone upon which our destinies are built.

I acted out of compassion by extending a helping hand to a colleague in need. Little did I know that this simple act of giving would become an investment in the unseen currency of divine providence. Therefore, I urge you, dear reader, to embrace every opportunity, no matter how small, with the understanding that it could be a stepping stone to your destiny. Never underestimate the power of a kind gesture, a helping hand, or a word of encouragement. As you continue your journey, remember that every act of kindness, no matter how small, is a seed sown into the fertile ground of God's master plan for your life.

Upon hearing the joyous tidings, my husband suddenly became a pillar of support, his enthusiasm as palpable as the midday sun. He bustled around, orchestrating the logistics of our relocation with a vigor that belied the undercurrents of our strained relationship. This support was a bittersweet salvation to my apprehensive heart; relief was tinged with the sharp aftertaste of uncertainty. I eventually took a leap of faith to relocate back to the West, and we agreed he would also find a job in the West and later join me and the children.

As I packed our boxes and suitcases, I could not help but wrestle with the specter of doubt. Long-distance relationships are like tightrope walks over gaping chasms, fraught with the winds of suspicion and the tremors of loneliness. How treacherous would this path be for us, whose marital fabric was already frayed at the edges? Nevertheless, there was a still, small voice—a whisper of divine assurance that this was the hand of God at work.

So, with a heart brimming with gratitude and eyes set on the horizon of career progression, after eight years of faculty career in the eastern part of the country, I stepped forward to career progression into an esteemed university in the West. This was the affirmation of my faith, the acknowledgment of my worth, and the proof that all things work together for good to those who love God and those who are called according to His purpose (Romans 8:28).

As the dust of our relocation to the West began to settle, we found shelter in the warmth of old friendships. My childhood friend, whose memory now dances in golden lights, opened her home and heart to us. We crossed the threshold of her abode, seeking a temporary haven, but found so much more.

Her home was a hub of life, brimming with the energy of the young people she mentored and the guests she entertained with open arms. However, I realized that behind her radiant smile and the laughter that filled the rooms, there was an undercurrent of strife—a silent storm that raged behind the calm of her demeanor.

One day, driven by curiosity and concern, I questioned her about her laissez-faire attitude toward her private space, her sanctuary invaded by the constant parade of visitors. Her reply was a lesson etched in the stone of my consciousness. She spoke with the simplicity of a sage: "There is nothing worth holding onto in this world." She professed a truth that reverberated with the teachings of Matthew 6:19-21, where Jesus admonishes against laying up treasures on earth, urging instead for treasures in heaven, where neither moth nor rust destroys. My friend embodied this teaching, loosely holding her possessions and prioritizing relationships and service.

She illustrated her point further, saying, "If I were to leave this world today, people would still enter this room, organize my farewell, and claim everything I had zealously guarded." Her words call for a reevaluation of our attachments and priorities. They underscored the fleeting nature of our earthly possessions and the futility of obsessing over them. With profound clarity, she illustrated the essence of life: the temporary nature of our earthly existence and the pointlessness of clinging to material possessions.

Let this counsel the reader: Life is a wisp of vapor, a brief dance in the grand ballroom of eternity. Let us not be consumed by the temporal but invest in the eternal. Ultimately, it is not what we have but what we give, not the breadth of our possessions but the depth of our legacies that truly endure.

Tragically, the cruel shadow of cancer recently crept into her life, and we lost her to its merciless grip. The shock of her passing will forever linger like a persistent fog, a reminder of the fragility of life. As I dedicate this chapter of my life to my beloved friend, I implore you to embrace the screenings that may seem like mere inconveniences but are, truthfully, silent guardians against a hidden foe.

Let this be a clarion call for self-care, especially for women who often place themselves last on the list of priorities. Please do not wait; it promises nothing but the present's passing. Cancer is an indiscriminate foe that can be held at bay with vigilance and regular health screenings. Mammography and other preventive measures are not mere appointments but lifelines we must grasp firmly. The Bible speaks of our bodies as temples (1 Corinthians 6:19-20), and we must honor them with the care they deserve. Regular check-ups, a balanced diet, and exercise are acts of self-preservation and reverence for the divine breath within us.

In memory of my beloved friend, whose identity remains hidden within these pages but whose spirit is eternally inscribed in the Book of Life, I take a moment to reflect. Let us anchor ourselves not in the fleeting allure of material things but in the enduring grace of God. This divine grace remains untouched by the inexorable passage of time and stands as our most lasting legacy. Let us endeavor to live our lives to the fullest, love with profound depth, and create a lasting impact that is measured not by our worldly possessions but by the hearts we have warmed and the lives we have enriched with our presence.

Grace in the Shadows

TWENTY-ONE

Pathways of Promise

Change is the law of life. And those who look only to the past or present are certain to miss the future.

John F. Kennedy

As I settled into the rhythm of my new job back in the West, I felt the comforting embrace of structure and stability, which had often eluded me in years past. The university suddenly became a vessel of hope, ferrying me toward a horizon of opportunities and personal growth. The environment was conducive, supportive, and nurturing for the intellect and soul.

Our children, ages around three and six, quickly adapted to their new environment. I enrolled them in a private school nestled within the verdant embrace of the campus and secured a modest apartment that mirrored the tranquility of my new workplace.

This New Haven was a far cry from our previous dwellings; here, neighbors were friendly, and colleagues became friends, each offering a supportive nod or a helping hand, embodying the proverbial village it takes to raise a child. The campus environment was nurturing, offering a community where the values we held dear were respected and celebrated. My husband visited biweekly, and with each visit, I clung to the belief that the familiar landscape and proximity to our extended families would rekindle more of a sense of responsibility in him.

His journeys, though consistent, left a hollow echo in the chambers of my heart. I should have been grateful, perhaps, for the peace that his absence granted me, for the space to live without the shadow of fear or another unexpected pregnancy. Nevertheless, I was terrified that this separation might only unravel my husband further and loosen the tenuous threads that bound him to decency and duty. This felt less like freedom and more like a vacuum, pulling at the seams of my spirit, whispering that distance could be the chisel chipping away at the fragile sculpture of our marriage.

So, each day, as I walked the paths of the university, working hard to make my mark as one of the few women in the computer science field, I never forgot to send up silent prayers for my marriage. I prayed not just for change but for the courage to face whatever the future held, knowing that the most excellent Author was still writing our story of all, who, in His wisdom, had brought us to this place of hope and new beginnings.

In quiet moments of reflection, my thoughts often drifted back to a tumultuous chapter in my birth family's history. It was a period marked by my mother's courageous yet contentious decision to pursue a more lucrative career opportunity in a far-off city. Fueled by aspirations for a brighter future, which included the allure of potential travel abroad, she embarked on this new path with a heart full of hope and ambition.

However, rather than being seen as a bold step toward personal and professional growth, her absence was viewed as a breach of communal expectations, a deviation from the unspoken norms that bound our tight-knit society. This disapproval swelled into a tide of hostility, enveloping our family in a dense cloud of judgment. The pressure for her to return was immense and unyielding, to the extent that even my father found himself powerless against it.

Amidst the echoes of my mother's past choices, I harbored a growing fear that a similar storm of judgment might soon engulf my marriage. The parallels between my mother's experience and my current situation were evident, and the patterns were too similar to dismiss. It seemed as though history was not merely repeating itself but was almost taunting me, deriding my efforts to forge a better future for my family.

In African communities, where traditionally the burden of maintaining the smooth running of the family often disproportionately falls on the woman, I was acutely aware of how quickly people might shift their gaze from my husband's shortcomings to my own decisions.

There was a lingering apprehension that any flaws in our marriage, any rifts that might emerge due to our geographical separation, would be attributed to my ambition and choice of career. This societal perspective, often quick to assign blame to women for marital issues, weighed heavily on my mind. I feared being perceived as the architect of my marital distress, much like my mother was viewed when she sought a better life for us all. This added layer of cultural scrutiny only intensified my anxiety, casting a long shadow over my aspirations and the choices I made for the sake of my family's well-being.

To the reader at the crossroads of career and family, personal growth, and communal expectations, I offer this counsel: tread carefully but boldly. Your journey is your own, and while the voices of community and tradition are loud, the quiet stirrings of your truth are worth listening to. Remember that emotional or physical distance can be both a balm and a poison. It can heal, giving space for growth and reflection, or erode, leaving a trail of estrangement and misunderstanding in its wake.

The Bible offers its wisdom on such matters. Proverbs 31 showcases the virtues of an industrious woman and attentive to her household, yet nowhere does it suggest that her endeavors be limited by proximity. In the strength of the Proverbs 31 woman, we find an affirmation for those who, like my mother—and indeed, like myself—seek to balance personal aspirations with familial duties.

> “Our journey is our own; tread it with integrity and courage, for each step composes the melody of your life's song.

The decisions are weighty, and their consequences are long-lasting. Hold them up to the light of prayer and introspection. Seek counsel not from the crowd's chorus but the still, small voice guiding you toward wisdom. Your path may diverge from expectations and may carve through uncharted territories, but it is yours to walk. Walk it with integrity, courage, and the knowledge that each step is a note in the song of your life, a melody that only you can compose.

Considering these reflections, I knew that the emotional architecture of a marriage cannot be sustained on the pillars of presence alone. It requires the mortar of trust, the reinforcement of communication, and the shared vision of a future where both parties are fully engaged in the tapestry of family life.

As the chapters of our life turned, a decision bloomed on the horizon that promised to stitch our fragmented family tapestry back together. My husband's years of service were nearing the moment he could claim retirement benefits. This gave me a beacon of hope, a potential end to the biweekly commutes that left a trail of worry in their wake. My discomfort with his travels was not the sole catalyst for this change; guilt also gnawed at me. Each time he left his station to stay a couple of days with us, I could not shake the feeling that I was pulling him away from his duties or the Church assignments back in the East. This tug-of-war between his professional obligations and our family needs was becoming another burden that weighed heavily on my thoughts: could I eat my cake and have it all the time?

I tried to convince my husband to retire from the government service, and hopefully, with his presence with us locally, he could find a more efficient way. I was not very concerned about the financial implications of this change, as I had already become accustomed to solely supporting our family financially without any contribution from my husband. It may raise curiosity about where he spent his money, but it no longer mattered to me; my determination remained unwavering. Instead, I directed my efforts toward a new venture - a printing and publishing business. Much to my satisfaction and with divine grace, the business began to thrive, establishing solid roots within our new community.

During his visits, my husband would bring a supportive presence that breathed new life into the enterprise. His contributions, once intermittent, became a steady force as the good news arrived: he had submitted his retirement letter, ready to join us in permanence. The prospect of him channeling his energies into our family business full-time was a refreshing turn of events.

Encouraged by his imminent transition, I nudged him toward academic advancement—enrolling in a Ph.D. program at the university that had become my professional harbor. In this whirlwind of change, the pieces of our life puzzle finally found their rightful place. However, as life has often taught me, the appearance of order can sometimes be a prelude to further lessons and trials. I held onto faith, the conviction that through the ups and downs, we were being shaped, molded by Potter's hands into vessels fit for His purpose.

Meanwhile, another pastor had been chosen to lead the parish that we had lovingly nurtured in the East, and thanks to the grace of God, it continues to flourish to this day. So, as a pastor with experience, the church ministers eagerly welcomed my husband to their midst. Thus, with his adeptness for influence, it was not long before he began to weave himself into the framework of the church's leadership. His ability to make himself seem indispensable was a skill and, I realized, a subtle stratagem. The currents of change that had brought us to this point now carried whispers of a familiar stir within the congregation—a murmur of a new calling, a new parish in need of leadership.

Without hesitation or seeking my input, my husband embraced this calling. In any case, I felt indifferent toward being excluded from the decision-making process. My main desire was unity and a connection beyond mere roles and responsibilities. Thus, I again accepted my role as a pastor's wife despite lingering doubts about my calling. I was resolute in one conviction: this path would afford me the privilege of being a conduit of positive change. With each opportunity to interact and influence, I sought to inspire and empower the women around me, to be a beacon of transformation, kindling the flame of empowerment, wisdom, and grace in as many lives as possible.

It is crucial to underscore that appointing a pastor is a task of profound spiritual importance and should not be rushed. Discerning the readiness and the motivations of those called to serve is critical. Leadership within the church goes beyond the charismatic presence or a willingness to serve. However, it requires a heart aligned with the will of God, a life reflective of the teachings of Christ, and a spirit guided by humility and servitude. The scriptures advise patience and discernment; as 1 Timothy 5:22 warns, "Do not be hasty in the laying on of hands, nor take part in the sins of others; keep yourself pure." The Scriptures specifically provide wisdom in 1 Timothy 3:6 by cautioning against appointing a recent convert or someone inexperienced in faith to leadership positions, lest they become conceited and fall under the same judgment as the devil. Similarly, James 3:1 reminds us that teachers will be judged more strictly, underscoring the gravity of such roles.

Therefore, church leaders must be vigilant, seeking God's guidance through prayer and communal counsel before appointing pastors to lead. Through such careful and prayerful consideration, we can maintain the integrity of the church's leadership, ensuring that those chosen are genuinely called to serve, not for their glory, but for the glory of God.

To the women stepping into the role of a pastor's wife, I extend a word of caution grounded in both experience and a heart for service: this journey is not one of prestige nor personal gain. It is, primarily, a call to service—a commitment that is as noble as it is demanding. The mantle you are considering will challenge you, mold you, and require the complete surrender of your ego at the altar of servitude. It is about pouring out oneself for others, about embodying the servanthood exemplified by Christ Himself.

Regrettably, the true essence of this calling has been misunderstood and, at times, misused to wield power or secure material benefits. Such actions tarnish the individual and can cast a shadow over the entire ministry.

As you step into this role, do so with humility and the earnest intention to serve God's people with love, patience, and integrity. Let your actions reflect the Proverbs 31 woman, who leads with strength and dignity, extending her hands to the needy and speaking wisdom with kindness on her tongue. Embrace this opportunity to make a positive impact, to support and uplift, and to serve as a pillar of faith and compassion within your community.

Years later, as I can testify, the relationships you forge, particularly with your congregation, will be a testament to your influence and heart for service. The bonds you cultivate through genuine care and shared growth will endure, outlasting transient accolades or momentary gains. To serve in this capacity is to plant seeds of change and hope that will flourish long after your active role has shifted, leaving a legacy of love and a community strengthened by your dedication.

By the grace of God, the enduring bonds and the lives I have been blessed to influence serve as a testament to this sacred service. To the glory of God, from my time as a pastor's wife to the present, I have formed deep connections with countless women who attest to the impact of a heart committed to God's work. This profound reward surpasses any fleeting honors—the legacy of lives transformed through service offered in love.

TWENTY-TWO

Grace in Abandonment

The most beautiful people we have known are those who have known defeat, known suffering, known struggle, known loss, and have found their way out of the depths.

Elisabeth Kübler-Ross

My husband's assimilation into our life back in the West was smoother than I had hoped. He took over the reins of our fledgling publishing business, and under his stewardship, it flourished, blossoming into a lucrative enterprise. There were moments, fleeting yet significant, where he would let slip, almost subconsciously, that his earnings from this venture far exceeded what he had ever made in his government position.

I recall one such instance, vivid as if it were yesterday. With a light-hearted chuckle, he boasted about his newfound financial prowess. I could not help but jest, "Well, that is quite a revelation, considering I never really knew how much you made in your government job!" This remark was wrapped in humor, but years of financial opacity and unspoken frustrations lay beneath it.

Even amidst this period of burgeoning prosperity, a familiar pattern persisted - a testament to the adage that the more things change, the more they remain the same. My husband's unwillingness to contribute financially to our household needs was as resolute as ever. Excuses were always at the ready, each more creative than the last. One day, he would claim that an unexpected expense had arisen at work, necessitating all his spare funds. Another time, he might insist that he was saving for a significant but mysteriously unspecified future investment that would benefit us all.

His ever-changing and conveniently timed justifications pointed to one consistent behavior: his persistent avoidance of contributing to our joint responsibilities as parents. This included a glaring lack of financial support for our children's tuition and school needs and a complete absence from their everyday school life. He neither engaged in school pick-ups or drop-offs nor attended parent-teacher meetings, sports days, or any school-related events.

The irony of my situation could have been the subject of a tragicomedy. There I was, a computer science faculty adept at navigating complex academic theories yet grappling with the seemingly simple task of securing paternal involvement in my household. My husband had become a shadowlike figure in our children's lives to the extent that even outsiders started to take notice. He was practically nonexistent in the eyes of the teachers at our children's schools.

During one of those crisp weekends, I hired a private tutor for my son to bolster his mathematics skills. On her first visit, she arrived ready to transform our living room into a vibrant educational space while my son awaited her guidance with barely contained excitement. The lesson proceeded smoothly until an unexpected figure entered: my husband. His arrival, rare and unannounced, caused a palpable shift in the atmosphere. The tutor, caught by surprise, paused mid-sentence, her expression a mix of astonishment and confusion.

As she was about to leave for the day, she approached me with a hesitance that spoke of a delicate question she was about to ask. "I hope you do not mind me saying this," she began, her voice tinged with uncertainty, "but I had always assumed you were a single mother." Her assumption, though initially startling, reflected the narrative that had inadvertently been woven around my family life. "What made you think that?" I inquired, even though I had a sinking feeling about the answer.

She fumbled for words, clearly uncomfortable. "I just... I have never seen their father around. Moreover, you seem to handle everything so well on your own. I am sorry, I did not mean to presume..."

I could not help but smile, albeit with a tinge of sadness. "No need to apologize. It is a reasonable assumption, given the circumstances."

As I watched the tutor leave, her earlier words echoed. It was a slight, almost humorous misunderstanding, but it underscored a deeper, more profound truth about the dynamics of our family life. A truth where I played dual roles – mother and father, provider and nurturer – while my husband, though physically present, was absent in every other sense that truly mattered.

Another vivid memory that lingers is the episode with our malfunctioning refrigerator. Realizing the fridge was beyond repair, I took time off work to manage the situation, as my husband seemed indifferent.

After purchasing a new refrigerator, I faced the challenge of transporting it to our upstairs apartment. I found myself negotiating with the taxi driver, not just for the ride but also for his assistance moving the fridge in exchange for a token of extra payment. Ironically, as we labored to maneuver the bulky appliance up the stairs, my husband's contribution was to grumble about the distraction our efforts caused. At that time, I could not help but notice the driver's fleeting glances toward my husband. His body language was subtly telling – a mix of surprise and a specific unspoken understanding of the dynamics within our household.

Though these instances might seem trivial in isolation, they painted a broader picture of the weirdness of our relationship. In African culture, where gender roles are often clearly defined, such neglect by a husband is not only frowned upon but also seen as a failure to uphold his responsibilities. The African proverb, "The man is the head of the home," underscores the expectation of men to be proactive and responsible for their family's well-being. However, these roles were reversed in our household, and the burden fell heavily on me. His indifference failed to fulfill societal expectations and a deeper, more profound abdication of the partnership we were supposed to share.

The most glaring of these instances was during one of my academic sojourns abroad to attend a conference. Back home, my husband, ostensibly busy with his printing endeavors, had traveled out of the city to meet clients. The semblance of normalcy, however, was shattered with a single phone call to me in faraway Italy to inform me that our car had broken. The car was stranded there, on the side of the road. Moreover, he wanted me to call the mechanic to handle it.

The sheer impracticality of his request left me speechless for a moment. Despite being thousands of miles away, he expected me to address a mechanical breakdown in our homeland. With a sense of resignation and the knowledge that my children and I would be the ones to bear the brunt of any further damage to the vehicle, I put aside all my activities to tackle the issue.

The situation was complicated: the car had broken down in a remote area between Lagos and Ibadan highway, and my husband had left it there. With no roadside assistance services like AAA[30] in my country, I was left to coordinate the recovery efforts from afar.

I instructed our mechanic to locate and tow the car to his workshop for repairs. My husband only gave me a vague description of the car's location. The mechanic's charges were steep, but I reluctantly agreed as I arranged for the car's rescue and repair.

> “In the face of abandonment, I found my strength, transforming echoes of neglect into a symphony of resilience and grace.

As I lay in my hotel room that night, the weight of the day's events pressed heavily on my soul. It was not just the car or the mechanic. It was the pattern, a series of deliberate acts that stretched back through the years. My husband's financial stinginess and his blatant disregard for his duties as a husband and father seemed to be more than just apathy. It was a calculated withdrawal, a form of silent retribution. He saw my strength, my determination to keep our family afloat, as a defiance of his authority, a challenge to the traditional norms he clung to.

It was as if he was punishing me, retaliating for my resilience and my refusal to give up on our marriage despite the overwhelming odds. He, perhaps, believed that the weight of these responsibilities would crush my

[30] AAA service is a membership-based roadside assistance and vehicle-related services provider, offering aid for car troubles such as flat tires, battery failure, and towing needs.

spirit and force me to capitulate. Nevertheless, I grew more robust and resolute with each challenge and every burden he thought to impose upon me. My resolve to protect and provide for my children became an unbreakable vow, a testament to my unwavering commitment as their mother.

TWENTY-THREE

The Spiritual Awakening

Sometimes God allows what he hates to accomplish what he loves.

Joni Eareckson Tada

As time progressed, my strength and determination only grew in the face of each new challenge and burdened my husband sought to impose upon me. Weeks melted into months, and the situation seemed only to worsen.

During those trying times, I yearned for a semblance of the connection and belonging that should exist between a husband and wife and, more so, as co-parents to our children. I repeatedly implored my husband to change, to recognize me not just as his wife but as the mother of his children. However, my husband remained stubbornly unyielding, ensconced in a delusion of adequacy. His defense was always the same, rooted in the belief that he was a good man. He justified this by pointing out that he is not a physically violent man, as if the absence of physical abuse was enough to qualify his behavior as appropriate.

This perspective highlights a crucial yet often misunderstood facet of intimate partner abuse. Abuse is not always physical. Emotional and psychological neglect, the refusal to acknowledge a partner's needs and contributions, can be equally damaging. His justification, based solely on the absence of physical harm, failed to account for the emotional and psychological neglect that was eroding the very foundation of our marriage.

Holding onto a deep and fervent hope, I reached out to the power that surpasses any earthly force. I turned earnestly to prayer, fasting, and heartfelt supplications, yearning for a celestial intervention to heal the fractures in my relationship and to restore the love I had always cherished with the man I held dear.

In its profound wisdom, the Bible speaks volumes about the transformative power of prayer - of how faith, as small as a mustard seed, could move mountains. Philippians 4:6-7 urges, "Do not be anxious about anything, but in everything by prayer and supplication with thanksgiving, let your requests be made known to God." In the depths of my despair, I clung to these promises, hoping they would seep into the essence of my reality as a much-needed balm to my troubled soul.

The heavens seemed silent as days bled into weeks and weeks into months. Once filled with fervor, my prayers began to feel like whispers lost in a void. The silence was deafening, and doubt crept into my heart like a stealthy intruder. Was my faith lacking? Were my prayers not fervent enough? The questions plagued me, casting a shadow over my unwavering belief in the power of prayer.

Meanwhile, I was ensnared in a moral and spiritual conundrum. The teachings of the Bible, which I held dear, emphasized the sanctity of marriage, the power of forgiveness, and the virtue of prolonged suffering. However, where does one draw the line? At what point does enduring become enabling?

While extolling the virtues of a patient and forgiving spouse, the Scriptures do not condone abuse or neglect. 1 Corinthians 13:4-7 speaks of love as patient, kind, and never self-seeking. Was I then, in my patience and forgiveness, inadvertently enabling his self-seeking behavior?

This spiritual dilemma is not unfamiliar in the Christian journey. The Bible is replete with stories of faithful believers who faced prolonged periods of silence from God. Job's unwavering faith in the face of immense suffering, David's soulful pleas in the Psalms, and even Jesus' cry of abandonment on the cross ("My God, my God, why have you forsaken me?") echoed my sense of divine silence.

As I navigated through this spiritual wilderness, I began to understand that sometimes, the silence of God is not the absence of God. Perhaps, in His infinite wisdom, God spoke to me in ways I had not understood. Could this silence be an invitation to deepen my trust, relinquish my desire for control, and embrace a faith that does not rely solely on visible answers?

It was in this barren landscape that my faith underwent a metamorphosis. It transitioned from faith-seeking visible miracles to a faith rooted in the invisible yet unshakeable assurance of God's presence and purpose. This shift was not immediate but a gradual awakening, a dawning realization that sometimes the most incredible miracles are not in changing circumstances but in transforming the self. Thus, I began to see a different form of God's response in the stillness of my unanswered prayers. It was not the dramatic change in my husband I had hoped for, but a subtle transformation within me. My faith was being purified, stripped of its naivety, and fortified in the fire of trials. This spiritual metamorphosis was not devoid of pain but necessary for my growth.

> "God's silence is not an absence but a sacred space where your faith is being molded, strengthened, and prepared for a deeper encounter with the Divine.

At this juncture, I offer this perspective to you, dear reader. In your moments of spiritual silence, when prayers seem unanswered, remember that you are not forsaken. The silence is not an absence but a sacred space where your faith is being molded, strengthened, and prepared for a more profound encounter with the Divine. Embrace your own 'night of the soul,' knowing that it is part of a larger plan of the Almighty God who works in mysterious ways. Your cries in the wilderness are not in vain; they are the birth pangs of a deeper, more resilient faith. Most importantly, in this journey, you are not alone.

As you would recall, my husband's explicit reservations about discussing family matters with outsiders had long been a chain around my neck, silencing my cries for help. This enforced silence became my norm; a suffocating shroud veiled the turmoil.

However, there comes a time when the soul, burdened beyond endurance, yearns for liberation. The turmoil within my home had intensified to a crescendo that rendered my fears of exacerbating my husband's irritation insignificant compared to the pressing need for external support. In this moment of acute desperation, I shamed the heavy shackles of enforced silence. I contacted friends and pastors, seeking the help I desperately needed.

Some might wonder why it took me so long to seek help, why I endured in silence for as long as I did. The potential social stigma in my country, especially within the church community, loomed large in my mind. The fear of being judged, misunderstood, or, worse, ignored was a powerful deterrent. This fear and the hope that things might change for the better kept me silent.

The stigma of failed or struggling marriages in a Christian context can be a heavy shroud. It is a paradox that wounds deeply—the church, a place of refuge and healing, can sometimes become a court of judgment and isolation. This contradiction is a deviation from the very essence of Christ, who exemplified unconditional love and acceptance, but it also exacerbates the suffering of those in need. It often leads to silence and solitude. Instead of finding support, many endure the cold shoulder of judgment.

I offer this reflection to the congregations: Embody Christ's love. Extend a hand of support, not a finger of judgment. Remember, the church is not a museum for saints but a hospital for sinners. Embrace those struggling in their marriages with empathy and understanding, not with whispers and stares.

Church communities must transform their approach toward struggling marriages. Rather than ostracizing, we must offer a safe space for open dialogue and support. This shift requires a deep understanding and acceptance that no marriage is immune to challenges, and these struggles are not a reflection of spiritual failure but a part of the human journey. By breaking the chains of stigma and judgment and replacing them with love and support, we not only uphold the teachings of Christ but also nurture a community of healing and strength.

Church workers and congregations must be educated and equipped to handle marital issues with sensitivity and wisdom. Workshops, seminars, and counseling services should be staples in church activities, providing preventative and supportive resources for couples. Let us be the hands and feet of Jesus, bringing healing where there is hurt, love where there is loneliness, and hope where there is despair. In doing so, we uplift the burdened souls and fulfill our divine calling to be a light in the world's darkness.

Those traversing similar paths know that reaching out for help, often perceived as a sign of weakness, is, in truth, a testament to strength. Marriage is not a journey to be walked alone in the shadows of fear and silence. The partnership thrives on communication, mutual respect, and the wisdom of shared counsel. Breaking free from the imposed silence of a troubled marriage is about aspiring for a life where you thrive. The decision to seek help is a declaration of self-worth, a refusal to be trapped in the echo chamber of one's despair. Acknowledging that your voice matters, your pain is valid, and your well-being is paramount.

Let this be a message of hope to you, dear reader. In your struggles, may you find the courage to seek the light, break the silence, and embark on a journey of survival, flourishing, and rediscovery. Remember, in Psalm 46:1, "God is our refuge and strength, an ever-present help in trouble." Your voice is your strength; you will find your path to healing and peace in its echo.

Eventually, I realized that my fear, however valid, was not a reason to suffer in silence. The cost of silence was too great, and the need for healing too urgent. While not every individual or institution within the church community may understand or be equipped to handle such situations effectively, genuine people and frameworks still support those in dire circumstances like mine.

In seeking help, I found unexpected sources of solace and understanding. The individuals I reached out to, firmly rooted in their faith and compassion, became my pillars of strength during this tumultuous period. They endeavored to intervene, offering support and guidance to mediate the situation with my husband.

Despite their best mediation efforts, my husband remained unyielding to external intervention. Not only did he refuse to engage constructively with their attempts to help, but he also began to react with increasing disrespect and anger toward me. He was particularly incensed about me sharing our private matters with outsiders.

I eventually understood that his reaction was part of a deliberate and manipulative strategy. He aimed to instill fear in me and create a wedge between me and those offering their support. By openly showing disrespect to my confidants and directing his anger toward me for seeking assistance, he was actively working to foster an environment of isolation around me.

This approach is a well-documented tactic in relational manipulation and control, as noted by Bancroft (2002). Abusers often employ anger and intimidation to exert control, thereby inhibiting their partner from accessing the strength and support that might enable them to confront or exit the abusive situation. By recognizing these actions as deliberate and calculated rather than spontaneous reactions, those affected can better navigate their situations, seek appropriate support, and make informed decisions about their relationships.

As someone who has walked this path, I urge anyone experiencing similar challenges to hold onto their support systems and not be swayed by attempts to instill fear or isolation. True healing and resolution often require the intervention of unbiased, external support, and it is essential to persevere in seeking this despite any resistance or backlash from the partner.

TWENTY-FOUR

When Grief Meets with Solitude

What we have once enjoyed we can never lose. All that we love deeply becomes a part of us.

Helen Keller

As the days melded into years, my husband's neglect—both emotional and financial—began to etch itself not only on my heart but also on my body. The constant stress and the unrelenting emotional turmoil found a tangible expression in my deteriorating health. I became a living testament to the adage, "The body keeps the score." My physical ailments reflected the internal chaos, a manifestation of the unseen scars etched deep within my spirit.

The connection between chronic stress and physical health has been extensively studied in the field of psychoneuroimmunology. A study by McEwen (1998) has long established the connection between chronic stress and a range of physical disorders. Prolonged stress, especially psychological stress, can disrupt nearly every system in the body, impair the immune system, disrupt hormonal balances, and contribute to a range of health issues, from heart disease to autoimmune disorders (Segerstrom & Miller, 2004). In my case, the findings were not just statistics but a reality I lived with every waking moment.

The words of Proverbs 17:22, "A cheerful heart is a good medicine, but a crushed spirit dries up the bones, became my reality. My spirit was not just crushed; it was hammered under neglect and betrayal. My body began to speak the language of pain and exhaustion, a silent cry for help. Headaches became a constant companion, and my immune system seemed to have surrendered, leaving me vulnerable to a series of infections.

Despite the physical toll, I endeavored to maintain a semblance of normalcy. In the face of the domestic storm that was my life, I found solace and purpose in my academic career. It was a realm where I could exert control, achieve success, and feel accomplished. As I climbed the ranks in my faculty, I was simultaneously profoundly entrenched in my Ph.D. program, a lifeline that kept me afloat amidst the turbulent waters of my personal life. I was also elected to the executive council of the national body of my professional organization. I saw this as a distraction from the raging storm back home.

However, this pursuit required an unwavering dedication and a commitment that transcended the typical boundaries of a regular. It required whisking me away from the familiar confines of home to various academic conferences, symposiums, and collaborations. Unfortunately, the repercussions were heartbreakingly evident in my children's lives.

Their father, ensconced in his world, failed to bridge the gap my absence created. In their formative years, the children needed more than just a figure; they needed a nurturing presence, an emotional anchor — something their father was unable or unwilling to provide. My heart ached with every achievement, knowing that my success came at the cost of moments lost with my children.

To those walking a similar path, know that balancing career and family is fraught with bittersweet symphonies. The highs of professional success often coexist with the lows of personal sacrifices. As you strive for excellence in your career, remember the silent stories of those at home whose lives are inextricably linked with yours. Your story is not just one of professional triumphs but also a tale of resilience, love, and unspoken sacrifices that paint the complete picture of a working mother's life.

Amidst the whirlwind, I received news that pierced through the usual chaos like a bolt of lightning - my father was gravely ill, lying in a coma in our hometown. This news set off a chain of urgent actions, a frantic race against time. I hastily arranged for an emergency trip to our town, my heart heavy with trepidation and hope. Would I be too late? Would I get another chance to see my father, hear his voice, and feel his comforting presence?

> " The highs of professional success often coexist with the lows of personal sacrifices.

Arriving at the hospital, I was greeted by the sight of my father, a once-vibrant man now lying motionless, tethered to the lifelines of medical machinery. However, amidst the hospital's sterile beeps and hushed tones, there was a flicker of hope – he was still breathing. This fragile thread of life propelled me into action, arranging for his immediate transfer to the city where I worked, confident in the capabilities of the teaching hospital at my university.

For three long months, the teaching hospital became a second home for my mother and, by extension, for me. Her constant presence in the hospital corridors transformed them into a place of hope and resilience. Night after night, she endured the discomfort of sleeping on those hard floors while my father's slow journey back to health unfolded under the watchful eyes of caring doctors and nurses.

During this trying period, the outpouring of concern and support from friends, colleagues, and church members was a balm to my weary soul. They came in droves, their presence a comforting reminder that I was not alone on this journey. However, amidst this whirlwind of support and care, there was a glaring, incomprehensible absence – my husband. His failure to appear, even for a single day, to see my ailing father was a blow that words fail to capture. How could one, bound by the sacred vows of marriage, display such callous indifference? Was his heart so devoid of compassion, so bereft of empathy, that not even the dire circumstances could stir a semblance of concern?

In the depths of this bewildering neglect, a question haunted me: Had I been hypnotized into holding onto a marriage that seemed not to exist? The resilience of my spirit and the unwavering commitment to my marital vows perplexed even me. Despite the storm that raged, my decision not to give up on the marriage was a paradox that defied logic. It was as though I was locked in a dance with destiny, where each step was guided by an unseen hand, leading me through the web of pain and perseverance.

To the glory of God, my father's health improved sufficiently for him to be discharged, though he never fully regained his physical strength. We took him back to our hometown, where my elder brother continued to take on the mantle of his care until his passing.

As I navigated the murky waters of grief following my father's passing, the absence of my husband's support was, regrettably, no longer a surprise. Grief is a road often walked alone, but the journey becomes even more solitary without a supportive partner. Each condolence, each sympathetic glance from friends and family, was a reminder of what was missing at home: a shoulder to lean on, a hand to hold, a presence to share in the sorrow. When the day of my father's burial arrived, my husband did make an appearance. Nevertheless, his presence felt more like a ceremonial gesture, a superficial compliance with social expectations rather than a genuine sharing of the burden of grief.

This part of my story is shared not to evoke sympathy but rather to offer solidarity to those who might find themselves in a similar situation. My journey through grief, while solitary in many ways, was also a period of profound personal growth and deepening faith. It was a reminder that even in the darkest times, one can find an inner wellspring of strength and grace.

Thus, in my period of mourning, my resilience was put to the test. I had no choice but to gather the shards of my broken heart and continue forward. The void left by my partner's emotional absence was filled, not with bitterness, but with a renewed focus on the love and support of those who truly stood by me – my children, colleagues, friends, and the unwavering strength of my faith.

Most importantly, my father, a man of great humility and kindness, has left an indelible mark on my life. His presence was a constant source of strength and inspiration. In his memory, I dedicate this chapter to celebrating the virtues he embodied and the legacy he left behind.

My father's humility was his crown. He navigated life's challenges with a grace that never wavered, never succumbing to anger or conflict. His peaceful demeanor was a testament to the strength of gentle spirits, teaching us that true strength lies in the ability to remain calm amidst the storm.

No matter the disrespect or the disregard he faced, my father's response was always one of peace. He was a man who cherished harmony above all. He believed sincerely in the power of reconciliation and practiced it with every breath.

His commitment to education was unwavering. Despite limited resources as a teacher, he stretched every resource to ensure that his children and extended family received the best education possible. In times of personal crisis, he remained steadfast despite societal pressures. His sacrifices were a silent yet powerful expression of his love and hope for the happiness of everyone around him. My father would go to great lengths, sacrificing his comfort to meet the needs of others. He was so selfless that he often went hungry or borrowed money to meet the needs of others. He lived not for himself but for those around him, a living embodiment of altruism and compassion.

Tragically, my father passed away before he could witness the fruits of his selflessness, a moving reminder of the often-unseen impact of a life lived for others. He fondly called me "doctor," a term of endearment and belief in my potential, but sadly, as fate would have it, he could not wait to see the fulfillment of this title as I earned my Ph.D. after his passing.

A Poem for My Father:

In the stillness of the night,
I pen these lines with tearful sight,
For a father whose love was a guiding light,
A beacon of peace, shining ever so bright.

Gentle in word, humble indeed,
In every heart, he planted a seed,
Of love and hope, he was the creed,
A selfless soul, in thought and deed.

In trials and storms, he stood so tall,
A rock of peace, amidst it all,
In his silent way, he answered the call,
To lift us whenever we would fall.

"My Doc," he'd say with pride in his eyes,
A dream unfulfilled, beneath the skies,
Yet, in his legacy, his spirit lies,
Guiding my path as I rise.

Though now you're gone, your memory stays,
In every dawn and twilight's rays,
Your teachings guide my life's maze,
In my heart, your love forever blazes.

Farewell, dear father, your journey's at peace,
In the heavens above, where all sorrows cease,
Your life, a masterpiece of love's release,
In our memories, your essence will never decrease.

- In memory of Mr. Michael Ojo Longe.

TWENTY-FIVE

The Unseen Hands of Grace

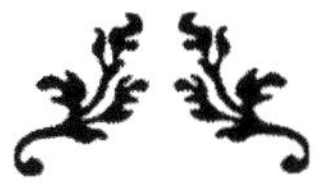

Life is not about waiting for the storms to pass. It's about learning how to dance in the rain.

Vivian Greene

In the wake of my father's funeral, life resumed its relentless march, pulling me back into the embrace of my professional and familial duties. I returned to these responsibilities with a heart laden with grief yet fortified by the same unwavering determination that had long been my compass.

During this tumultuous period, my academic career was a cornerstone of my identity amidst the emotional whirlwind. Balancing a demanding role as a full-time faculty member while pursuing my Ph.D. as a full-time student at another university was an immense undertaking. This deep commitment began to extend its toll on the emotional well-being of my children. Their father, though physically present, was always absent in spirit, leaving a void that began to erode the tender fabric of their young souls.

Throughout this tumultuous period, my academic career was a cornerstone of my identity amidst the emotional upheaval. Balancing a full-time faculty role while pursuing a Ph.D. as a full-time student at another university was a profound commitment. This intense dedication, however, began to take its toll on the emotional well-being of my children. Their father, though physically present, was often absent in spirit, leaving a gap that gradually wore away at the delicate fabric of their young lives. I strove to maintain a balance in everything, but being neither a machine nor an artificial intelligence, something inevitably had to give way.

The direct consequence was a delay in the progress of my Ph.D. program, which was initially intended to span three years. Sometimes, I missed seminar presentations or found myself unprepared for my own. The path I had envisioned, which once seemed clear and direct, now stretched out, marred by interruptions. As much as I desired, taking a break from home responsibilities to focus solely on my research, or even a leave of absence from work, was a luxury I could not afford.

Around the fifth year of my Ph.D. journey, a glimmer of hope appeared in a twist that felt like a divine intervention: my university selected me to receive the prestigious MacArthur Foundation Grant Award (MacArthur, 2009). This accolade opened the door to an invaluable collaboration opportunity with a leading university in Canada. The opportunity felt like a biblical liberation, akin to the freeing of Zion described in Psalms 126:1.[31]

However, with this blessing came a significant crossroad. It demanded a sacrifice I had never contemplated: six months away from my children. Torn between my dual roles as a career woman and a mother, I faced a heart-rending decision. My career progression, crucial for the future security of my children, cast a long shadow over their immediate needs. To soften this impending absence, I turned to my mother for assistance, hoping her presence in our home would provide a nurturing environment for my children.

As I embarked on an essential journey to Canada to further my Ph.D. research, fortified by a resilience ingrained in me by my mother, I was not overly concerned about my husband's behavior in my absence. I had grown accustomed to his ability to present a façade of kindness and perfection,

[31] Psalm 126:1 "When the LORD brought back the captives to Zion, we were like men who dreamed."

particularly in front of others. He had mastered the art of wearing a mask, adeptly portraying himself as the ideal husband whenever outsiders were involved. Therefore, I trusted that he would maintain his best behavior while I was away.

At the airport, amidst the comforting presence of friends, my farewell to my husband was a mosaic of complex emotions. Our parting kiss, a customary gesture, was tinged with an undercurrent of hope and despair and fraught with unspoken fears and uncertainties.

I found myself questioning the future of our marriage - would this journey be a turning point? Concern for my children's well-being in my absence clouded my thoughts. Their faces haunted me, stirring a whirlwind of anxiety and doubt.

As I boarded the plane to Vancouver, my husband's motives at the airport remained an enigma. Were his gestures of farewell genuine signs of affection or merely his way of preserving a semblance of normalcy in our strained marriage? Was his goodbye kiss a genuine token of love or a performance staged for our pastor and friend who escorted us to the airport? The ascent of the plane mirrored my rising anxiety – about my marital future, my children's well-being in my absence, and the unknowns that awaited me in Canada.

Each mile that separated me from my homeland intensified the storm of thoughts. I reflected on John Gottman's insights about the complexity of emotions in a relationship, wondering what our future holds. As the plane cleaved through the clouds, my heart mirrored its journey, soaring amidst a tumult of emotions. Anxiety and fear were my silent companions, as tangible as the seat beneath me, yet invisible to the world. The steady hum of the aircraft's engines constantly reminded me of the growing distance from the familiar – from the embrace of my family. Visions of my young sons appeared like delicate mirages against the stark backdrop of the cabin – my four-year-old's eyes wide with innocence and my seven-year-olds earnest face, both unaware of the intricate tapestry of emotions their mother was weaving high above the clouds.

Around me, fellow passengers found refuge in the rhythm of the flight, succumbing to sleep or the distractions of in-flight entertainment. In contrast, I was enveloped in a cocoon of introspection and prayer. The silence of the cabin, punctuated only by the occasional murmur or shift of a fellow traveler, formed a stark canvas for the fervent appeals emanating from the depths of my soul. I prayed not just for protection and guidance but for divine strength to navigate the uncharted waters of my life that lay ahead.

The pilot's voice announcing our descent into Vancouver interrupted my reverie, signaling the end of one journey and the beginning of another. Below, the city lights of Vancouver twinkled like stars in a tapestry of hope and possibilities, casting an ethereal glow over the landscape that awaited me.

This was my maiden voyage into the Western World, a leap into realms unknown. With its majestic landscapes and the vibrant tapestry of its multicultural fabric, Vancouver beckoned with promise and uncertainty. However, even amidst the thrill of new exploration, a part of my heart remained anchored in the home I had left behind.

During the descent, my thoughts drifted to the flurry of random emails and social media messages I had sent weeks earlier. It was a digital casting of my net into the vast ocean of the internet, a hopeful attempt to find a connection, a guide, or a compassionate stranger in this new land. I reached out to various communities, churches, and individuals, casting my net wide, yearning for a familiar face or a kind-hearted soul in Vancouver.

However, the silence that greeted my digital outreach was a profound echo of isolation, each unanswered email and ignored social media message slipping silently into the abyss of the internet. In the back of my mind, a nagging question persisted: had my Nigerian identity influenced this silence? The global stigma attached to 'Nigerian scammers,' a label unfairly borne by the honest majority due to the actions of a few, loomed over my outreach efforts like an ominous cloud.

This experience points attention to an important message that needs to be echoed across the globe: not all Nigerians fit into this negative stereotype. Countless Nigerians, like me, strive for integrity and endeavor to contribute positively to the global community. This journey was a step toward dispelling these misconceptions, a showcase of the true spirit of Nigeria – one of resilience, integrity, and unwavering faith. It was a call to those tarnishing our nation's reputation to cease their deceitful activities, which cast an undeserved shadow over our beloved country.

As the plane prepared to touch down, a realization dawned on me. Perhaps I had placed too much faith in earthly assistance in the arms of flesh, expecting human intervention to ease my path. The words of Jeremiah 17:5[32] reminded me to realign my trust away from the fallibility of humans and toward the unwavering strength of my faith.

With the plane's wheels gently kissing the tarmac, a serene calm enveloped me. I turned to prayer in expressing gratitude to God for the safe journey. I also sought His protection over my family left behind and implored His guidance in navigating this new chapter of my life.

Indeed, the answer to my prayers came unexpectedly: a vivid testament to God's miraculous and serendipitous workings.

As I navigated through the crowd, a peculiar sight caught my eye—a woman standing confidently, holding a placard that read 'Yoruba woman.' Intrigue mingled with skepticism in my mind as I initially walked past. The idea that this sign was meant for me amidst the anonymity of the crowd seemed implausible. Nevertheless, an inner nudge, gentle but persistent, drew me back. Approaching her, I masked my curiosity with a practical question about taxi directions, hardly daring to believe our paths were meant to intersect.

To my astonishment, she mentioned my university and asked if I was the expected visitor from there. Upon my confirmation, her face lit up with excitement and warmth, as if we were reconnecting after a long separation. She revealed that she and her husband had been waiting to offer me shelter and comfort. I stood, rooted to the spot, my mind struggling to grasp this surreal twist of fate. Who were these strangers, and how did they know of my arrival? A wave of exhaustion from the journey subdued my swirling questions, allowing me to embrace this unexpected but welcome turn of events.

As I joined them in their car, an amusing thought crossed my mind – could they have mistaken me for someone else? However, deep within, I

---

32 Jeremiah 17:5: 'This is what the LORD says: "Cursed is the one who trusts in man, who draws strength from mere flesh and whose heart turns away from the LORD" '

recognized this as the divine response I had sought, a serendipitous alignment in my time of need.

Then, to my utter delight, they presented me with a surprise—a meal of traditional food, still warm, waiting in the car. My long-honed caution gave way to overwhelming gratitude as I savored each bite. I was here miles from home, yet being nourished with familiar flavors by individuals quickly transforming from strangers into kindred spirits. It was a moment of divine providence, affirming the power of prayer and the mysterious ways in which God meets our needs. Their literal and figurative embrace was a spiritual affirmation that I was not alone, that my prayers were heard, and that even in the most unlikely scenarios, the grace of God shines brightly.

I was eager to settle into the apartment I had carefully selected from afar. However, the couple who unexpectedly became my angels in this new land expressed concerns about the neighborhood's safety. Despite my initial skepticism, their apprehension piqued my caution, and I agreed to see the place myself. The reality was a jarring contrast to the idyllic images online.

The neighborhood, rather than the palace I had envisioned, was draped in discomfort, its streets marked with apparent realities of public drug use. Their earlier warnings now rang true, sincerely reflecting their concern for my well-being. We promptly decided to abandon this initial plan and seek a safer abode.

As we drove away, our conversation bridged the gap from strangers to something more akin to friends. Curiosity overcame me, and I asked how they knew of my arrival. Their shared story was so beautiful – my email had reached a community member, and it touched their hearts, compelling them to reach out to me, a stranger from across the seas.

As we drove away from the disquieting neighborhood, faced with the unsuitability of my initial choice, my alternate option to find a hotel accommodation was overshadowed by financial worries, given my tight budget. Amidst these swirling thoughts, the couple, who had unexpectedly become my guardians in this foreign land, turned to me with an offer that was as astonishing as it was generous.

"You know, we have a home," the husband began, his voice laced with a warmth that felt like a comforting embrace. "It is not a huge citadel but filled with love and laughter."

His wife chimed in, her eyes reflecting the kindness in her heart. "We have four children, two boys and two girls. Our daughters would not mind sharing their room. Would you be comfortable until you find a more suitable place?"

I was speechless. Their offer was like a ray of sunlight piercing through the clouds of my anxiety. The irony of the situation was not lost on me. All my meticulous plans, laid out precisely, had crumbled in the face of reality. Furthermore, now, here I was, being offered a haven by people who were practically strangers yet felt like family.

I chuckled softly, more to myself than to them. "It is as if a divine scriptwriter has taken over my story," I mused aloud, my heart swelling with gratitude and disbelief. "Your offer... it is more than I could have hoped for. I would be honored to stay with your family."

As we drove toward their home, the couple's easy banter and the laughter of their children, whom they called to share the news of my arrival, filled the car. It was a symphony of warmth and welcome, a stark contrast to the loneliness that had begun to seep into my bones.

For the following two weeks, I found physical shelter and a deep sense of belonging and connection in the warmth of this family's embrace. Their unwavering support helped me navigate the initial challenges of settling into a new country, providing physical comfort and spiritual nourishment.

Despite coming from different religious backgrounds, with them being a devoted Muslim family and me a Christian, they received me with immense warmth and acceptance. This embrace was a living testament to the Yoruba adage "iwa lesin,"[33] which translates to 'character is the true religion.' Their genuine kindness and open-heartedness transcended the boundaries of our different faiths. They defied stereotypes and shattered barriers, embodying a universal truth that often, the most profound expressions of faith are found not in our rituals but in our actions and attitudes toward one another. Their conduct

> “The most profound expressions of faith are found not in our rituals, but in our actions and attitudes towards one another.

[33] "Iwa lesin": A Yoruba phrase from Nigeria, which emphasizes that one's character and conduct serve as the truest reflection of their faith or spirituality, rather than the mere practice of religious rituals.

was a living echo of the biblical verse 1 John 4:8, revealing that true faith manifests in how we treat others, irrespective of our diverse beliefs.

They introduced me to the local transport system, ensuring I felt confident and secure in navigating my new environment. Sundays transformed into a beautiful blend of faith and fellowship. They would drive me to my church, return to pick me up from it, and then share a meal with their children and me afterward, creating a harmonious blend of interfaith, understanding, and respect.

This chapter in my life, shared with a family who started as strangers and became my guardians, taught me the power of human kindness. It vividly illustrated the unexpected ways we can experience God's love and provision through the hands and hearts of those around us.

I eventually secured accommodation near the campus, yet the home of my unexpected guardians remained a haven of comfort and warmth. Weekends at their abode, I have transformed them into a symphony of delightful culinary experiences and rich cultural exchanges. Within their walls, we wove a bond that defied the conventional bounds of friendship, blossoming into an extended family knit together by a fabric of love and mutual respect.

The lessons I learned from this encounter went beyond academic knowledge. They taught me about the power of kindness, the strength of faith, and the beauty of human connection. These lessons were the true gifts of my journey, treasures I carried with me as I continued to navigate the challenges and opportunities ahead.

This chapter of my life taught me that divine providence can emerge in the most unexpected forms in the most challenging situations. This realization echoes the words from Isaiah 55:8 (NIV): "For my thoughts are not your thoughts, neither are your ways my ways," declares the Lord. In this unexpected journey, I witnessed the miraculous unfold, reaffirming my faith in the unfathomable and gracious ways of the divine.

Amidst this whirlwind of change and adaptation, my thoughts often returned to my children. Their images, imprinted in my heart, constantly reminded me of the purpose behind my sacrifices. Every success in my research was a step closer to providing a better future for them. However, each day apart from them was tinged with a mother’s longing as I clung to the phone calls, videoconferences, and messages as precious lifelines connecting me to them.

TWENTY-SIX

Crossroad of Opportunity

God sometimes takes us into troubled waters not to drown us, but to cleanse us.

Author Unknown

As my research stay in Canada neared its end, I stood at a significant crossroads. The experiences and knowledge I had gained were invaluable, yet an undeniable sense of incompleteness clung to me like a persistent fog on a morning landscape. During this period of introspection and yearning for more, I discovered an opportunity that seemed to call out to me—a research lab in the USA, specifically at the University of Pittsburgh. Known for its pioneering work in my field, this lab promised to be the lighthouse guiding me to the unexplored depths of my research ambitions.

This opportunity, however, was shrouded in financial uncertainty. My grant, the lifeblood of my research endeavors, was depleted. However, the familiar adage "opportunity comes but once" reverberated, reminding me that certain moments in life are pivotal and can profoundly alter our paths.

Amidst this tumult of uncertainty and aspiration, I found pillars of strength in two crucial communities—my host family in Canada and my church family. Their support transcended mere kindness; they rallied around me, offering moral support and practical aid, bolstering my resolve to journey to the USA.

The farewell with my host family in Vancouver was deeply emotional. Our connection had evolved far beyond the initial act of kindness; we had become a family, woven together not by blood but by shared experiences, meals, and countless heartfelt conversations. Their home had been a crucible of transformation, leaving an indelible imprint on my life's journey. In keeping with my commitment to privacy, their names are not disclosed in this narrative. However, our bond has only strengthened over time, becoming a profound familial connection. Their children, whom I have watched grow into remarkable men and women, hold a special place in my heart, reinforcing the familial bonds that feel as accurate and enduring as any ties of blood.

To this family, whose names are unspoken in these pages but whose spirit and love shine like beacons in my heart: your acts of kindness are etched deep within me, a testament to the profound power of empathy and selflessness. You have taught me that true charity seeks no accolades and knows no boundaries. In your everyday lives, you have embodied the essence of the Biblical verse from 1 Corinthians 13:13[34], demonstrating that among faith, hope, and love, the greatest is indeed love. Although your names remain veiled in this story, I believe they are celebrated in the heavens, and I pray the generosity you have shown me returns to you in multiple folds.

In the spirit of the promise from Psalm 23:6[35], I hope the same goodness and mercy you bestowed upon me would bless every day of your lives, illuminating your paths and enriching your existence as profoundly as you have enriched mine.

This acknowledgment does not diminish the immense impact and support I received from my nurturing community in British Columbia, especially my congregation. Their embrace was a lifeline, providing warmth and support that constantly calmed my troubled spirit. These relationships, tenderly cultivated in a land far from my own, have blossomed into a cherished and enduring facet of my life's journey. In their presence, I found echoes of my

---

[34] 1 Corinthians 13:13: "And now these three remain: faith, hope and love. But the greatest of these is love."

[35] Psalm 23:6: "Surely your goodness and love will follow me all the days of my life, and I will dwell in the house of the LORD forever."

homeland, a soothing solace reminding me that even in distant lands, one can discover kindred spirits and a sense of belonging. They reaffirmed my belief in the goodness of people, the power of faith, and the unending grace that carries us through life's journey.

Upon arriving at the research lab in Pittsburgh, USA, I was greeted by a world of intellectual vigor and collaboration, where I worked with brilliant minds in recommender systems. Together, we embarked on numerous research endeavors, resulting in joint publications and a robust global network with whom I still collaborate.

Reflecting on this journey, I see it as a testament to the power of faith and resilience. Faced with financial limitations and uncertainties back home, I could have succumbed to doubt and hesitation. Instead, I chose to listen to my inner voice and embrace the opportunity as a pathway to growth.

As the days seamlessly wove into weeks, the conclusion of my six-week research sojourn in the United States marked a period of profound fulfillment and thankfulness. My academic boundaries had been broadened, and I had cultivated relationships destined to endure well into the future. The connections I established within my research cohort and the vibrant church community in Pittsburgh emerged as foundational support, offering strength and camaraderie for the journey ahead.

Finally, the time came for me to return home. Exhaustion was etched into my bones, but it was overshadowed by an eager anticipation of reuniting with my family. I yearned to see my children's faces, to hold them close and share the tales of my journey. Moreover, deep in my heart, there was a flicker of hope – hope that my husband, too, had transformed during my absence.

As the plane descended and I set foot on the familiar soil of my homeland, I felt an overwhelming sense of transformation. The trials and triumphs of my journey in North America had molded me into a vessel of resilience and faith. I was returning as a scholar who had broadened her academic scope and a woman who had been refined in the crucible of life's challenges.

"Welcome home," whispered a gentle voice within me, which seemed to echo the divine assurance of my faith. I carried with me lessons of compassion, kindness, and the profound human connections I had forged, treasures that were now inseparable parts of who I had become. They were my guiding stars, illuminating the path as I navigated the intricate dance of reuniting with my family and reclaiming the life I had left behind.

Regrettably, the success of my endeavors abroad starkly contrasted with the unchanged, strained dynamics awaiting me at home. While my academic achievements reached new heights, my family life remained ensnared in unchanged complexity.

It is important to remember that my mother, the unsung heroine of our family saga, had become a pillar of stability and care for my children in my absence. As expected, my new academic achievement also required more responsibilities and dedication to my career. I also needed to prepare for the final defense of my thesis, which required a deep level of commitment. God bless my mother. She became the lighthouse in the storm for my children. I remember her tireless mornings, waking before dawn to ferry the kids to school in her old Nissan, the backseat always filled with the comforting aroma of her lovingly prepared breakfasts. Yet, beneath the surface of this domestic harmony, she faced a deluge of disrespect from my husband.

My mother carried this burden silently, choosing to preserve the facade of peace within our 'godly' household. I was completely unaware of these tensions. However, the day the reality of her suffering was revealed to me remains indelibly etched in my memory. I was at home, unbeknownst to my husband, when I witnessed an unbearable scene – my husband, in a rare loss of control, verbally lashing out at my mother.

In that pivotal moment, I faced a sobering introspection regarding the essence of my commitment – was it indeed the scriptural injunction to uphold the sanctity of the family that anchored me to this marriage, or was it merely fear? Was my perseverance driven by the well-being of our children or by the biblical counsel to steadfastly defend the covenant of marriage?

When the time came to address these concerns with my husband, his apologies were superficial and solely aimed at placating me, leaving my mother's wounded dignity unaddressed. While delivered with a veneer of calmness, his words fell short of offering any genuine solace or restitution for the hurt inflicted.

I contemplated whether my mother's presence was exacerbating our marital conflict. So, I broached the topic to my husband's hearing. To my amazement, he swiftly agreed that we send my mother away from our home. His readiness to send my mother away, the very person who had been instrumental in the stability of our children, was sickening.

I decided to talk with my mother about this dilemma, which unfolded with unexpected lightness. Her words, laced with humor and wisdom, belied the gravity of our situation. "My child," she said, "I have weathered greater storms. This is but a breeze." Her resilience, her ability to place the well-being of her grandchildren and daughter above her own, was a profound lesson in selfless love and sacrifice. She was willing to downplay her discomfort, prioritizing the well-being of her grandchildren and my health over her ego. Her sacrificial love was a powerful lesson in resilience.

Considering my mother's unyielding support, I was faced with a problematic paradox in my marriage. My career advancement necessitated having my mother's support more than ever. Yet, the thought of leaving her alone with my husband, fearing an act of sacrilege such as harm coming to her in my absence, was unbearable. It was clear that her welfare and peace of mind were paramount, and I could not, in good conscience, subject her to the potential heartache of living under the same roof with him, especially when it was evident that he preferred her absence. Thus, I devised a solution that would allow me to have the best of both worlds—a solution that felt akin to eating my cake and having it too.

Thus, I took a decisive step and secured a two-year lease on an apartment within our neighborhood. This was a bittersweet victory, offering my mother proximity and the ability to continue supporting us without subjecting her to the daily tensions of our household.

It was no longer a surprise that my husband instantly agreed to this arrangement. The most important thing to me at that time was that I had managed to shield my children from the marital discord, ensuring their grandmother's love and support enveloped them. At the same time, I grappled with the complexities of my relationship with my husband. Though far from ideal, this setup offered peace and stability. It was a poignant reminder of the wisdom found in Proverbs 17:1, highlighting the sometimes painful pursuit of peace over conflict, even at a personal cost.

In her new residence, my mother thrived. She remained the indomitable force of support for my children and me, her strength undiminished. Driving her car, she took on the responsibility of picking up and dropping off the children for school runs and providing good meals, ensuring their days began and ended with the comfort of her presence.

Meanwhile, I continued to navigate my domestic challenges, trying to shield my children from the discord. At the same time, my mother provided not just food but a stable, loving environment for them.

I have penned a poem for my mother in homage to her unspoken bravery, relentless spirit, and the boundless love that has been our guiding light. This poem is a tribute to the strength, love, and sacrifice that defines my mother. It is a testament to the unspoken trials she has endured and the silent victories she has won. Through these lines, I seek to give voice to her sacrifices, celebrate her resilience, and acknowledge her indelible impact on our lives.

In the quiet strength of your silent toil,
You nurtured a garden in rocky soil.
A heroine unsung, with love so grand,
Bearing burdens only hearts understand.

In my absence, you were the guiding light,
Keeping their worlds joyful, warm, and bright.
School runs, meals made with a tender touch,
In every act, you gave beyond so much.

The veil lifted, your trials came to light,
A warrior's heart veiled by night's plight.
Mum, your love, a beacon ever so true,
In every step, I carry a piece of you.

For the sacrifices seen and unseen,
For the love, the care, unspoken, serene,
This poem is but a humble token,
For words unspoken and vows unbroken.

Thank you, Mum, for being our steadfast shore,
In your strength, we find so much to adore.
In this life's tapestry, you are the thread,
Golden and robust through every path we tread.

TWENTY-SEVEN

Triumph Amidst Trials

"Trials teach us what we are; they dig up the soil, and let us see what we are made of.

Charles Spurgeon

In the unfolding drama of life, we often find ourselves cast in roles for which we never auditioned. Yet, through faith and wisdom, we can author a new script that reflects our deepest values and acknowledges our inherent worth as beloved children of God.

The curtain rose on a new chapter: I triumphantly completed my Ph.D. in Computer Science after a challenging six-year journey marked by marital discord, academic diligence, and a relentless pursuit of spiritual equilibrium. As the scripture in James 1:12 offers solace, "Blessed is the one who perseveres under trial because, having stood the test, that person will receive the crown of life that the Lord has promised."

However, despite my apparent progress, the financial gaps remained unfilled. My husband's withdrawal from our family life deepened, leaving me to continue to manage our domestic sphere single-handedly. This was in addition to the challenge of sustaining two households—my own and my mother's.

I accepted two additional part-time teaching roles at different universities to bridge the financial gap. This demanding schedule pushed me to the brink of physical and mental exhaustion, leaving me ensnared in a relentless cycle of travel, sleep deprivation, and the unending demands of academic responsibilities.

I then began to question the nature of my husband's detachment. It was as if he was punishing me, though for what transgression I could not fathom. His disconnection from me and the children, coupled with the financial strain he was putting on me and his nonchalant attitude toward my family, felt like a systematic effort to push me to my limits. Moreover, indeed, my limits were being tested. My health started to deteriorate, a clear sign that this situation was unsustainable.

His addiction, once a shadowy presence, now loomed more significant than ever. I would find him night after night, lost in a digital world, his eyes transfixed on the screen, in a world that excluded me, excluded our family. The constant strain of juggling professional responsibilities with the challenges of my personal life began to manifest in various undiagnosed ailments.

"But why, Lord?" I often found myself asking in the quiet of the night. "Why this path? Why this burden?" However, in those moments of despair, I would feel a gentle whisper in my heart, a reminder of His promise, a reminder that I would find the courage to press on in His strength.

With each passing day, as I balanced lectures, research, and family, I held onto this newfound resolve. The journey was far from easy. There were days when exhaustion clouded my vision, the financial burdens seemed insurmountable, and the loneliness of my marital void felt overwhelming. However, in each of these moments, I found strength in my faith, in the unwavering belief that God was with me, molding me and shaping me into a vessel of His grace and strength.

Thus, clutching my Ph.D. in Computer Science like a shield, I navigated through the tumultuous waters of a troubled marriage, holding fast to the one thing that seemed unshakable. My career was my sanctuary, a realm where I exercised control, where my capabilities and intellect were recognized and respected. Unlike the instability of my personal life, my professional journey was a testament to my resilience and a reflection of God's grace.

My academic pursuits took me beyond my country's borders, offering me opportunities to engage with scholars worldwide. These journeys became a pilgrimage of enlightenment. Each conference and collaboration opened my eyes to the world beyond my struggles, reminding me of a larger purpose. They ignited a passion in me to give back and be the mentor I never had, guiding young minds toward a prosperous future with possibilities.

Upon my return from an overseas trip that had broadened my horizons and deepened my understanding of global technology trends, I was inspired to establish an initiative that would become one of the cornerstones of my career and a beacon of hope for many: the Geek Girls Collaborative (GGC),[36] a network of like-minded people, with the vision of boosting the confidence of young girls by igniting the passion for technology and motivating more females into the technology workforce.

So, just as the servants in the Biblical parable of the talents (Matthew 25:14-30) were entrusted with their master's wealth, I felt entrusted with knowledge and experience that I was duty-bound to multiply. The GGC community was my way of investing in these 'talents,' ensuring they yielded fruit in the lives of young women who aspired to make their mark in technology. Moreover, I saw it as a beacon of hope amidst my turbulent waters, a refuge to channel my energies into something profoundly positive and impactful.

This project, conceived and nurtured in the halls of academia, was the fruit of countless hours of brainstorming, planning, and unwavering dedication, not just from me but from a remarkable team of my students and colleagues.

These extraordinary individuals were the accurate engines driving this initiative, each a powerhouse of knowledge and enthusiasm. Together, we shared a common vision – to empower African girls and women to confidently step into the world of technology and equip them with the skills and confidence needed to navigate and excel in a field historically dominated by men. Our mission was clear: to dismantle the barriers, dispel the stereotypes, and lay a solid foundation for future generations of women in tech.

GGC was not just about teaching coding or software development; it was

---

[36] www.ggc-global.org

about fostering an environment of support, mentorship, and encouragement. My former students, now emerging as leaders and mentors, brought fresh perspectives, innovative ideas, and a passion for change. Their contributions were invaluable, turning this community into a vibrant, dynamic space where learning was intertwined with empowerment.

My colleagues, too, played a pivotal role. Their expertise in various computer science and technology fields enriched the program. They volunteered their time and knowledge, proving that the path to gender equality in tech Is paved through collective effort and shared responsibility.

As the years passed, the Community grew beyond our initial vision. We watched with pride as it expanded, touching the lives of thousands of young people. Our students and mentees achieved remarkable feats – winning competitions, following their academic passions, graduating from college, securing internships, and launching their own companies. Each success story was a testament to the power of mentorship and the impact of a supportive community.

However, perhaps our most significant achievement has been witnessing the transformation of these young girls into confident, skilled individuals ready to take on the world.

In sharing this journey, my intention is not to bask in the glow of these achievements but to shine a light on the collective effort that made it all possible. It is a tribute to the tireless work of my former students and colleagues, their belief in a cause greater than themselves, and their commitment to shaping a more inclusive and equitable future.

Ironically, my two boys became statutory members of the Geek Girls Collaborative. Their involvement was initially convenient, solving the logistical challenges of juggling my professional and personal responsibilities. However, what began as a practical arrangement became something far more significant. Their passion for technology not only flourished but multiplied exponentially as they grew. They were living proof nurtured in an environment that encouraged exploration and innovation; young minds could transcend traditional gender roles in technology and science.

I share this not to boast but to encourage anyone reading this memoir. If I, amidst my struggles, could find the strength to impact lives positively, then so can you. It is about recognizing your potential, harnessing your inner resilience, and asking God's grace to guide you.

However, the sunnier my career became, the darker the clouds over my personal life grew. My husband's indifference and the physical toll of maintaining a façade of perfection was wearing me down. My health continued to decline, but I continued to don the mask of a happy, healthy pastor's wife amidst this. It was a role I played to perfection, a performance for the world that belied the reality of my situation.

> "If I, amidst my struggles, could find the strength to impact lives positively, then so can you. It is about recognizing your potential, harnessing your inner resilience, and asking God's grace to guide you.

To my dear readers, it is crucial to remember that appearances can be deceptive. It is essential to seek help when needed, be honest about your struggles, and understand that it is okay not to be okay. As a community, we need to foster environments where vulnerability is not seen as a weakness but as an opportunity for growth and support. Remember, our worth is determined not by how well we keep up appearances but by the authenticity and courage we face our challenges.

The escalating situation drove me again to seek guidance from our leaders, but my husband's respect for pastoral authority had waned as much as his regard for our vows. I found it unbelievable that he was dismissive of the pastors' counsel. "There is nothing wrong with our marriage," he would say, "every marriage has its cross to bear."

In Ephesians 5:25, the Bible instructs husbands to "love your wives, just as Christ loved the church and gave himself up for her." This scripture underlines the expectation of selfless, nurturing love, not the passive acceptance of neglect or emotional abuse. Life's experience has taught me that misinterpreting the scriptures can perpetuate unhealthy dynamics in relationships. It is crucial to understand that biblical teachings on marriage advocate for a partnership grounded in love, respect, and mutual support.

Furthermore, 1 Corinthians 13:4-7, which defines love as patient, kind, and not self-seeking, offers a counter-narrative to the notion of enduring mistreatment under the guise of carrying one's cross. Love does not dishonor others, nor is it easily angered; it rejoices with the truth and always protects. These verses challenge the misguided belief that suffering in silence is a hallmark of a solid Christian marriage.

This phase of my life was a crucible, testing my faith and resilience. It was a period of deep introspection and learning when I had to differentiate between the true tenets of my faith and the distorted versions used to justify unfair treatment. It was a painful but necessary journey toward understanding that my value and worth were not contingent upon enduring a one-sided relationship.

TWENTY-EIGHT

Seeking Transformation

Change is the law of life. And those who look only to the past or present are certain to miss the future.

John F. Kennedy

The chapter of my life that followed was marked by a desperate search for solutions, a quest to salvage the disintegrating situation of my family life. During this tumultuous period, an idea began to germinate in my mind—an idea both audacious and fraught with uncertainty. I wondered if a change in the environment, a transition to the Western world, could be the catalyst needed to transform my husband into the spouse and father he had failed to be.

This perspective was informed by recognizing how environmental and cultural exposure can significantly shape individual behaviors and attitudes. Drawing upon contemporary sociological insights, Gladwell (2006), in his exploration of success and societal influences, posits that the fabric of society and its cultural norms play a pivotal role in molding individual actions and perspectives. Thus, I harbored the aspiration that immersion in a society where women's rights and gender equality are more profoundly entrenched would inspire my husband to renew respect for me and our children.

With a heart full of prayer and a mind armed with faith, I embarked on a quest to secure an opportunity for postdoctoral studies abroad. I hoped this would be a lifeline, a chance to immerse my family in an environment that would inspire positive change. I longed to see my husband touched by a culture that valued mutual respect and equality, a society where the consequences of one's actions were clearly understood and adhered to.

The divine hand of providence seemed to guide my endeavors as I began to submit applications for postdoc abroad. I soon received the news that the Schlumberger Foundation had selected me for a postdoctoral fellowship opportunity in the United States. It was a moment of overwhelming gratitude and cautious optimism. Here was a chance to escape the stifling confines of our current life, an opportunity to introduce my family to a world where respect for women and accountability in relationships were part of the societal fabric.

In preparing for our move abroad, a stark reality unfolded before me, echoing the trials of many women who bear the weight of their family's future. Securing international passports for my husband and children, arranging visa appointments, and managing the myriad logistical details became my sole responsibility. It was as though an invisible mantle had been placed upon my shoulders, a mantle I carried with determination and a sinking heart.

My husband's attitude during this process was a complex amalgam of indifference and an unspoken expectation that I would, as always, shoulder the burden alone. His passive participation was not just a lack of physical involvement; a form of emotional blackmail, a silent assertion that regardless of his inaction, I would persevere because I had no other choice.

Reflecting on my experiences, I understand that this subtle yet deeply impactful form of manipulation is frequently overlooked in relationships. Dr. Susan Forward, in her groundbreaking book Emotional Blackmail, delineates this as a potent manipulation tactic where perpetrators employ fear, obligation, and guilt to dominate their victims (Forward, 1997). In my situation, the unspoken yet intense fear revolved around the potential disintegration of our family's prospects for a brighter future. The sense of obligation was rooted in my identity as a wife and mother; roles that society often implicitly suggests should be synonymous with self-sacrifice and ceaseless duty. The guilt operated as a pervasive whisper, implying that any shortcomings in fulfilling these roles would be my burden.

On the day we ventured to the immigration office for the passport applications of my husband and children, I found myself at the helm, literally as I drove us to the venue for fingerprinting and capturing and metaphorically as I navigated our family's future. Sitting behind the wheel amidst the bustling traffic and burdened with contemplative thoughts, the irony of the situation struck me profoundly. I was, in every sense, propelling our family forward on this journey toward a new beginning, while my husband seemed merely to observe from the passenger seat. This one-sided relationship has undoubtedly crossed into the realm of emotional exploitation.

To readers finding themselves in similar situations, I urge you to recognize the signs of emotional blackmail and to understand that you have a choice. Setting boundaries, seeking support, and communicating openly about distributing responsibilities in relationships are essential. Remember, a marriage is a partnership, a joint journey where both parties share the load, navigate the challenges, and celebrate the successes together.

Embarking on the formidable journey to secure the 'J'[37] visas for my family's relocation to America presented a significant challenge that deeply tested my faith and resilience. The visa application process demanded concrete proof of financial stability, a hurdle that seemed insurmountable. While my fellowship grant sufficiently covered my expenses, financially supporting my husband and two children in this venture fell squarely on my shoulders. Those days were marked by a frenetic quest to amass the required funds, which proved exhausting and enlightening.

Despite my husband's publishing business experiencing a period of prosperity, his contributions to this crucial fund were negligible. He alternated between professing a shortage of funds and citing business-related

[37] The 'J' visa, often referred to as the Exchange Visitor Visa, is designed for individuals approved to participate in work-and study-based exchange visitor programs in the United States

expenditures, such as purchasing materials or making strategic investments, as reasons for his inability to contribute. This stark discrepancy between his business's success and his claimed financial incapacity was not just ironic; it was a source of deep frustration for me.

Polite refusals and closed doors marked the quest for loans and cash gifts among friends and acquaintances. In our culture, lending substantial sums for such ventures is often hesitant. This cautiousness, while prudent, often leaves those in dire need with few options.

Left with no other option, I turned to the banks. Securing a loan was a necessary evil, a step taken with a heavy heart. I also made the painful decision to sell my car, a sacrifice that felt like parting with a piece of my independence. Additionally, I took a loan from the cooperative fund at my campus. Despite these efforts, the money I had managed to gather still fell short of what we needed. However, my husband remained apathetic, his inaction a silent rebuke of my frantic efforts.

One weekend, I overheard him conversing with one of his suppliers, who owed him significant money. To my utter disbelief, my husband instructed the supplier to hold onto the payment. His rationale? He wanted to save the money as a fallback for when we returned to Nigeria. This decision left me dumbfounded. How could he prioritize an uncertain future over our immediate, pressing needs? It was as if he was blinded by a negative psychology that prioritized self-preservation over collective family welfare.

In a moment of quiet desperation, as I grappled with the turmoil that had become my daily existence, a thought whispered through the chaos of my mind: to leave my husband in Nigeria, to seize the fellowship abroad as an opportunity for respite from his cruel behavior, to breathe in a year of peace. However, embarking on such a path without divine guidance was a step I hesitated. So, I prayed to the Lord, my heart pouring out in a torrent of silent tears that night. Amidst the despair, I sought a sign from God, a beacon to illuminate my path, pleading for a miracle to avert the impending shame.

In the aftermath of my prayer, a divine conviction settled upon me. The idea of leaving, though momentarily enticing, did not align with the Lord's plan at that moment. It was a reminder that "God's ways are not our ways" (Isaiah 55:8-9). Indeed, He often uses the "foolish things of the world to confound the wise" (1 Corinthians 1:27). That night, the Lord guided me to the story of the Israelites under Pharaoh's harsh rule, illustrating a more profound purpose within my suffering. Through this biblical parallel, He revealed that my journey, akin to the Israelites, was still unfolding. I was being prepared for a glory yet unseen, a future radiant with promise beyond my current afflictions.

This revelation, though difficult to grasp in the throes of my struggle, hinted at a more profound spiritual warfare at play, one that transcended mere human understanding. It underscored the conviction that my current trials were not merely obstacles but divine preparations, sculpting me for a future filled with purpose and promise.

I am eternally grateful for heeding those whispered directives from God at that time. This decision, rooted in faith rather than immediate relief, underscored the complexity of my situation. This spiritual conundrum may not be immediately comprehensible, but it would unfurl its wisdom as readers journey through this memoir with me. In this narrative of faith and resilience, the layers of spiritual significance behind my decision reveal a story of survival and preparation for a destiny yet unveiled.

> "God interacts with each of us individually, considering our strengths, weaknesses, and the specific purpose He has ordained for our lives.

At this juncture, I feel compelled to offer a word of caution: God's plan for us is as unique as our fingerprints. The path He has guided me on, marked by trials and revelations, is deeply personal and tailored to the lessons I needed to learn and the growth I needed to experience. It is crucial to understand that my story, while a testament to faith and perseverance, should not serve as a universal yardstick for decision-making in the face of adversity.

While my narrative may resonate with many, it is essential to understand that my choices, especially in the face of marital challenges, were guided by a personal conviction and an intimate dialogue with God. I have certainly made my share of mistakes along the way, but it was through holding onto His grace and patiently waiting on His timing that I navigated through those tumultuous waters.

God interacts with us individually, considering our strengths, weaknesses, and the specific purpose He has ordained for our lives. The way He has led me through my challenges reflects His unique plan for my life and the spiritual lessons I was meant to learn.

Therefore, I urge you, dear readers, to seek God's guidance in your life with open hearts and minds. Let my experiences serve as a reminder that while we may draw inspiration and find solace in the stories of others, our own stories are being written by the hand of the Divine Author, who knows our end from our beginning. Seek His guidance, listen for His whispers, and remain open to the unique path He has charted for you. For in the grand tapestry of life, each thread is woven with a purpose, each color with a lesson, all contributing to the masterpiece that is your life, as envisioned by the Creator.

Thus, after earnestly dialoguing with God, a profound sense of calmness enveloped me, leaving me with a steadfast belief that God was about to orchestrate a surprise in my life. Moreover, a miracle unfolded before me, true to that divine anticipation.

In what can only be described as a breathtaking orchestration from above, I was greeted with credit alerts from the two universities where I had been offering part-time lectures. They had been owing me a considerable amount of money for some time. The long overdue payments had accumulated to an amount that could resolve our financial quandary. It was as if the heavens had conspired, aligning the actions of these two institutions to come to my aid in my darkest hour.

This unexpected financial windfall was a sign from the Almighty. It reinforced my belief in the power of divine timing and the mysterious ways God orchestrates events in our lives. As the Bible says in Ecclesiastes 3:11, "He has made everything beautiful in its time."

I reflect on this experience as a powerful illustration of the importance of faith and perseverance. It teaches us that our steadfastness and trust in God can open doors we never thought possible when faced with seemingly insurmountable challenges. It also serves as a poignant reminder that while we may not understand the ways of the Divine, faith can lead us through the darkest valleys to emerge more robust and resilient.

TWENTY-NINE

Divine Detours

The only limit to our realization of tomorrow will be our doubts of today.

Franklin D. Roosevelt

As I navigated the jumble of challenges in preparation for our sojourn abroad, little did I know this journey would unfold according to a divine script, far different from what I had envisioned. The process was fraught with a whirlwind of physical exhaustion, emotional turmoil, career uncertainties, and health scares.

These struggles stretched me to my limits, threatening to derail our plans. However, rather than breaking me, each hurdle only solidified my resolve. I choose not to delve into the exhaustive details of these trials–To recount them would be an overwhelming narrative. However, an occurrencc too significant to overlook emerged on the eve of our pivotal interview. To avoid delays, I meticulously booked a hotel room near the embassy and arranged a chartered taxi to take us to Lagos. This was a deliberate choice to mitigate the stress of navigating the lengthy journey myself—a task my husband habitually deferred to me during long-distance travels.

I had a straightforward task I thought he handled: to place his passport in the folder with the rest of us, ensuring all our crucial documents were consolidated. Regrettably, my faith in this simple act being carried out was misplaced.

The realization hit me like a tidal wave at 4 a.m. on the day of our appointment. Amid the pre-dawn silence of our hotel room, a frantic search revealed the unthinkable—our passports were absent, inadvertently left behind on our bedroom table. The panic that ensued was palpable. I was considering commencing a postdoctoral job in just two weeks. Missing this appointment carried the heavy consequence of potentially waiting months for another chance.

My husband's response, initially seeming empathetic, took a turn toward resignation as he suggested that perhaps it was God's will for us not to attend the interview. This declaration, which I perceived as a misinterpretation of divine intent, ignited a fire within me. In this moment of desperation, our first son, wise beyond his years, proposed that we pray for a miracle. His innocent suggestion, stark in its simplicity and wisdom, was a beacon of hope that contrasted with my husband's resignation to fate. Together, we clasped hands and lifted our voices in prayer, seeking solace and a tangible miracle.

Our situation seemed insurmountable, with the embassy appointment looming and our passports lying on a table miles away. The congested roads of Nigeria, notorious for their unpredictability, loomed as a formidable barrier between us and our lifeline. Yet, in that moment of collective prayer, I felt a peace that fortified me with the courage to confront it head-on. What followed was a race against time.

I paused, taking a deep, steadying breath. My mind raced through potential solutions until a glimmer of an idea surfaced. The taxi driver who had taken us to Lagos the day before—by some stroke of foresight, I had saved his number, a decision that now seemed fortuitous. Frantically scrolling through my phone, I found his contact and dialed, my heart pounding with each ring.

When he answered, I hastily reintroduced myself, the desperation in my voice palpable. "We met yesterday. I am the one you drove to Lagos," I began, my words tumbling out in a rush. "I have an enormous favor to ask of you," I continued, outlining our predicament. The passports critical for our visa appointment were forgotten at home. I implored him to undertake a mission bordering on the miraculous: retrieve them from our home and deliver them to us in Lagos within three hours. His initial response was a resigned skepticism. "It is impossible," he said.

Though I echoed his sentiment of impossibility, surrender was not an option. I clung to a sliver of hope, refusing to relinquish it until all possibilities had been exhausted. Thus, faced with my persistent plea and the allure of generous compensation, the driver relented, agreeing to attempt the feat. However, he stopped short of promising success within our tight timeframe.

Divine providence seemed to weave into our narrative just days before our ordeal, as my mother-in-law and brother-in-law had unexpectedly decided to visit us. Initially, their timing felt like an added layer of stress to an already tense period. Yet, as the situation unfolded, their presence transformed from an inconvenient timing to a serendipitous blessing. Grasping at this newly revealed lifeline, I dialed my brother-in-law's number, my voice laced with urgency. I explained the dire situation and the crucial role he now played in our desperate bid against time.

Without hesitation, my brother-in-law sprang into action, securing the precious folder from our bedroom and ensuring it was ready for the driver's critical mission. In an act of solidarity and determination, he even offered to accompany the driver back to Lagos, a testament to the strength of family bonds in times of crisis.

As the phone call ended, a fragile hope was rekindled within me. What had initially seemed an insurmountable obstacle now appeared as a daunting yet navigable challenge, thanks to the unexpected alignment of circumstances and the collective effort of unlikely allies. The race against time had begun, underpinned by prayers, pleas, and the power of human resolve.

With a mixture of hope and determination, I began orchestrating our preparation for the embassy visit, clinging to the hope that the driver would meet us there in time. Upon arrival at the embassy, I implored the security officers with a sincerity and urgency that could not be feigned. With tears, I presented them with all our documentation, save for the crucial passports, explaining our predicament. The officer was compassionate. He granted us entry, understanding that I would be permitted to step outside to retrieve the passports upon their arrival.

Miraculously, by 7 a.m., the driver had already made it to Lagos, navigating a path miraculously clear of the usual traffic snarls that plague the highways due to perennially poor road conditions. This unusual ease of travel reignited my faith, convincing me of divine intervention at play. However, as my spirits were lifting, they faced a daunting obstacle. The driver and my brother-in-law were ensnared in the notorious traffic on the Third Mainland Bridge, the critical artery connecting Lagos mainland to Victoria Island, where the U.S. embassy stood. For two grueling hours, they remained almost stationary, the promise of their arrival growing dimmer with each passing minute.

The tension was palpable as I constantly communicated, each update further cementing their stationary plight. Amidst this, my husband's patience wore thin; he criticized my refusal to acquiesce to what he deemed impossible. However, I could not entertain his defeatism. My resolve was unwavering, fortified by the belief that determination could pave the way where none seemed to exist.

In the face of dwindling time and fading hopes, I contemplated a decision that would be deemed reckless under any normal circumstance. It was nearing 9 a.m., and our interview slot was fast approaching. The prospect of admitting defeat was intolerable. In desperate resolve, I stepped outside, informed the officer that our passports had "arrived," and ventured beyond the embassy's premises.

Outside, I sought the services of a motorcycle transporter, locally known as an "okada." These riders are infamous for their perilous navigation through Lagos' congested streets, especially on the highways where their daring maneuvers often flirt with danger. After a harrowing experience years ago, one that had occurred while I was pregnant with our first son, I had sworn off ever using their services again. However, here I was, poised to entrust my safety to an okada in what felt like a life-or-death gamble, all to secure my family's future.

With my heart in my throat, I uttered a swift prayer for divine protection and approached the nearest rider. I explained the urgency of my situation and promised him a substantial reward if he could get me to the Third Mainland

Bridge, where my brother-in-law and the driver were stuck in traffic. The rider's initial glance was disbelief, perhaps marveling at the audacity of a woman willing to undertake such a risky endeavor. It seemed the notion of facing oncoming traffic on one of Lagos' most notorious highways was as daunting to him as it was to me.

However, driven by the promise of payment — and perhaps sensing the desperation in my plea — he agreed. For once, I agreed with the okada's typically cavalier attitude toward safety. At that moment, any semblance of rationality seemed to desert me, replaced by a singular focus on the mission. Nevertheless, despite the apparent madness of the decision, a deep, unwavering conviction sustained me. I believed that God was watching over me with every fiber of my being.

Embarking on what could only be described as a mission fraught with peril, I found myself clinging to the back of an okada, racing against the clock through the labyrinthine streets of Lagos. The motorcycle riders, known for their uncanny ability to navigate even the most daunting traffic jams, lived up to their reputation. Thus, amidst the cacophony of honks and shouts, we pressed on, driven by an urgent mission to retrieve the most valuable possession of the moment.

Miraculously, we arrived at the infamous Third Mainland Bridge within mere minutes. There, amidst the sea of immobilized vehicles, we located the taxi carrying the crucial documents. The retrieval of the passports felt like a heist against time itself, a fleeting victory snatched from the jaws of defeat. With the documents secured, we made our hasty return to the embassy. My gratitude toward the bike rider, a silent guardian angel of the asphalt, was immense. Upon our arrival, I rushed to the officer, passports in hand, my heart pounding with relief and anticipation. Gratitude filled me as he accepted them, just in time for our interview.

Shortly after that, it was our turn to stand before the immigration officer. With bated breath, we awaited the verdict, a thick veil of uncertainty that could only be pierced by the immigration officer's decision. Then, like the first rays of dawn dispersing the night, the words we yearned to hear were spoken: J1 visa approved for me and J2 for my husband and children. The relief and joy was indescribable.

The ordeal underscored a crucial lesson: In pursuing our dreams, we are often called upon to take leaps of faith to embark on journeys that test our resolve and courage. It reaffirmed the belief that when faced with seemingly insurmountable obstacles, the human spirit, fueled by determination and faith, can achieve the extraordinary.

As readers, you are invited to reflect on the broader implications of this story. It serves as a reminder that behind every successful endeavor are human stories of struggle, resilience, and the unyielding desire for a better life. I hope to inspire, inform, and perhaps even educate by sharing this tale. The path to achieving our goals is rarely straightforward or risk-free. However, it is through confronting these challenges head-on, armed with faith and trust in God, that we forge our destinies, one daring ride at a time. Through all of these, one thing remained constant – the unwavering grace of God, or 'Golden Grace,' as I have come to recognize it. This divine grace was my anchor, sustaining me when the waves of adversity threatened to capsize my resolve.

THIRTY

Crossing Thresholds

The only impossible journey is the one you never begin.

Tony Robbins

Upon returning home, our family's status had unmistakably transformed. The distinction of obtaining a U.S. "J" visa, a symbol of opportunity and prestige, profoundly resonated with my husband. Surprisingly, he made a significant gesture that marked a departure from his usual detachment from our financial affairs. For the first time, he actively participated by contributing 150,000 Nigerian Naira—roughly equivalent to $750 at that time—toward our travel expenses.

In the broader context of our financial requirements, this contribution might have seemed insignificant, barely covering half of his ticket cost. However, the act itself resonated deeply with me. It could have been the gravity of the impending journey or perhaps the honor of having an American visa stamped on the untouched passport that inspired him. Whatever the motivation, this contribution, though small, represented a ray of hope, a sign of potential progress in our shared path.

From a psychological viewpoint, this significant shift in behavior within our story may be understood as a manifestation of narcissistic tendencies triggered by a perceived increase in status. The prospect of relocating to a developed country like the United States might have bolstered his self-esteem and sense of self-importance. This interpretation aligns with findings in the field of psychology that suggest narcissistic individuals often respond positively to situations that they perceive as enhancing their status or prestige (Twenge & Campbell, 2009).

Thus, with the visas secured and the date of departure drawing near, I held onto a cautious optimism. Perhaps, just perhaps, this journey to a new land would be the crucible in which my husband's character would be reshaped.

As we embarked on this new chapter, I could not help but reflect on 'Golden Grace'– the unmerited favor and divine assistance that had carried me through the darkest days. It was this grace that I leaned on, hopeful yet realistic about the potential for change. The journey ahead was shrouded in uncertainty, but one thing was clear – it would be a journey of discovery, not just of a new world, but also of ourselves and the potential for transformation within each of us. Only time would reveal the true impact of this transition on our lives and on the man who had been a conundrum to me for so long.

As the news of our impending journey to America spread amongst friends, family, co-workers, and most notably within our church congregation, it was met with a chorus of congratulations and best wishes. The church leadership extolled our dedication and commitment to church growth, their words painting a picture of unwavering faith and exemplary service.

Standing amidst the congregation, listening to the church leaders sing praises of my husband, my mind was awash with a storm of emotions. I found myself lost in a sea of thoughts, envisioning a future where these praises would align with a transformed version of my husband. This version would embody the virtues and commitment celebrated that day. I imagined us returning to Nigeria spiritually renewed, with my husband finally embodying the qualities the church leadership extolled. These thoughts were a silent prayer, a plea to God to mold him into the man he was being publicly lauded to be.

As the senior pastor addressed our congregation, a flood of emotions swept over me, drawing my thoughts back to the modest edifice that cradled our church community. This building, a symbol of faith and collective endeavor, stood mainly due to my financial contributions, which filled me with a deep sense of purpose and gratitude.

This moment of reflection transported me back to a pivotal chapter in my life. Shortly after earning my Ph.D., I was honored with the Commonwealth Foundation grant, a recognition that propelled me into a four-month research collaboration in the United Kingdom. My work, centered on artificial intelligence for gaming, not only advanced my academic career but also came with a generous stipend. With a commitment to frugality, I chose a simple living arrangement and a modest diet in the UK, all intending to save as much as possible. This was not just for my gain but was a strategic move to contribute significantly to improving our collective lives back home.

Upon my return, I brought back substantial savings, a financial cushion that promised comfort and security. True to form, my husband, ever the advisor on expenditure but seldom the contributor, had his plans. He suggested using the money to purchase a piece of land to build our property. Though this sounded reasonable, I remember chuckling inwardly at his eagerness to spend money he had not earned. However, I insisted on pausing to seek God's guidance, believing in the wisdom of Proverbs 21:5, "The plans of the diligent lead to profit as surely as haste leads to poverty."

Our church congregation, which I led alongside my husband, was then facing its crisis. We had been using a classroom in a local primary school for Sunday worship, but suddenly, we were asked to leave. This left us stranded, without a place to call our spiritual home. Around the same time, an opportunity presented itself - a plot of land available for lease in our neighborhood. However, this solution came with a price tag that our congregation, barely scraping by, could not afford.

Then, the purpose of my savings from the UK became clear. Perhaps God had orchestrated my Commonwealth-funded trip for my academic and financial gain and a more significant cause - to provide a home for our congregation. With heartfelt prayer and conviction, I allocated much of my savings, and with my husband's support, we constructed a modest yet decent structure for our church.

The irony was not lost on me - the resources I had garnered through personal sacrifice were now the cornerstone of our church's physical presence. Though I often referred to this as a 'we' effort, in truth, it was my financial contribution that made it possible. However, I maintained the illusion of a joint endeavor in the spirit of humility and unity.

Leading the congregation in that space was a source of profound fulfillment. There, amid our new church building, the announcement of our family's sojourn to America was made. The congregation erupted in a triumphant shout of "Hallelujah," piercing through my reverie and pulling me back to the present. The pastors beckoned my husband and me for prayers, and as we walked forward, I reflected on the miraculous sequence of events that had led us to this moment.

Not long after we had built a modest yet comfortable sanctuary for our congregation, another divine opportunity presented itself. A plot of land in a prime location in our neighborhood became available. My husband quickly dismissed it as an expensive venture as unworkable, considering we had just invested hugely in the church property. However, armed with the golden grace of God, I was undeterred.

Though significantly depleted due to the Church building, the savings from my UK trip were enough to deposit on the land. Coupled with a bank loan, I gathered the necessary resources for this new land. It was a testament to Philippians 4:13, which states, "I can do all things through Christ who strengthens me."

I vividly recall the day my husband, tasked with making the first installment payment, returned with a receipt bearing solely his name. His defense was rooted in the traditional notion that what belongs to the husband also belongs to the wife and vice versa. I could not help but respond with a touch of irony, "Why not put only my name instead, so what belongs to me also belongs to you, especially since you have not contributed financially?" This exchange led me to a request for a new receipt

> "Wisdom is the principal thing; therefore, get wisdom: and with all thy getting get understanding. — Proverbs 4:7

that reflected our joint ownership—a decision that, unbeknownst to me then, would become significantly crucial in the years to come.

This episode underscores the importance of wisdom and foresight in matters of joint ownership, even within the sacred bonds of marriage. The scriptures advocate for wisdom in all things, as Proverbs 4:7 states, "Wisdom is the principal thing; therefore, get wisdom: and with all thy getting get understanding." Ensuring joint ownership was a protective measure, safeguarding against future unforeseen complications. It serves as a poignant reminder for readers to approach such decisions with prudence and informed judgment, remembering that the veneer of marital unity should not cloud the practical aspects of financial and asset management.

The resounding "Amen" from the congregation jolted me back to the present as I was lost in these reflections. As we stood there, receiving prayers and blessings, I could not help but ponder the journey ahead. It was a journey marked by faith and resilience, a testament to the belief that even the most daunting challenges can be overcome with God's grace.

I felt a surge of hope and determination as we returned to our seats. I believed the prayers we had received would be replete with God's grace—a grace I trusted would continue to guide and sustain me through all the trials and triumphs that lay ahead.

Grace Amidst Trials

THIRTY-ONE

New Beginnings

Faith is taking the first step even when you don't see the whole staircase.

Martin Luther King Jr.

As the wheels of change began to turn, ushering my family and me into an entirely new chapter abroad, I found myself navigating the vast, digital expanse of the internet with a purpose. My quest was singular: to find a Christian family, a friend, a colleague, or even a benevolent Samaritan who could ease our transition into this foreign realm. This search had evolved into a sacred ritual for me, each venture a leap of faith into the unknown, bolstered by the scripture from Matthew 7:7[38] that whispered promises of guidance and providence. With unwavering belief, I trusted that the same divine orchestration that had navigated my path in Canada would manifest again.

In what felt like a brush with the miraculous, an answer came, reshaping the trajectory of our lives. A senior pastor from an international parish of our church reached out, offering to be our beacon in the vastness of America. This congregation would soon envelop us in spiritual kinship, becoming our

[38] Matthew 7:7: "Ask, and it will be given to you; seek, and you will find; knock, and the door will be opened to you."

sanctuary.

Thus, on a crisp autumn night, filled with the anticipation of new beginnings and the quiet hum of adventure in the air, my family and I embarked on a journey that promised to redefine our lives. With our two sons in tow, we boarded the flight that would carry us across the skies to Boston, a city that shimmered with the promise of becoming our home for the year ahead.

Awaiting our arrival at the airport were the senior pastor and his wife. This elderly couple extended the first signs of warmth and welcome in this new and unfamiliar territory. They assisted us with our luggage and drove us to our Airbnb accommodation, providing a comfortable and nurturing environment from when we landed.

They even prepared delicious meals, taking care of every detail to ensure our seamless transition into this new setting. Upon meeting them, a voice inside me quietly acknowledged that I had been graced with a new set of parental figures in this foreign land. The pastor's gentle demeanor and the wisdom in his eyes evoked memories of my late father, whose presence I missed daily. However, in the pastor's nurturing gaze, I found a semblance of the fatherly love and guidance I longed for.

True to my intuition, the pastor and his wife went above and beyond to ensure our smooth transition. They helped us secure and settle into a rented apartment, helped us navigate the choice of school for our children, and even mobilized church members to assist us in finding our feet. This outpouring of love and support was overwhelming. The members of the church, with their diverse backgrounds and stories, formed a mosaic of God's love, each one playing a unique role in easing our transition.

In those early days, I could never have imagined how deeply intertwined our lives would become with that of the pastor and his wife. As time unfolded, they walked with me through the darkest valleys of my life. They became my steadfast support, my guiding lights, navigating me through tumultuous times I could never have anticipated. The kindness of our church community, embodied in gifts, prayers, and moral support, eased the burden of settling down. At this juncture, I must emphasize that I am eternally grateful to all the brethren for being true keepers of the faith.

As I signed the contract for our house rent, I could not help but feel the familiar pressure of the financial burden settling on my shoulders again. It was a role I had known only too well back in Nigeria, and here I was, continents away, about to replay the same script.

As usual, my husband, with his deceptive charm and seemingly gentle demeanor, had a way of endearing himself to people, especially within the church community. His manipulative tendencies, a recurring theme in my memoir, were no secret, but to the unsuspecting eye, he was the epitome of a devout man of God.

Sadly, his entry into our new congregation's leadership in America was as smooth as I had feared. His physical presence, years of pastoring, and talent for saying the right things allowed him to quickly ingratiate himself with the church members and leadership. It was a pattern I had witnessed time and again. However, a part of me clung to the hope that in this new environment, under the scrutiny of a developed society, he might shed his old ways and embrace the sincerity and integrity true faith demands.

The Western world, emphasizing accountability and consequences for one's actions, seemed like the perfect setting for him to realize the importance of genuine commitment and respect in family and spiritual life.

However, as readers of my story, you must brace yourselves for the unfolding drama. The journey ahead was laden with unexpected turns and revelations. The smooth transition into the church was merely the calm before the storm, a deceptive lull that masked the turbulence ahead.

Looking back, I understand that true transformation comes not from external changes in geography or society but from a profound, internal revolution of the heart and mind. While I held onto hope, the realities of life taught me that real change is from the inside and often requires more than just a change of environment.

On a beautiful Sunday afternoon after church service, I vividly recall standing in the grocery store aisle, my hands as full as my heart, methodically placing each item into the cart and moving toward the cashier to pay. At the same time, my husband remained passively on the sidelines. A creeping shadow of doubt began to engulf me. "Am I destined to replay the narrative of my life from back in Nigeria?" The specter of being a 'single, married woman' seemed to have traversed continents with me. This seemingly mundane moment was laden with deeper meanings, reflecting a past where I shouldered the financial responsibilities of our family alone.

The bright fluorescent lights of the store felt like a spotlight on my predicament, intensifying the realization that, perhaps, I was on the brink of reliving my old life in this new world. At the same time, I clung to the flickering hope that my husband would find employment soon and share in our domestic responsibilities. However, deep down, a part of me braced for the possibility that this hope might be in vain.

On a more positive note, I settled into my career, where my research group's warm hospitality and stimulating environment buoyed me. There was an undeniable sense of accomplishment and optimism as I navigated my new role. I also had the opportunity to teach two computer science courses as an adjunct faculty, meaning I could make extra income while relishing the intellectual rigor of my research. This assured me that my children and I would be fine, whether my husband had a change of heart or not.

Soon, a glimmer of hope emerged as my husband secured a work permit and began working at a care facility. This should have been a turning point, a chance for him to share the financial responsibilities that had long been mine alone. However, old patterns resurfaced instead of the expected equilibrium, casting longer shadows over our family dynamics.

I clearly remember the evening I decided to broach the subject of shared responsibility. It was a typical evening during the Fall. I observed falling leaves through the window, painting a picture of change. I hoped this change would seep into our conversation.

His reaction, however, was dishearteningly predictable. He deflected whenever I broached the subject, finding ways to evade the conversation. On the rare occasion when he did get engaged, it was not with the spirit of cooperation I longed for but instead with complaints and a litany of grievances about the hardships of our home country and the challenges he faced in his new job.

Understanding that this narrative is not meant to diminish or criticize my husband is essential. Every person is a complex amalgamation of virtues and flaws. However, a troubling shadow from our past persisted, casting a dark pall over our daily existence. My husband's addiction to pornography and his indulgence in various forms of sexual immorality continued unabated.

Amid this turmoil, I recognized the critical need for professional intervention. I earnestly pleaded with him to seek help, believing that in a country like America, where mental health and addiction therapy are more openly discussed and accessible, he might feel less stigmatized and more open to receiving the assistance he desperately needed. However, each of my pleas seemed to dissolve into the air, unheard and unheeded, like echoes in a vast, empty canyon.

Not only did I urge him to pursue professional counseling, but I also implored him to seek spiritual healing. My faith has always been a beacon in the darkest of times, and I believed fervently that divine intervention, coupled with professional help, could lead him toward a path of recovery. "Please," I would beseech him, my voice often trembling with desperation and hope, "consider seeking guidance from a pastor or even a deliverance ministry. Our faith can heal, but we must take the first step."

However, my appeals seemed to vanish before they could reach his heart. Each day, as I watched him retreat further into his world, a world marred by the chains of addiction, my heart grew heavier with a sense of helplessness.

As a minister of the gospel, I understand addiction is not merely a physical dependence; it is a multi-faceted issue that encompasses mental, emotional, and spiritual aspects. The Bible speaks to us about freedom from bondage in Galatians 5:1: "It is for freedom that Christ has set us free. Stand firm, then, and do not let yourselves be burdened again by a yoke of slavery." However, the healing journey is often fraught with obstacles and resistance, especially when the individual grappling with addiction is in denial. The book of Proverbs offers wisdom in dealing with such challenges. Proverbs 12:15 says, "The way of fools seems right to them, but the wise listen to advice."

As I navigated this treacherous path, balancing my role as a supportive spouse with the need to protect my spiritual and emotional well-being, I clung to my faith and resolved to constant praying and fasting. Despite the deafening silence that met my pleas, I believed God's voice could still reach the depths of my husband's heart. Moreover, in that belief, I found the strength to keep hoping, praying, and advocating for a change that seemed distant.

THIRTY-TWO

Fire For Fire

I know God won't give me anything I can't handle. I just wish he didn't trust me so much.

Mother Teresa

In all my trials, did I mention that the torchbearer of our family altar was none other than myself? Despite my husband's apparent devotion to the church, he was invariably reluctant to spearhead this crucial aspect of our family life. However, I never let that deter me. After all, as the technical breadwinner of the family, it seemed only fitting that I should also be the 'prayer winner.' There is a small quantity of humor in that, is not there? The one who brings home the bacon (or, in this case, the daily bread) also leads the prayers to bless it!

Maintaining our family altar and ensuring we had daily devotionals became not just a routine but a lifeline for me. Just as my parents had passed on the legacy of faith to me, I was determined to instill the same values in my children. The importance of a family that prays together was a principle I held dear, knowing its power to bind us together, even in the most tumultuous times.

Each time I gathered our children for prayer and to learn from the Bible, I could not help but feel a mix of pride and wistfulness. This ritual should have been a shared responsibility, yet it had fallen into my lap again, like many other things in our marriage. However, rather than dwell on what was lacking, I focused on the opportunity it presented.

The family altar and daily devotionals in Christian homes are rooted in the Biblical principle of teaching and nurturing faith within the family. Deuteronomy 6:6-7 emphasizes the importance of incorporating faith into the daily rhythm of family life. This ensures the word of God is a constant presence in our interactions and decisions, stating: "These commandments that I give you today are to be on your hearts. Impress them on your children. Talk about them when you sit at home, walk along the road, lie down, and get up."

Maintaining the family altar in the face of my husband's apathy was challenging. There were days when it felt like a solitary endeavor. However, I drew strength from the conviction that I was laying a foundation to serve our children throughout their lives. As Proverbs 22:6 teaches, "Train up a child in the way he should go, and when he is old, he will not depart from it." This assurance fueled my commitment, giving me the resolve to persevere even when it felt like I was the sole spiritual anchor of our household.

> "Indeed, the path to raising God-fearing and responsible children in the land of America, with all its complexities, can only be successfully navigated with God's

The family altar was also a personal refuge for me, a space where I could pour out my heart to God, seeking guidance, strength, and wisdom in navigating the complexities of our family dynamics. It was a haven of peace during turmoil, where I could connect with God and find solace in His promises.

The daily investment of prayers and the sowing of God's word into my children's hearts have borne remarkable fruit. Despite the complexities of our family dynamics and the cultural challenges in America, God's grace has been evident in their upbringing. Their growth into God-fearing and responsible young men is a beacon of hope and a clear sign of the Lord's steadfast presence in their lives.

Indeed, the path to raising God-fearing and responsible children in the land of America, with all its complexities, can only be successfully navigated with God's guidance. It is His grace that has sustained us, His wisdom that has directed us, and His love that has kept us. In this journey, notwithstanding my husband's choice, the family altar has been a compass, leading my children through the vicissitudes of life and keeping them centered in God's will. The fruits of this spiritual labor are not just for the present; they are eternal treasures, shaping their future and impacting the world for the better.

As the days turned into weeks and weeks into months, the strain of my husband's unresolved issues began to take a heavier toll on my health. His continued indulgence in pornography and immoral behavior, coupled with a glaring lack of empathy toward our children and me, was eroding the very foundation of our family. It became increasingly clear that these were not mere personal failings but manifestations of a deeper spiritual battle, a sinister force at work.

I recognized the need to confront these issues with a more fervent and focused spiritual approach. I intensified my prayer sessions, asking for divine intervention in battling the malevolent forces threatening our family's peace. "Lord, You know the struggles we face. I pray not for vengeance but for Your divine intervention. Change his heart, Lord, and lead us out of this valley of darkness," I would beseech. I also redirected our family's communal prayers, turning our collective spiritual efforts toward warding off the enemy's influence.

Despite my prayers, heaven's door seemed shut as the situation deteriorated. Thus, I turned to the Scriptures for more guidance and reflected on instances where God's judgment and wrath were directed toward the enemies of His people. One such instance that resonated with me was in Psalm 35:1, where David cries out to God, "Contend, O Lord, with those who contend with me; fight against those who fight against me."

My contemplations also led me to Psalm 109:8, which states, "May his days be few; may another take his place of leadership." Although the wording may appear severe, it underscores a plea for transformative change — a divine recalibration to excise detrimental influences from our lives.

As I studied the scriptures, I became increasingly aware that, although pursuing justice is a natural inclination, the responsibility of judgment and retribution ultimately rests with God. This is affirmed in Romans 12:19, which counsels: "Do not take revenge, my dear friends, but leave room for God's wrath, for it is written: 'Vengeance is Mine; I will repay, says the Lord."

One morning, during our family prayer, there was a palpable sense of solemnity. Then, I brought forth a prayer point inspired by David's entreaties for divine intervention against his foes. "Lord, in the same way, David sought Your aid against those who opposed him, we too beseech You to confront any forces of darkness aiming to inflict harm upon us," I entreated. "We rely on Your unwavering promise of safeguarding and rescue. Please engage in battle with any demonic entities endeavoring to undermine our family unity," I concluded, invoking the name of Jesus with faith in His protective embrace.

The children, ever receptive to the spirit of prayer, responded earnestly with 'Amen.' However, my husband's reaction was totally different. He sat there, unmoved, his lips sealed in a firm line, and he left for the bedroom before the prayer was over. I later prodded him to ask why he left the prayer session before we finished. His response left me bewildered and deeply troubled.

"Why should we pray against our enemies?" he questioned, his voice laced with an unsettling calm. "The Bible teaches us to pray for our enemies, not curse them." His words, referencing Matthew 5:44 – "But I say to you, love your enemies and pray for those who persecute you" – were technically correct, yet they missed the essence of the spiritual warfare we were engaged in.

This incident was a glaring revelation of the depth of my husband's spiritual crisis. His refusal to acknowledge the enemy's work in his life and our family was alarming. I realized that instead of improving, his condition had deteriorated, plunging us into a deeper state of spiritual warfare.

Faced with this daunting reality, I decided to double down on my prayers, seeking wisdom and strength from above. I understood this battle was not just about confronting my husband's behavior but engaging in spiritual warfare against the forces that sought to destroy my destiny. Ephesians 6:12 calls for spiritual vigilance against the forces of darkness: "For we wrestle not against flesh and blood, but against principalities, against powers, against the rulers of the darkness of this world, against spiritual wickedness in high places." I braced for the battle ahead, which I knew could only be won by spiritual armor.

I remember vividly attending Church for Bible Study on a Tuesday evening. The topic was seemingly simple yet deeply complex: How do Christians approach the concept of 'enemies' in our prayers? As the conversation unfolded, my husband, ever the provocative conversationalist, stirred the waters with his assertive stance that we are called to pray for, not against, our enemies.

My husband's argument, fueled by his characteristic energy, reflected the ongoing struggle within our family and personal agenda, given our private circumstances. Though seemingly rooted in Scripture, his words felt like an indirect attempt to shield his actions from any spiritual scrutiny or intervention. I am confident the experiences of that evening would resonate deeply with those who shared in this journey and were present in the church that night.

While theologically sound in its call for love and forgiveness, this perspective overlooked the complexities of dealing with persistent negative influences, especially those threatening a family's spiritual and moral fabric. My heart ached with the irony of his words, considering the turmoil his actions had brought upon our family.

Thankfully, our pastors and fellow congregation members were well-versed in the Scripture and adept at navigating these intricate theological waters. They acknowledged the importance of Jesus' teachings on love but also emphasized the need to recognize our spiritual battles and the necessity of prayer in combating these forces.

THIRTY-THREE

Balancing Act

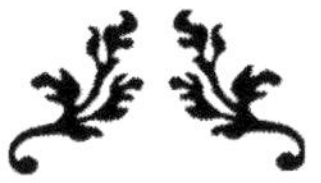

The key is not to prioritize what's on your schedule, but to schedule your priorities.

Stephen Covey

As you already know, my days were a delicate balance between managing my health, tending to my family saga, pursuing my postdoctoral work, and adjunct teaching responsibilities. Each task demanded a piece of me, yet somehow, by the grace of God, I found the strength to give.

Despite adequate income from my postdoctoral job, I worked extra hours to make more income. A larger vision fueled this commitment. The building project in Nigeria loomed in my mind as a symbol of stability and hope for our future. The thought of returning to Nigeria and not having to live as tenants again was a powerful motivator. It was a dream I had nurtured since our days in Nigeria. So, despite the frailty of my health, I pushed myself, working double time, driven by the dual forces of necessity and aspiration.

Before long, my body, weakened by the emotional storms I had weathered, began to betray me. Hospital visits became a haunting routine, a series of harrowing journeys from one lab test to another, from one diagnosis to another, and from one referral to yet another specialist.

While navigating the stormy seas of my health, which was failing, juggling the relentless demands of family responsibilities, and upholding my professional commitments, an unexpected beacon of support flickered to life from my husband. He displayed a newfound readiness to contribute financially toward completing our dream building project in Nigeria, which held fragments of our shared aspirations.

This seemingly small gesture transported me back to when that dream was just a blueprint in my hands. I recalled the countless hours I had invested, the substantial sums of money I had poured into purchasing the land, procuring the raw materials, and paying the laborers who toiled to bring our vision to life, brick by brick, up to the decking level. Those were days fueled by hope and tireless dedication, days before our departure to America, when the dream seemed within reach, and our future seemed a canvas of endless possibilities.

Now, as my husband stepped forward with his contribution, albeit modest in comparison to the sacrifices already made, it felt like a bridge being built over the chasm that had widened between our realities. The project, a four-apartment structure with two apartments on each floor, was nearing completion. My husband's decision to contribute, albeit a relatively small amount, was a welcome and unexpected gesture.

His contribution fueled my determination to ignore my health dynamics and ensure the building was fully set before our return to Nigeria. It was cheering to see him, perhaps inspired by the visible progress of the construction, extending a helping hand. Though his financial input was modest compared to the overall expenses, I saw it as a significant stride. It was a step toward a more collaborative effort. It signified a potential shift in our dynamics, a possibility of more shared responsibilities and mutual support.

While we busied ourselves with our plans and projects, a more outstanding design was unfolding that would take us down a path we had not anticipated. It was a reminder of the old saying, "Man proposes, God disposes." Unbeknownst to me, God had different plans for our family.

As I navigated the treacherous waters of my health, family, and career, the sands of time were rapidly slipping through the hourglass of my fellowship year. The impending end of this chapter felt like the shuttering of a haven, a respite from the storms that awaited back in Nigeria. The thought of returning, of re-entering a world where my struggles were magnified and my support diminished, was a specter that haunted my days and nights. Each clock tick reminded me of the looming transition I felt ill-prepared to face.

In the quiet solitude of my room, where the only sound was the soft ticking of the clock and the occasional distant laughter of my children, the weight of impending change felt overwhelming. My health, already a fragile vessel battered by the relentless waves of hospital visits, seemed ill-equipped to navigate the tumultuous journey ahead. The thought of relinquishing the stability and progress I had made during my fellowship year to plunge back into an environment fraught with challenges and scant support was daunting.

So, I found myself wrestling with questions that seemed to have no answers, prayers that felt echoing into a void. The duality of my life was stark — professionally advancing yet personally faltering.

And then, a ray of hope pierced through the gloom. An email notification chimed, its arrival seemingly mundane. Yet, it carried with it the potential to alter the course of my life when I saw that it was from the Schlumberger Foundation, the organization that sponsored my postdoc fellowship. With a trembling hand, I opened the message, and there it was — the news that my project was one of the select few granted a one-year renewal.

The relief that washed over me was palpable, almost physical in its intensity. It was as if a massive weight had been lifted off my chest, allowing me to breathe freely for the first time in months. This extension was a professional accomplishment and a lifeline, a divine intervention granting me a reprieve from the impending storm.

> “ Isaiah 43:2, "When you pass through the waters, I will be with you; and when you pass through the rivers, they will not sweep over you."

I could not help but see the hand of God in this. It reminded me of Isaiah 43:2, "When you pass through the waters, I will be with you; and when you pass through the rivers, they will not sweep over you." At that moment, I felt the truth of these words deep within my soul. It became apparent to me that the Lord was charting my path and providing sanctuary amidst life's tumult.

This was a testament that even in our darkest hours, when all seems lost, God can open doors that we did not even know existed. It reminded us that our plans are not always His, and our timing is not always His. As Jeremiah 29:11 says, "For I know the plans I have for you, declares the Lord, plans to prosper you and not to harm you, plans to give you hope and a future."

So, with a heart swelling with gratitude and eyes gazing toward a horizon filled with promise, I embraced this extension of my fellowship not just as a professional boon but as a divine provision—a year of grace. It was a golden opportunity, allowing me more time to heal, grow, and fortify myself for the challenges awaiting my return to Nigeria.

However, the path to this newfound opportunity was strewn with bureaucratic hurdles, emblematic of the challenges many young professionals face in developing countries, including Nigeria. Amidst this newfound hope, a formidable hurdle loomed before me. My home university in Nigeria only granted me a year of study leave for the postdoc. I emailed my university, announcing what I considered good news, only to be met with a challenging reality: Extending this leave was fraught with bureaucratic complexities and would not be as straightforward.

The requirement from my home university to return in person for an extension application was the first of these obstacles. The logistics and practicalities of this demand were daunting, a vivid reflection of the systemic barriers that often impede academic progress in many developing nations.

My request for a second year of study leave with pay was understandably denied, but I was allowed to take a leave of absence without pay. However, in taking the leave of absence, I still had to sign a bond, a commitment to return to my university post-fellowship. My academic career and work nurturing the Geek Girls community were a testament to my dedication and passion for research and development in my home country. I was not ready to forsake this path I had carved with tenacity and perseverance, so I signed the agreement without hesitation.

The more challenging hurdle, however, was the requirement to manage my classes back home during the fellowship. With every faculty member's workload at capacity, no one could cover my classes. This dilemma presented me with a stark choice: to either shoulder the responsibility of teaching these classes without remuneration or forgo this prestigious fellowship and return home.

Opting for the former, I committed to an exhausting and logistically complex schedule. It was a challenging yet sensible decision. This meant undertaking an arduous six-week journey back to Nigeria during my fellowship's second year, teaching triple hours to cover an entire semester's workload, and then returning to the USA to complete my fellowship. It was a Herculean task, yet it was the only path that allowed me to extend my stay in the USA, where I could access advanced medical care and stabilize my health while making giant strides in academia.

This situation highlights a pervasive issue in my country. Young professionals often face bureaucratic hurdles and systemic challenges that impede their career advancement. The concern of my university was not unfounded; many academics who travel abroad for study or fellowships often do not return, seeking greener pastures in more developed nations. This brain drain is a significant issue, depriving countries of valuable expertise and talent.

This phenomenon calls for a reevaluation of policies by government and university administrations. There is a pressing need for systems that support continuous academic development without imposing unreasonable demands on scholars.

My advice to academics facing similar dilemmas is that it is crucial to weigh the long-term benefits against the immediate challenges. We must navigate these challenges with integrity and commitment. It is about balancing personal advancement with a sense of responsibility. Universities and governments in developing countries need to create more supportive frameworks and policies. These could include flexible leave policies, better integration of international experience into home institutions, and incentives encouraging professionals to return and contribute to their home country's development.

So, I signed the agreement with a deep sense of duty and integrity, demonstrating my commitment to my home university. While the road ahead was daunting, it underscored my resolve to rise above the limitations of my environment and seize opportunities for advancement despite the systemic challenges. Philippians 4:13[39] continued to be my mantra, a source of strength and conviction as I navigated the complexities of academic bureaucracy and personal challenges.

After completing the necessary paperwork, I returned to the USA to embark on the second year of my fellowship. Per my commitment, I traveled back to Nigeria the following semester. For six intense weeks, I immersed myself in teaching the courses assigned to me, grading, and submitting results. Upon completing my teaching stint in Nigeria, I returned to the USA, utterly fatigued but ready to dive back into my research activities.

It is essential to highlight that this entire undertaking was self-funded. No institutional resources were allocated for this purpose. Thus, I had to dig deep into my finances and credit cards to cover travel, accommodation, and other related expenses. This decision placed me in a tight financial spot, but it was worth the endeavor.

By the time I returned to the USA, the accumulated toll of this relentless stress manifested in a stark and undeniable fashion. My health, which I had taken for granted, faltered grievously. I found myself ensnared in the grip of weakness that demanded a complete withdrawal from the world, confining me to my home for nearly two weeks. It was a period of enforced solitude that became a crucible for introspection and decision-making.

During my time of recuperation, I realized that I could no longer rely solely on the system in my home country. I needed to be proactive and prepare for any eventualities. After much prayer, research, and soul-searching, I discovered the possibility of applying for my family under the second-preference employment category (EB-2) National Interest Waiver (NIW) category.

For readers unfamiliar with this term, the EB-2 NIW is a United States visa category. It allows individuals with exceptional ability in their field of expertise and whose employment in the US would greatly benefit the nation to seek permanent residency without the usual job offer or labor certification requirement. This category particularly appeals to professionals like me who wish to leverage their skills and experience in a developed country's more

[39] Philippians 4:13: "I can do all things through Christ who strengthens me."

resourceful and stable environment.

The EB-2 NIW appeared as a potential pathway to stability and security for my entire family. It represented an opportunity to build a future in an environment where my professional aspirations could be realized without the constant battle against bureaucratic inefficiencies and financial constraints. More importantly, in case of any eventuality, it would put me near reliable health infrastructure to navigate the hurdles.

In pursuing this path, I envisioned a future where my children could thrive without the limitations and struggles that often hindered my journey. It was a decision grounded in a blend of pragmatic foresight and the relentless pursuit of a more fulfilling and stable life where my health, career, and family could flourish.

Meanwhile, my duties at home remained unchanged. I continued to shoulder most domestic responsibilities, including bills, rent, and household needs. At the same time, under the guise of contributing to our family's needs, my husband continued to channel a fraction of his income toward putting the finishing touches to our building project in Nigeria.

THIRTY-FOUR

The Cost of Aspiration

Do not let what you cannot do interfere with what you can do.

John Wooden

Reflecting on my journey, I realize the extra workload, driven by a noble vision of stability and hope, came at a significant personal cost. It was a decision that would come to haunt me in the future. In my pursuit of securing a better future for my family and avoiding the status of tenants upon our return to Nigeria, I pushed myself beyond my physical limits. This was my lifestyle during our time in Nigeria, and I continued the same pattern in America, driven by a blend of necessity and aspiration.

Looking back, I understand this approach was not sustainable and detrimental. As much as we aspire to achieve our goals, it is crucial to prioritize our health and well-being.

The consequences of pushing oneself excessively, especially in the face of ill health, are profound. Studies have consistently shown that overworking, particularly when coupled with health problems, can lead to severe physical and mental health issues and long-term repercussions (Schulte, 2015).

The book of 1 Corinthians 6:19-20 (NIV) also reminds us of the importance of taking care of our physical well-being as a form of reverence to God: "Do you not know that your bodies are temples of the Holy Spirit, who is in you, whom you have received from God? You are not your own; you were bought at a price. Therefore, honor God with your bodies."

Furthermore, Psalm 127:2 states, "In vain you rise early and stay up late, toiling for food to eat—for he grants sleep to those he loves." This verse highlights the futility of overworking and neglecting rest, a principle I wish I had heeded.

The lesson here is profound yet simple: While hard work and dedication are commendable, they should not come at the expense of our health. It is essential to listen to our bodies and recognize our limits. As I pushed myself to work double despite my health challenges, I failed to heed these warnings. This oversight was a mistake that haunted me for many years after that.

In hindsight, I advise readers to avoid the same trap I fell into. It is crucial to strike a balance between your aspirations and your health. While working hard for your family's future is commendable, it should not be done at the cost of your physical and mental health.

Remember, taking care of yourself is not just a personal responsibility but a spiritual one. It is about honoring the temple God has entrusted you and recognizing your physical body's limits. Balancing work, health, and family responsibilities is challenging but essential for a fulfilling and sustainable life. As you strive to achieve your goals, do so with a mindful awareness of your health and well-being.

It is a lesson I learned the hard way, and I hope my experience can be a lesson for others to avoid making the same mistake. It is difficult for me to recount all the details of those dark days, even now. The memories remain etched in my mind like scars, and the emotions they evoke are still raw. However, it was a battle, a fierce struggle for survival, where the line between life and death grew thinner with each passing day.

However, in these darkest hours of my life, I found myself navigating the hazardous waters of sickness and despair all alone. I had always known my husband as a cold and disinterested partner, and it seemed there was no limit to the cruelty he could inflict. Thus, as I struggled to care for our children while my health deteriorated, the weight of the world seemed to press down on my shoulders.

As I was getting weaker and weaker, my husband's toxicity grew to such a monstrous proportion, and his callousness reached new depths. There came a night when I felt the life draining out of me, my breaths shallow and labored. It was around 11 pm, and I knew something was seriously wrong. Desperation filled my voice as I pleaded with my husband to take me to the hospital. Nevertheless, his response was chilling in its indifference. He told me to take some medication because he wanted to sleep; after all, he had work early in the morning.

The realization struck me like a thunderbolt. There I was, on the precipice of life and death, and my husband could not be bothered to care. I knew driving myself to the hospital was out of the question; I might pass out on the way. So, reluctantly, I mentioned taking an Uber. To my astonishment, he agreed without a hint of concern. When the Uber arrived, I glanced at my children's room, tears in my eyes, and silently prayed to God for healing so I could return to them alive and healthy.

I stepped into the Uber, my heart heavy, knowing I was on the brink of something life-altering. I asked the driver to take me to the nearest available hospital. Little did I know this decision would be the turning point. That night, I underwent treatment for severe anemia and exhaustion.

In the early morning hours, I was discharged, my body still weak, but my spirit unbroken. When I returned home, I saw my husband sleeping soundly, snoring without a care in the world.

As the sun began to cast its rays that morning, I solemnly vowed to myself. The marriage was beyond redemption, and if I wanted to be alive for my children, I had to escape from the clutches of this man, who seemed either sick, crazy, or a manifestation of pure evil. I prayed fervently for God to grant me the strength needed for the trials ahead and to seek the light at the end of the tunnel. My first step in this journey toward liberation was to prioritize my health, for I knew that only in a state of physical and mental wellness could I effectively fight the battles that lay before me.

As my health continued to spiral downward, the realities of my condition became starkly apparent. I was no longer the energetic researcher and the dynamic professor who engaged students with a passion for knowledge. An

Array of medical appointments, referrals, and diagnoses had overshadowed my once-vibrant personality. The relentless progression of my illness had left me in the shadow of my former self, unable to fulfill my professional obligations.

Thus, as my health deteriorated, the joy and fulfillment I found in my professional duties faded into a distant memory, compelling me to step away from my work. It was a heartbreaking decision but one necessary for my survival. The complexity increased adversely by the time my second year of fellowship ended, as the steady income that had been a lifeline for our family's financial stability ended with it. Thus, here I was, on a leave of absence without pay from my home university and without a financial backbone to rely on in America.

As I no longer had any means of income and could no longer work due to my health condition, The burden of being the sole breadwinner now fell squarely on my husband's shoulders, a role he had skillfully evaded throughout our sixteen years of marriage. Despite knowing my situation, he adopted a stance that disappointed me. He limited his contribution to our household finances by agreeing to pay only the monthly rent bills for our apartment, leaving me to grapple with the remaining expenses. It was a stark and painful revelation of how much he would go to shirk responsibilities.

In an unfathomable display of selfishness, my husband began to buy food for himself alone. He would sneak it into the house, hidden in his backpack, retreating to our bedroom to consume it in solitude. Behind that locked door, he isolated himself, indulging in meals while our children's stomachs growled with hunger. This act of blatant betrayal is more profound than any financial strain.

> “ The resilience of the human spirit, often tested in the fires of adversity, was something I experienced firsthand.

Desperate to shield them from the gravity of our situation and preserve the semblance of normalcy, I turned to credit cards. These plastic lifelines became my means to put food on the table, keep the lights on, and pay for the necessities my husband blatantly disregarded.

Nevertheless, with each card swipe, I sank deeper into a quagmire of debt. I had no savings to fall back on; every penny we had once possessed had been funneled into completing our building project in Nigeria—a venture that now seemed like a distant dream. The minimum payments on the credit cards were a monthly reminder of the financial precipice on which I teetered, yet my husband remained indifferent to my plight. Whenever confronted with the growing mountain of bills, his default reaction was a dismissive complaint, claiming that his financial contributions were already maxed out by covering the rent.

In this crucible of hardship, I bore the weight of financial pressures, the relentless assault of illness, and the emotional burden of holding together a family that was being silently eaten away by discontent and despair. My days were a blur of managing symptoms and nurturing children oblivious to the storm around us.

The resilience of the human spirit, often tested in the fires of adversity, was something I experienced firsthand. As I navigated through these trials, my faith, though battered, became the anchor that kept me grounded. The journey was arduous and fraught with obstacles, but I was determined to emerge stronger, wiser, and more resilient from this crucible.

However, in the quiet moments of introspection, I could not help but question my chosen path. Why did I remain tethered to a man who wanted to choke my life out of me? Why did I continue to uphold a marriage that was already crumbling from day 1? Was my unwavering commitment to our sacred vows, or was the fear of societal judgment shackled me to this façade? While unique in its details, my story was a universal tale of struggle, resilience, and the undying quest for grace amidst life's trials.

My heart goes to anyone in similar circumstances as I write these words. I share my story as a testament to my journey and a beacon of hope for others. May my experiences remind me that even in the darkest times, the human spirit can endure, adapt, and triumph.

THIRTY-FIVE

Between Health and Duty

"Health is a state of complete harmony of the body, mind, and spirit.

B.K.S. Iyengar

Recall the arduous process of obtaining approval from my home university for the second year of my fellowship. It was a feat that required perseverance and negotiation, and ultimately, signing a bond that mandated me to return to my home university after the fellowship. However, as the fellowship ended, I found myself in profound confusion, torn between the urgency of my deteriorating health and the binding commitment to my career.

Compelled by a fierce determination to preserve my health and the dignity of my career, I reached out again to my home institution with a plea for compassion. I presented my case with earnestness, explaining the impending diagnoses, surgeries, and the necessity of focusing on my treatments. The request was a desperate bid for understanding, hoping they would extend the grace I so urgently needed by keeping my position for me while I extended my leave of absence.

Unfortunately, my request was denied. The bond I had signed with the university was a chain that bound me to my responsibilities, allowing little room for deviation, even in a medical emergency. While understandable from an administrative standpoint, this mandate overlooked the nuanced challenges of health and wellness that are so prevalent yet often unaddressed in similar settings.

This situation is a pointer to the systemic challenges many in my home country face. The delicate balance between career progression and personal health can become skewed in a landscape where academic and professional commitments are often paramount. Institutions, driven by a need for continuity and adherence to regulations, may inadvertently overlook the human element, the essence of their existence.

A profound lesson lay at the heart of this ordeal: Institutions must cultivate a more empathetic approach toward their constituents, especially in developing regions. It underscored the importance of flexible policies to accommodate the unforeseeable challenges of life, particularly health-related ones. My story, therefore, serves as a clarion call for a paradigm shift, for a balance that harmonizes the rigors of professional duty with the undeniable realities of human fragility.

Despite my precarious health, teetering on the brink of collapse, and my family's future hanging in the balance, I made a decision that would test the very limits of my endurance. Leaving my family behind in the USA, I traversed oceans and continents. I embarked on a journey back to my native land, driven by a singular mission: to prove my dedication to my academic career and dispel notions of abandonment.

Upon my return to Nigeria, my physical state had deteriorated to a point of alarming fragility, instilling a deep-seated fear of the repercussions of my recent decisions. My hands shook uncontrollably as I completed the necessary official documents. With the formalities out of the way, I submitted letters from my American doctors, which painted a vivid picture of my dire health situation and underscored the critical need for my swift return to the US for upcoming surgeries. However, the path to securing medical leave entangled me in the complex web of bureaucratic inefficiency. I faced a bureaucratic behemoth, its procedures mired in a quagmire of red tape and dilatory tactics. Time, an increasingly precious commodity, seemed to elude me, slipping through my trembling fingers while the stress exerted a relentless assault on my already compromised health.

In an unexpected turn of events, my predicament caught the attention of my university, prompting them to offer me a leave of absence. Though this gesture offered a semblance of relief, it was a double-edged sword; the extension would be unpaid, stripping me of any financial lifeline. This reality struck fear into the core of my being, for I knew all too well the absence of a financial safety net. My support system was virtually non-existent, significantly, as my husband's behavior toward me had deteriorated from bad to untenable.

Upon receiving approval for my leave of absence, I departed from the campus, flanked by friends whose steadfast support had been a beacon of light throughout this harrowing journey. As we walked, the vibrant world around me began to dim, its colors and contours melding into a featureless fog. The firm ground beneath me seemed to dissipate in an instant, and the icy grip of unconsciousness ensnared me. My body, devoid of strength, yielded to the encroaching shadows, collapsing as delicately as a leaf succumbing to autumn's first frost.

In this critical moment, my friends emerged as my protectors, swiftly carrying me to the nearest hospital in a desperate bid for aid. However, we encountered a healthcare system in crisis, unresponsive and inaccessible. The public and teaching hospitals, which should have been healing sanctuaries, stood incapacitated, their operations halted by a nationwide strike. This calamity held patients and medical personnel in a stranglehold, leaving us facing the stark reality of a system at a standstill.

This situation illuminates a grim facet of life in Nigeria, where industrial actions within the healthcare sector frequently abandon the most vulnerable to the whims of destiny. The impact of such strikes transcends mere statistics; they embody vivid narratives of lives hanging in the balance, aspirations postponed, and hope eroded. In these times, the fragile boundary separating survival from demise becomes agonizingly clear—a precarious balance many are forced to maintain without a safety net.

Driven by an urgent need for medical care, I found myself at a private hospital. Surrounded by the antiseptic ambiance of white walls and the persistent drone of medical machinery, I was brought back from the brink and stabilized. Although relief washed over me, it was shadowed by a stark awareness of my fragility. It was then, from the depths of vulnerability and a close encounter with mortality, that I resolved unequivocally to return to the USA immediately.

I purchased a next-day ticket to embark on a pilgrimage toward healing and survival. As I stepped onto the plane, the weight of my circumstances pressed down on me. I recognized that not everyone trapped within the constraints of an overstretched and underfunded healthcare system would be as fortunate as I was to evade death's clasp. Many remain ensnared in the relentless machinery of a healthcare landscape plagued by scarcity and strain in my home country.

As my plane soared into the skies, leaving the familiar landscape of my homeland far below, I found myself enveloped in a sea of introspection. Below me lay a nation where, for many, healthcare remained an elusive luxury, a distant dream in contrast to the fundamental right it should be. This transition marked a shift from a realm where healthcare deficiencies and bureaucratic indifference were commonplace to a context where medical services, though imperfect, were more readily available and not taken for granted.

My health saga clearly illustrates this broader crisis, mirroring the struggles faced by countless individuals trapped within healthcare systems incapable of addressing their most basic medical needs. This experience, grounded in the bitter truth of global health inequities, underscores the vital importance of access to timely and adequate medical care—a matter of life and death for many and a determinant of chronic illness for others.

That December, I underwent a minor surgical procedure, serving as a precursor to a more substantial operation slated for January. The intricacies of my health situation, the diagnosis I received, and the treatments that followed, while deeply personal and confidential, were in absolute contrast to my prior experiences within Nigeria's healthcare system. This chapter of my journey, laden with its complexities and intensely personal revelations, is one I hold closely, choosing to keep the intimate details within the confines of my reflection. This is not done out of secrecy but out of a desire to maintain a personal sanctuary around these profoundly transformative experiences.

As the days went by, I grappled with the realization that the journey to recovery would be long and solitary. I contacted my home university again, requesting an additional year's leave of absence. Unfortunately, my request was met with a response I had not hoped for; my extension was declined. At that critical juncture, I faced a daunting decision: my career or wellness. After much contemplation and heartache, I chose the latter, deciding to retire honorably from the university. This meant committing to repay the penalty for breaking my bond. It was a sacrifice I was willing to make to focus entirely on my treatments without the distractions of my job back in Nigeria. This decision, though difficult, felt right. With my experience and qualifications, I knew that I could always secure a better future with good health and God on my side.

In grappling with this reality, I was compelled to reflect on the broader implications for my home country and other developing nations. How many talents are lost in this cycle of fear and mistrust? How many opportunities for collaborative growth and development are missed?

As I pen these thoughts, I realize my story is a single thread in the realities of global talent mobility. It is a narrative that highlights the need for trust, understanding, and policies that recognize the value of global exposure while nurturing the bond with one's homeland. It calls for balancing individuals' aspirations with their home countries' needs, fostering a world where talents are nurtured and celebrated, not restrained by borders or fears.

Nevertheless, it is essential to acknowledge the role of my home institution in my journey. Their initial support and the opportunities they provided were crucial stepping stones in my career. My decision to leave was not a reflection of their shortcomings but a necessary step for personal and health-related reasons. The Bible's teaching that all things work together for good (Romans 8:28) assured me that every experience, whether challenging or uplifting, shapes us and directs our path in ways we might not immediately understand.

In my heart, I felt gratitude for my roots and the experiences that shaped me. While I had to make a difficult choice, it was done with a deep respect for my home institution and with the hope that my journey might, in some way, contribute positively to the future.

THIRTY-SIX

Unwavering Alone

"The human spirit is stronger than anything that can happen to it.

C.C. Scott

Alone, like a solitary figure in a vast, empty landscape, I faced the daunting prospect of my initial medical procedure that December. My husband had preoccupied himself with a self-imposed need to work extra hours under the guise that he needed to make extra income to meet the responsibility of our house rent—a responsibility I had transferred to him due to my ailment. He leveraged this as an excuse for not accompanying me to the hospital for the surgery, leaving me to navigate the cold corridors of the medical facility by myself. It did not bother me much because I had already accustomed myself to his absence and emotional detachment.

This self-reliance in adversity only underscored my growing resilience and ability to face challenges head-on, even in the most vulnerable moments. Moreover, the procedure was minor, not necessitating a companion's presence. However, deep down, the realization that I was navigating this critical juncture of my life without the support and companionship of my partner underscored a profound need to rethink the relationship.

As the date of my major surgery in January loomed, I found myself imploring my husband to be present. The hospital had a strict rule: a family member must accompany the patient, or the surgery would be postponed. Reluctantly, he agreed to be there. However, his insensitivity reached new heights on the morning of the surgery. I woke him early, only to be met with his groans for more sleep, his body languidly sprawled across our bed, indifferent to the ticking clock and my escalating anxiety.

Realizing the gravity of the situation, that waiting for him would jeopardize the surgery, I took matters into my own hands. With a heart heavy yet determined, I drove myself to the hospital. I called him as I approached the hospital, hoping he would meet me there, but his words were like a cold splash of reality - he was at the train station, had missed his bus, and claimed there was no money for an Uber. It was a moment of desperate realization; the man I had married, the partner who should have been my rock, was indifferent to whether I lived or died.

In a desperate move, I reached out to an elder from our church who lived near the hospital. This woman, whose name remains unspoken in this memoir for privacy, has been a maternal figure to me, a beacon of support and love. When I arrived at the hospital, she was already there, a guardian angel in human form. She stood by me, offering prayers and comfort as I handed over my items, preparing to be wheeled into the operating room.

It was then, in that moment of vulnerability, that my husband appeared, his arrival too little, too late. A silent affirmation crystallized as I gazed at him: our marriage was over. However, first, I needed to reclaim my health.

This narrative is not an exposé of my husband's failings but a hope that one day, he might read these words and see himself through the lens of my experiences. Perhaps, in this mirror of truth, he might find the impetus to change, to become the person he could be.

To the elderly church member who stood in his place, who embodied the love and support that should have come from a spouse, I offer my deepest gratitude. Her name may not be written here, but her actions are in my heart. She is the unsung hero of this chapter of my life, and I imagine her nodding in affirmation as she reads about the critical role she played. She was more than just a stand-in; she was a lifeline, a reminder that angels are among us even in our darkest hours.

This experience, painful and illuminating, reinforces the notion that we are the architects of our destiny. In moments of crisis, our actions, our decisions to choose life and health, define us. As I lay on that operating table, I knew my journey was mine to walk, a path of resilience and self-empowerment, lit by the grace of those who genuinely cared.

To the glory of God, the surgery was a success. As I left the hospital, driven home by my husband, a whirlwind of thoughts and emotions swirled within me. I gazed out the window, the world passing by in a blur, reflecting the turmoil inside me. I pondered over the fragility of life and the complexity of human relationships.

Six months later, with no improvement in my condition, I faced the prospect of a more significant medical procedure. This time, experience had honed my understanding – I would not involve my husband. Instead, I turned to the elders and pastors of our church, confiding in them that this was not just a medical battle but a spiritual warfare against the depths of darkness. They understood the gravity of my situation and pledged their support, maintaining discretion while committing themselves to intercessory prayer. Their priority, as was mine, was my well-being and recovery before any marital issues could be addressed.

The chasm between my husband and me had grown so vast that I no longer shared the same bed. I left our shared bedroom, transforming the living room into my makeshift sanctuary of comfort. However, even in this space, the addiction had consumed his sanity so much that I was not free from his intrusions. He continued to assert his 'marital rights,' forcing himself on me without regard for my health or consent. Each encounter left me contemplating legal action, but the thought of my children and my lack of employment held me back.

This revelation might seem unbelievable to some, yet those who have followed my journey from the beginning of this memoir would recognize the destructive pattern of his addiction. This part of my life, which I share publicly for the first time, is a clarion call to recognize the hidden struggles within relationships. It is an admonition to look beyond the surface and to understand that what you may be going through, as dire as it seems, might be an ordeal someone else is facing in an even greater magnitude. It reminds you that your story can be a beacon of hope and a catalyst for change in someone else's life.

For anyone reading this and experiencing similar challenges, know that you are not alone. Your experiences and voice are invaluable; seeking help is not a sign of weakness but immense courage and strength. The silence that often envelops issues of domestic abuse needs to be broken. As highlighted by García-Moreno et al. in their comprehensive analysis of the World Health Organization, the silence and stigma surrounding domestic violence serve only to fuel its persistence (García-Moreno et al., 2006).

It is a sobering truth that not everyone emerges from such trials with the opportunity to share their journey. No matter how insurmountable your circumstances may seem, there is a path forward. The initial and often most critical step is to seek assistance from friends, family, or dedicated professional services. Support networks play an indispensable role, offering emotional solace, practical guidance, and, when necessary, intervention.

The dawn of the surgery day finally unfolded with a somber, almost surreal quality on that quiet morning of June. As I watched my husband leave the house early in the morning for his self-proclaimed busy schedule, a cascade of emotions engulfed me. There he was, stepping out into the world, consumed by his own life, oblivious to the gravity of what I was about to undergo.

Turning away from the window, my gaze fell upon my children, the two beacons of light in my life. They were getting ready for school, their chatter piercing the heavy silence of the morning. I watched them with a heart full of love and trepidation, yearning to embrace them, to reveal the depth of my fears and hopes. However, I held back, masked by a façade of normalcy. They were still too young, their minds unprepared for the burdens of adult worries. My older child, on the cusp of fifteen, and the younger, a tender twelve, were oblivious to the magnitude of the day.

As they left, I went on my knees and pleaded passionately for God's mercy to see me through the surgery and help me to return home healthy. I vowed solemnly to right the wrongs I had unwittingly done by shielding my children from the truth of their father's abuse.

The Uber ride to the hospital was a path of fear and hope. I pondered over the choices that had led me here, the silent battles I had fought, and the resilience that had kept me afloat.

Upon arriving at the hospital, a wave of reassurance enveloped me. Our pastor, his wife, and the elder who had been my pillar of strength during my initial surgery were already there, forming a small, steadfast congregation of support. Their presence was a balm to my anxious heart. We prayed together, their words weaving a blanket of faith and love around me. They promised to continue their intercession until I returned, healthy and whole. In their eyes, I saw parental concern and an unwavering belief in my strength and the power of prayer.

As I lay on the hospital bed, enveloped in the sterile, impersonal environment, I could not help but reflect on my husband's lack of empathy. His failure to be present in my time of need was a wound deeper than any doctor's scalpel. However, as the anesthesia began to take effect, drawing me into a peaceful oblivion, I held onto the love and prayers of those around me. They were my actual family, who had shown me the true meaning of unconditional love and support. Their faces were the last familiar ones I saw, their prayers the last I heard before darkness gently closed in.

As I would later come to understand, the operation that day was an ordeal far beyond the expectations of even the most seasoned surgeons. What was initially projected as a two-hour procedure unfurled into a six-hour battle against unforeseen complications. I lost an alarming amount of blood, a critical situation that seemed to defy human efforts to save me. Nevertheless, in those perilous moments, I believe the sustaining power of the blood of Jesus kept me alive. The story inscribed on these pages might have never been told without this divine intervention. The intricate details of that operating room may remain undisclosed, but the outcome stands as a profound testament to the miraculous.

Meanwhile, as the doctors fought valiantly to save my life, the spiritual realm unfolded a different narrative. Amid the chaos, with the three elders pouring out their hearts in fervent prayer, I experienced a transcendental shift. My consciousness was transported beyond the confines of the sterile hospital room into a spiritual encounter that would forever alter my perspective on life and my purpose within it.

In this trance-like state, I faced what can only be described as a brush with death. It was a moment when the temporal veil was lifted, revealing the eternal realm. During this spiritual journey, I encountered God profoundly and deeply personally. While I choose not to divulge every detail of this experience, one aspect remains pivotal to my story.

I was given a glimpse of my mortality, a moment where I stood on the brink of eternal departure. However, it was not my time. God chose to breathe life back into me in His infinite mercy and wisdom. The reason for this divine intervention was twofold. Firstly, my mission on Earth was far from complete; humanity still needed the gifts and service I was destined to offer. Secondly, perhaps more importantly, I was to return to correct a grave error — the covering of iniquity within my household.

This revelation mirrors the Biblical narratives where God often calls individuals back from the brink for a greater purpose. Just as Jonah was given a second chance after his ordeal in the belly of the fish (Jonah 2:10),[40] or Lazarus was brought back to life as a testament to Jesus' power over death (John 11:43-44), my experience was a call to address the hidden truths and unspoken pain within my own family.

The book of Proverbs 28:13 states that "Whoever conceals their sins does not prosper, but the one who confesses and renounces them finds mercy." My trance was a divine mandate to bring to light the truths I had buried to protect my family. It was a call to confront and heal the wounds festering in the shadows, break the chains of iniquity, and set a course toward redemption and truth.

This encounter with the divine realm was a pivotal moment that redefined my purpose and mission. It was a clarion call to realign my life with God's will, embrace my role as an agent of change, and courageously step into the fullness of my calling.

[40] Jonah 2:10 - "And the LORD commanded the fish, and it vomited Jonah onto dry land".

THIRTY-SEVEN

Resilience in Recovery

The greatest glory in living lies not in never falling, but in rising every time we fall.

Nelson Mandela

As the anesthesia began to wear off, a sharp, almost visceral agony sliced through me. The pain was indescribable, a raw intensity that seemed to echo through every fiber of my being, leaving me gasping for breath and grappling with a reality far more excruciating than I had braced myself for. In this moment of overwhelming distress, the doctors and nurses around me were incredibly supportive, swiftly responding with the care and medications needed to ease my suffering. Once the pain had subsided to a more manageable level, I reached out for my phone with a trembling hand, intent on calling my husband.

A part of me quivered at the thought of informing him, yet I knew it was necessary. He was, after all, still my legal next of kin and the father of my children. As I dialed his number, a nagging thought haunted me: What if his presence in the hospital during the surgery could have somehow made things worse?

Indeed, considering the stark indifference he exhibited toward my well-being during my first two surgeries, it was not far-fetched to imagine that he would not have spent those tense hours praying for my recovery. Instead, his attendance might have introduced an undercurrent of negativity, an energy so potent that it could have tipped the scales in my favor in the delicate balance between life and death on the operating table.

This reflection led me to a deeper understanding: There are moments when wisdom must prevail over conventional expectations. It made me realize that the presence of a legal or societal bond does not always equate to a supportive or beneficial influence, particularly in times of vulnerability. Choosing not to inform my husband about this delicate surgery was a decision steeped in the understanding that sometimes, for healing to occur, one must carefully curate the energy that surrounds them. My survival, against all odds, underscored the subtle power of discernment, a reminder that knowing when to step forward and back is crucial in the dance of life.

“Sometimes, for healing to occur, one must carefully curate the energy that surrounds them.

When he picked up the phone, my voice was a faint murmur. With each word delicately laced with both relief and pain, I shared with him that I had undergone surgery, highlighting the procedure's success as a reflection of divine intervention. I also informed him of my need for an extended stay at the hospital to recuperate, my speech intermittently broken by sharp pangs of discomfort.

His reaction was as disheartening as anticipated. He mentioned an additional work shift he had taken on for the night, his voice carrying undertones of inconvenience at the prospect of my situation imposing on him. The irony struck me profoundly when he tepidly suggested he might ask for permission to visit me at the hospital. I wondered if he understood the severity of what I had just endured. With a quiet resolve, I assured him there was no need to alter his work schedule on my behalf. True to my expectations, he did not appear until the following day.

This revelation, though painful, was also liberating. It underscored the necessity of my journey toward self-reliance and healing. The ordeal was a profound awakening to the strength and resilience I possessed by the golden grace of God. In that hospital room, amidst the echoes of pain and revelation, I found a renewed sense of purpose and a determination to fulfill the purpose why God preserved my life, independent of the shadows cast by a faltering marriage.

During the five days I was sequestered within the cold, impersonal confines of my hospital room, my husband's presence was limited to a single visit, lasting no more than two hours. The indelible image of him unpacking his favorite Chinese noodles during that visit lingers in my memory. Under normal circumstances, the aroma of those noodles might have been inviting, but at that moment, it seemed to taunt me, filling the room with a scent that underscored my helplessness. He consumed them with a gusto that appeared wholly unaffected by the severity of my condition, a vivid and distressing contrast to my physical torment and the emotional anguish that enveloped me.

This seemingly trivial act represented his character, prompting me to reflect on the depths of his apathy. It was bewildering to consider how someone could be so oblivious to their partner's suffering, so detached from a fundamental sense of empathy. His capacity to seek enjoyment in such simple pleasures, even as I grappled with acute distress, revealed a painful truth—sometimes, having someone physically near can feel more isolated than their absence.

The conspicuous absence of my husband during those critical days served as a stark reminder of the lonely journey of recovery that lay ahead. My heart grew heavier as I realized that this path, fraught with challenges and introspection, was one I would predominantly navigate alone.

His fleeting visit, brief and disquieting, only served to solidify this understanding. He did not return; our sporadic interactions were limited to infrequent phone calls. During these calls, he either sought assistance for domestic quandaries he encountered in my absence or discussed his increased work hours, necessary, he claimed, to cover our house rent. This financial responsibility, one he had taken on in the wake of my illness after 16 years of shared life, left me pondering a painful question: Was this his way of exacting some form of retribution for the financial weight now placed upon his shoulders—a weight that I had singlehandedly carried until my health faltered.

Then, a few days before my scheduled discharge, he called with news that under any other circumstances would have been a cause for celebration: our green cards had arrived. This should have been a moment of joy, a significant milestone marking a new chapter in our lives. However, in my weakened state, the news failed to elicit its deserved response. Fragile and exhausted from the ordeal, my body and spirit could muster only a muted acknowledgment of this blessing.

As I absorbed the uplifting news of our green card approval, I was enveloped in a moment of deep introspection. My mind returned to the arduous endeavor I had embarked upon to secure this precious status. Crafting a comprehensive 58-page petition for the National Interest Waiver (NIW) within the Employment-Based Category (EB2) had been an imposing challenge. Undertaking this significant task alone, without legal assistance, was a decision dictated by circumstances rather than preference. The prohibitive cost of attorney fees and my husband's reluctance to provide financial support left me with no alternative but to tackle the intricate visa process independently.

I recall meticulously sifting through the extensive documentation, carefully ensuring every piece was ideally in place, and fully aware of the delicate nature of this petition. Despite the absence of legal guidance, the financial weight of the petition for our family of four was still substantial; I found charging most of the costs to credit cards. I knew my husband was taking advantage of my unwavering determination to persevere through the process, but I remained steadfast, driven by the promise of a brighter future.

In that hospital room, as I lay broken yet resilient, the green card represented tangible proof of what I could achieve through faith, grace, and relentless effort. Quietly, I thanked God for steering me through this arduous journey. The permanent residency (or green) card, a symbol of new beginnings, was a chance to rebuild and renew every aspect of my life. I envisioned myself rising, not just from the pain and betrayal I had endured but also from the ashes of self-doubt and fear. Thus, I vowed to emerge more robust, resilient, and ready to forge a path defined by my God-given choices and dreams.

I prayed for the strength to embrace the opportunities that lay ahead with the green card, to use it as a key to unlock doors that had been closed to me. I envisioned a future where I could stand independently, unshackled by the constraints of a marriage that had become a cage. With this green card, I saw a path to independence, a chance to forge a new identity rooted in my dreams and aspirations, guided by the golden grace of God.

The day of my discharge was a dawn of realization. It was not my husband who came to my aid but the compassionate pastors and the ever-present elder who had become my guardian angel. Their collective wisdom made them decide that, given my husband's nonchalant attitude, it was too risky to return home in my fragile state. Instead, they arranged for me to recuperate at the elder's home, a place where I could heal both physically and emotionally.

My husband's visit during my week-long stay at the elder's house was as brief as perfunctory. He appeared just once, and even then, as usual, his presence was devoid of genuine concern. It was during this rare visit that I decided to return home with him despite my still-weakened condition. Deep down, I knew a pressing mission awaited me - to reveal the truth about my marriage, a truth I believed God had restored me to life to confront.

Returning to what should have been my sanctuary, my home, I instead stepped into a realm as cold and desolate as my husband's demeanor. I continued using the living room couch instead of our shared bedroom. My most recent experience taught me that it would be better to grapple with the aftermath of my surgery in isolation.

Each morning, as dawn broke, I watched through half-closed eyes as my husband, cloaked in an air of feigned ignorance, avoided meeting my gaze. There were days when I would limp through the house, clutching at chairs and walls for support, while he sat comfortably in the living room, engrossed in a comedy show or savoring his meal, oblivious to my struggle.

One particularly harrowing day, I was in the restroom, battling agonizing pain as I attempted to use the toilet. The lingering pain from my surgery compounded the physical torment. My husband entered, not with words of comfort but with a callous request for me to hurry up because he was late for work.

When it came to my medication, his apathy knew no bounds. Requests for him to pick up my prescriptions from the pharmacy were met with excuses about strained finances, forcing me to hand over my credit card for a mere $5 copay. The depths of his insensitivity seemed to know no bounds.

As I navigated these days of isolation and neglect, I could not help but wonder: Who harbors such callousness but the devil in human form?

In stark contrast, the moments I treasured most were the mornings when our children would approach me. Their tender hugs, the gentle caress of their hands on my face, and their heartfelt prayers infused me with a strength I desperately needed. Their assurances, so full of innocence and love, were my daily dose of hope. I found solace in their presence, a balm for the aching loneliness my husband's indifference inflicted.

As I lay there, enveloped in the love of my children, my mind would often wander to the future. In those quiet, reflective moments, I could sense the golden grace God had deposited within me - a resilient spirit that refused to be extinguished despite the storms. It was as if each prayer from my children rekindled the flame of hope within me, illuminating a path forward.

I eagerly awaited their return from school each day, knowing their presence would bring a semblance of normalcy and care to my convalescence. They were my young caretakers, my little angels who reinforced my belief in a brighter tomorrow with every errand they ran for me.

Amid the chaos, my determination only grew stronger. I understood that my healing journey was about liberating myself from the confines of a marriage that had almost choked me to death. It was about confronting harsh realities with bravery and aspiring for personal restoration and wholeness.

However, I reminded myself to proceed with caution and patience amidst these revelations. Prioritizing my health was paramount; I needed to regain my strength and stability before I could address the wrongs that had been done, not only to myself and my children but also to the broader spiritual community I held dear. It was a time for careful healing, a period to gently peel away the layers of hurt and disappointment and gradually rebuild a foundation of well-being and dignity.

As I reclined on the couch, my thoughts drifted, weaving through a web of what-ifs—what if the elders had not stepped in? What if their compassionate intervention had not shielded me from the darkest outcomes of my surgery and recovery? In those moments of solitude, a profound sense of gratitude swelled within me, gratitude for the senior pastor, his wife, and the older woman who stood by me like unwavering pillars of strength and love. They embodied the essence of genuine family, stepping into the breach left by my husband, who was supposed to be my fortress.

As I awaited the return of my children, their imminent presence a balm to my weary spirit, I could not help but marvel at how the actions of these elders had altered the course of my destiny. Without their intervention, the narrative of my life could have veered into tragedy. Their unyielding support not only restored my health but also rekindled my faith. They showed me that in the face of life's most daunting challenges, there is always hope, a way forward, and grace to be found. For this, I am eternally grateful.

Their actions, marked by an unwavering commitment to my well-being, were light rays in my darkest hours. They did not merely perform acts of kindness; they saved my life, intervening in a way that only true parents would for their children. The depth of their empathy and the sincerity of their care transcended the bounds of biological ties, teaching me the true meaning of family. They stood by me when the burden of my condition seemed insurmountable, ensuring my access to necessary medical care, enveloping me in prayers, and providing the emotional sustenance that my soul so desperately craved.

This chapter may not carry their names, but it is a testament to their legacy—a tribute to their selflessness, unwavering support, and the sanctuary they provided when I was most vulnerable. It is dedicated to them, my spiritual parents, whose actions have left an indelible mark on my heart and the pages of this memoir. Their story, interwoven with mine, serves as a beacon for all who navigate the stormy seas of life, reminding us that we are never truly alone. I am deeply grateful to them, for they have shown me that grace and love can find us, lift us, and lead us home, even in our darkest moments.

THIRTY-EIGHT

Recovery and Realization

What lies behind us and what lies before us are tiny matters compared to what lies within us.

Ralph Waldo Emerson

In the aftermath of the surgery, the doctors had cautioned me that the road to recovery would be long, perhaps spanning six months to a year. However, as I embarked on this journey, I experienced an unexpected acceleration in my healing. This rapid progress was a clear manifestation of God's grace at work. It was as if Isaiah 40:31 had come alive in my life: "But those who hope in the Lord will renew their strength. They will soar on wings like eagles; they will run and not grow weary; they will walk and not faint." Indeed, under six months, I found myself not just physically recuperated but spiritually and emotionally fortified, ready to face the battles ahead.

This period also marked a turning point in my relationship with my husband. No longer could I allow myself to be subjugated, to be a silent sufferer of his advances. It was as if the scales had fallen from my eyes. I stood firm, resolved not to bend toward the indignities of the past. With this renewed vigor, my first thought was to secure financial stability.

Months passed, and with each day, my strength and determination grew. My physical and emotional recovery reached a point where I felt ready to dive back into the professional world—my passion for academia, which had never dimmed, reignited with vigor. I began my search for a full-time faculty position. This role would fulfill my career aspirations and provide my children and me with desperately needed stability.

The search was arduous, filled with moments of hope and despair. I reviewed faculty job listings, sent applications, and patiently waited for responses. However, this endeavor soon revealed the lingering fragility of my condition. Reality struck hard after two unsuccessful attempts at faculty interviews, where exhaustion clouded my performance during campus interview visits. I realized that I needed more time to recuperate. I learned firsthand that physical recovery and inner strength are distinct, and while one may flourish, the other may still require nurturing.

I decided to start small and thus began my journey back into the academic world as a part-time faculty member teaching a game design course at a nearby community college. Stepping into the classroom after about a two-year hiatus was filled with a mix of trepidation and exhilaration. The familiar scent of whiteboard markers, the eager faces of students, and the vibrant energy of academic life felt like a homecoming that filled me with nostalgia and newfound appreciation.

“ Physical recovery and inner strength are distinct, and while one may flourish, the other may still require nurturing.

The financial compensation from this role, however, was modest at best. It barely made a dent in the mountain of credit card debts that loomed over me. This reality nudged me to explore other avenues. With ample time, I turned to the digital world, searching for remote opportunities. During this exploration, a revelation dawned upon me: perhaps I was meant to be my boss, an entrepreneur charting her course.

The idea of utilizing my creative gift in fashion design, which had long been a dormant seed for a while, suddenly sprouted in my mind. Maybe, just maybe, this was the moment God had been preparing me for when He endowed me with this talent. Filled with a sense of divine purpose, I registered an online company. I ventured into selling African-inspired designs while coordinating remotely with African-themed designers from all over the world.

To my astonishment, the very next day, after listing my first designs, I made a sale. It was a small but significant victory, a beacon of hope during financial uncertainty. That small venture, born out of necessity and nurtured with creativity, not only helped me cover my basic needs but also continues to help me gradually lower my debts. With its ebbs and flows, this journey taught me that our gifts are often given to us long before we realize their purpose.

As I reflect, I see how each step, each decision, was a thread in the tapestry of my life, woven together to create a picture more extensive than I could have imagined. My journey underscores the truth in Jeremiah 29:11, "For I know the plans I have for you," declares the LORD, "plans to prosper you and not to harm you, plans to give you hope and a future." My small online business, a seed planted in a time of need, continues to thrive as a testament to God's grace and my journey of healing and self-discovery.

One afternoon, the world around me was a blur of creativity as I immersed myself in drawing sketches for my latest fashion styles. The peaceful rhythm of my work was abruptly interrupted by my husband's announcement. He casually mentioned his plans to travel to Africa to see his family. The news caught me off guard—not just for the suddenness of it, but for the sheer impracticality, considering our financial situation.

I remember looking up from my sketches, my hands still poised over my laptop as I processed his words. "Is not it too soon to be making such an expensive journey?" I asked, my voice laced with a mix of concern and disbelief. However, his mind seemed made up, his attitude nonchalant to the concerns evident in my tone.

At that moment, something within me shifted. The marriage, which I had long felt was teetering on the brink of collapse, seemed to be inching closer to the edge. However, part of me desired to fulfill all righteousness and benefit him from the doubt. So, I said to him, "If you decide to travel without us agreeing on this trip, then perhaps you should also inform your family that we are no longer together." His agreement to my statement was swift, almost too swift. It left me stunned, a mixture of disbelief and a peculiar sense of relief swirling within me.

In the aftermath of our conversation, I could not shake off the feeling that it was all a dark joke. The idea that our marriage had been reduced to this—informal negotiations about separation as casually as one would discuss the weather—was surreal. It seemed the journey would be easier than anticipated.

As I continued my work, the sketches before me became metaphors for my journey. The lines I drew seemed to mirror the lines of my life—intersecting, diverging, a complex pattern of choices and consequences. Moreover, somewhere amidst those lines, I found a reflection of my journey, a blend of resilience and grace, sorrow and strength, an ode to the chapters yet unwritten in the book of my life.

THIRTY-NINE

The Precipice of Change

The only way to make sense out of change is to plunge into it, move with it, and join the dance.

Alan Watts

As my husband was planning his departure to Africa, I continued to hold onto a sliver of hope while beseeching the heavens for guidance and clarity. Amid this spiritual odyssey, a practical voice within me whispered the need for caution and wisdom. It reminded me of the ancient saying, "Caesar's wife must be above suspicion." Determined to leave no stone unturned, I reached out to his family and friends, hoping to illuminate the depth of our marital crisis.

The responses I received were a mixed bag of reluctance, apprehension, and pleas for patience. Some knew all too well the complexity of his character, while others, out of love or a desire to see us reconcile, urged me to be patient. Throughout these conversations, I sensed a subtle acknowledgment that the well of my patience had long since run dry. I knew talking of patience at this time was a theatrical display of avoidance and denial as if it would somehow dissipate into thin air by not addressing the issue.

What I appreciated in their responses, despite the lack of a concrete solution, was the absence of blame. They played their roles as mediators and well-wishers, their words not of judgment but of concern and hope for reconciliation. In the end, in the echoes of their well-intentioned advice, I heard the unspoken truth that the end of my patience had been reached, a fact they perhaps recognized but found hard to articulate.

Then came a request from my husband that was as audacious as it was revealing. He asked me to assist him in paying for his flight using my credit card, promising to reimburse me in cash. The irony of the situation was not lost on me. Over the years, he had artfully evaded getting a credit card. The reason behind his avoidance of credit, a standard tool in modern financial transactions, was apparent to me now. I believe it was calculated to maintain control and opacity in our financial dealings.

However, I saw an opportunity in his request. If I handled his travel arrangements, I would know precisely when he would leave and return. It was like a tactical play in the chess game our marriage had become. Well, I ensured that the game rules were different this time. I demanded the cash upfront before I made any payments for his trip. The moment he transferred the funds to me, a sense of empowerment washed over me. It was a small but significant victory in the grand scheme of our relationship dynamics. I would no longer be at the mercy of his whims and fancies.

Amidst the turbulence, I was quietly laying the groundwork for a pivotal change—a strategic escape from a marriage that had become a valley of the shadow of death. The well-being of my children, who had innocently borne the brunt of their father's negligence, was the compass guiding my every move.

I was acutely aware that the road ahead would be challenging, especially as a single mother. Financial stability was not just necessary; it was the lifeline that would anchor us through the storm. I knew that securing a well-paying and regular job was crucial for our survival and independence.

Then, as if by divine intervention, an opportunity presented itself—a full-time faculty position at a reputable university nearby. It was a place where my skills and passion could genuinely flourish. The location was ideal; it was close to our home and my children's school, minimizing the disruption to their lives.

As I received the news of my appointment, relief and excitement washed over me. The role seemed tailor-made for me, aligning perfectly with my academic expertise and personal circumstances. It was the dawn of a new beginning, a pathway to independence and empowerment.

Signing the contract and preparing for my new role that Fall, I could not help but reflect on the journey that had brought me here. From the depths of despair to the heights of professional success, my journey was a testament to the power of faith, grace, and resilience of a mother's love. I stepped into the new role with a sense of purpose and a renewed commitment to provide my children with a stable, nurturing environment. It was the dream of any career woman, and by God's grace and mercy, it was now my reality.

Upon securing a stable and promising position, I knew the pivotal moment for a significant decision had arrived in my marriage. Delving into my husband's itinerary, I noted that his return was scheduled around Thanksgiving,[41] a time that serendipitously presented an opportunity. Then, a daring strategy began to form in my thoughts: to orchestrate a mock separation. This bold tactic aimed to confront him with the stark reality of our strained relationship, serving as a wake-up call to the seriousness of our issues.

With the stealth of a chess grandmaster plotting her next move, I orchestrated the plan. I packed our belongings and whisked our children away, leaving behind an empty home. As Thanksgiving approached, I envisioned him returning to our desolate apartment, the absence of laughter and warmth as a complete reminder of what he stood to lose.

However, I carefully shielded our boys from the truth of our exodus. They were young, innocent of the complexities of adult relationships and the heartache that accompanied them. To them, I painted a picture of a weekend adventure, a visit to my uncle, cloaking our departure in the guise of a festive getaway.

Upon our arrival at my uncle's place, I continued the charade, not yet ready to reveal the full extent of our situation. To him, we were there to

---

[41] Thanksgiving is a national holiday in the United States, celebrated on the fourth Thursday of November.

celebrate Thanksgiving, basking in the joy of family and the holiday spirit.

Then came the inevitable call from my husband, his voice a mix of confusion and surprise upon finding our home empty. My response was a mix of sorrow and resolve. "It is over," I said, trembling yet firm, "unless you are willing to change." The words hung in the air, a lifeline extended in the hope of salvaging what was left of our marriage. "Change," I repeated, "We deserve better. Our children deserve better. Show us you can be a better husband and father."

His response reverberated through the phone line like an icy wind, chilling me. His voice had no remorse, no trace of longing for reconciliation—just a severe, unyielding refusal to see the fractures in our marriage that were gaping wide open. His words, asserting he had given his best and saw no need for change, crashed over me like waves of finality. His casual acceptance of my decision to walk away struck me even more profoundly. "I am fine with it," he said, as if our years together, our shared history, were nothing but a fleeting chapter quickly closed.

I stood there, phone in hand, feeling a torrent of emotions. There was a piercing hurt, a deep sense of betrayal that the man I had spent nearly two decades with could so quickly let go. However, amid the pain, a fierce resolve began to stir within me. Unlike an insignificant leaf blown away by the autumn wind, I would not just walk away like this. No, there had to be more to this man, more to our story that had spanned almost eighteen years. I refused to let our marriage, our shared life, dissolve into a mere footnote.

At that moment, a wave of clarity washed over me. This was not just about walking away; it was about understanding and seeking the more profound truths beneath his indifference. I could not shake the feeling that there was more to his apathy, a hidden depth to the man I had once known so intimately.

I decided to delve deeper, to unearth the layers of our relationship that had been buried under years of routine and unspoken grievances. It was a quest for closure and understanding—for me and the children we had brought into this world. I knew it would be a journey fraught with pain and revelation, but I was determined to embark on it.

Thus, with a resolute heart, I began unraveling the webs of our marriage.

It was a journey that would take me through the valleys of our past, over the mountains of our conflicts, and into the heart of a mystery that had defined much of my adult life. Nevertheless, I was ready, for I knew the keys to my freedom, healing, and rebirth lay within this journey.

FORTY

Confronting the façade

The truth will set you free, but first it will make you miserable.

James A. Garfield

Returning to our city with the boys, I was torn between protecting my children from the harsh truth and the crushing reality of our disintegrating marriage. I chose not to return home. Instead, I checked us into a hotel, spinning a tale for the children of a five-star experience to reward their good behavior.

As the boys delighted in the hotel's luxury, unaware of the underlying turmoil I was going through, I began to make phone calls that would alter the course of our lives. I reached out to our leaders to inform them of the situation. As I relayed my decision to them, a part of me grieved for what could have been, even as another part braced for the uncertain journey ahead.

The situation was a huge concern to our senior pastor and his wife. They had been like parental figures to me since our arrival in America, providing guidance and support through their deep wisdom in life and the Word of God. I was aware that they had been making attempts to have a private conversation with my husband after noticing the abnormalities in our marriage. However, my husband artfully dodged their attempts to counsel him, using his work as a shield to fend off any discussion. I knew the truth was more straightforward and painful: he was not interested in help, nor did he want our marriage to be a subject of conversation, especially with the pastors.

The elders, wise and seasoned from years of navigating life's complexities, chose to address the situation directly. They reached out to my husband for an account of our family's well-being without revealing that I had shared our troubles. His response was a masterclass in pretense, projecting an image of normalcy and sidestepping the truth of our absence from the home.

Their disbelief was palpable. They could not fathom how he could effortlessly sidestep the significant matter of our departure. Sensing the gravity of the situation, they decided to visit us. They pleaded with me to come home the following morning for a candid discussion about the future of our marriage.

Leaving my children at the hotel, I approached this meeting with hope and trepidation. Perhaps, I thought, this might be the turning point. Maybe the intervention of these respected figures, whom he could not easily dismiss, might influence him toward a positive change. Maybe, just maybe, the revelation of his true nature to these third parties would catalyze his transformation.

As I stepped into our home, where the pastors were already seated with him, the atmosphere was thick with anticipation. The conversation began with a prayer, the pastors invoking divine guidance and wisdom. They turned to us, their faces etched with concern and empathy. "We have called this meeting," the pastor stated, "to understand how we can help heal and restore your marriage before it gets too late."

My husband, taken aback by the directness of the conversation, shifted uncomfortably. He offered a brief nod, his eyes avoiding mine. Then, he continued by sticking to his script and painting a picture of a contented family life. However, the pastors, wise to the ways of the heart, pressed further, gently peeling back the layers of pretense.

As the meeting unfolded, the room took on the air of a solemn tribunal, where my marriage's unspoken and long-buried truths were to be unearthed. My husband sat across from me, his eyes wandering to the window, tracing the light that seeped through the blinds. His gaze, however, carefully avoided mine as if direct eye contact would force him to confront the reality of his actions. It was as if the room itself had transformed into a confessional, where our marital woes were laid bare, scrutinized under the compassionate yet discerning eyes of the elderly couple.

And then, the pastor turned to me, inviting me to share my perspective, a flood of emotions welled up within me. I was about to unveil a reality cloaked in silence, a reality that readers following my story would find all too familiar. With a heavy heart, I began to unravel the tapestry of our marriage, thread by thread. Each word I spoke peeled back layers of emotional distance, neglect, and despair—constant companions in a relationship that had lost its way.

My husband's disposition was one of quiet resignation. He did not outright deny the accusations I levied against him; his responses were cloaked in delusional justifications. For instance, when confronted with his financial neglect, he retorted with what he must have believed was a clever defense that whatever money one of us has belongs to the other. The irony was not lost on anyone in the room. Here was a man who had shirked his financial responsibilities, and yet, in a twisted turn of logic, he sought refuge in the communal nature of marital assets.

" A family's finances are like a small boat in a vast ocean; without careful navigation, it is easy to lose direction.

Our stance on our financial arrangements recalled a nugget of proverbial wisdom that resonates deeply: " A family's finances are like a small boat in a vast ocean; without careful navigation, it is easy to lose direction." In our marital partnership, where I assumed the role of the primary provider, I was prudent in maintaining separate personal financial accounts. Our only joint financial venture was a shared business account dedicated to our publishing endeavors. This decision, reflective of cautious financial stewardship, emerged as a fortuitous strategy in the grand scheme of our relationship.

This narrative is a gentle admonition to readers about the importance of prudence and foresight in financial matters within a partnership or marriage. It underscores the need to maintain financial autonomy, not out of mistrust but as a strategy for safeguarding one's economic well-being and ensuring the stability of joint endeavors. It is a testament to the saying that while love may be blind, financial acumen should not be. In managing finances, as in steering a boat through the unpredictable seas, the wise captain anticipates storms, navigates carefully around potential hazards, and always keeps an eye on the compass, ensuring that even in tumultuous waters, the voyage continues toward a safe harbor.

Confronted with the accusation of abuse, my husband staunchly maintained that he had never been abusive toward me. In that moment, a profound understanding crystallized within me as I absorbed his words: emotional abuse is a pervasive yet often overlooked plague, its toxicity silently undermining the bonds of trust and love in a relationship.

His insistence on innocence, based on the lack of physical aggression, revealed a profound misunderstanding of the abuse's nature. It is imperative for those entangled in similar circumstances to recognize that emotional abuse bears equally, if not more, destructive power than its physical counterpart. Patricia Evans illuminates this in her seminal work, The Verbally Abusive Relationship (Evans, 2009), highlighting how emotional abuse's covert and manipulative tactics inflict deep psychological wounds. This brand of abuse, marked by patterns of manipulation, neglect, and emotional harm, can insidiously degrade one's self-worth and mental well-being, often leaving more lasting scars than physical maltreatment.

Building on the insights provided by Bancroft (2002), it becomes evident that behaviors exhibited by my husband are not isolated incidents but part of a deeply entrenched pattern that demands significant intervention for change. Regrettably, my husband's response to these revelations was one of stark opposition. This underscores a critical aspect frequently encountered in abusive dynamics: a steadfast state of denial and resistance to change. The reluctance to face and alter such behaviors not only sustains the cycle of abuse but also impedes the journey toward healing and growth, both on an individual level and within the relational dynamic.

For readers in similar circumstances, it is crucial to understand the importance of breaking the silence. While it may feel excruciatingly uncomfortable, bringing these issues to light is the first step toward healing and recovery. The shame associated with sexual abuse and pornography exposure within a marriage is not the victim's to bear. Opening up about such experiences, especially in safe and supportive environments, is vital for emotional healing and can also serve as a beacon of hope and guidance for others who might be suffering in silence.

Lastly, to those grappling with the complex web of sexual abuse within marriage, know that your story matters. Your pain is valid, and your voice deserves to be heard. Seek a safe space to share your burden, be it a counselor, a trusted friend, or a support group. Silence may offer temporary shelter, but healing begins with the courage to voice your truth.

Grace, Resilience and Redemption

FORTY-ONE

The Clash of Realities

Strength does not come from physical capacity. It comes from an indomitable will.

Mahatma Gandhi

As the meeting continued, my husband clung steadfastly to his delusional belief that he had given his best to our marriage, a stance that left me bewildered and frustrated.

His words struck me like a physical blow. How could he not see that his so-called 'best' was pushing me toward an early grave? It was only by the sheer grace of God that I had survived, but now, our marriage was irrevocably broken. However, he remained unmoved, cocooned in a blanket of self-righteousness. I countered his claims with a fervent insistence, my voice rising in volume and passion. "Your best could have led me to an early grave," I declared, the rawness of my emotions laid bare. "It is only by the grace of God that I stand here today, but this... this is unequivocally over."

And then, he shifted his strategy to a masterclass in deflection and blame-shifting. With an air of self-righteous indignation, he accused me of an "unforgiving spirit," attempting to paint me as the one clinging to old grievances. "You are always bringing up the past," he accused, his voice a mix of reproach and feigned dismay. However, I knew this was a mere diversion, a tactic to shift focus from his failings. However, his logic was flawed, a house of cards built on the shaky foundation of denial. I looked at him, my mind sharpened by the very pain he had caused, and retorted, "Forgiveness does not equate to amnesia."

I explained to him, with a clarity born of suffering and insight, that my memory was a ledger of our shared history. "Each incident, each moment of neglect, is etched in my memory, not out of spite, but because I was enduring the pain," I said firmly.

I conveyed to him that my preemptive decision to forgive any of his future actions was not a manifestation of vulnerability but an intentional act of self-care and empowerment. This approach aligns with the wisdom shared by Desmond Tutu and Mpho Tutu in "The Book of Forgiving" (Tutu & Tutu, 2014). They insightfully articulate, "Forgiveness is the journey we take toward healing the wounds of the past." This perspective underscores the transformative power of forgiveness, not as a conduit for forgetting or condoning unjust actions but as a pivotal step toward personal healing and resilience.

> “ the journey of forgiveness does not obligate one to erase the memory of the transgression.

I clarified that the gesture of forgiveness does not obliterate the past or negate the significance of the experiences that necessitated it. "The scars I bear are vivid testimonies of my trials. They are not to be dismissed or overlooked," I asserted.

Dear reader, as we traverse the narrative of my existence together, I wish to impart to you the pivotal role forgiveness has played in my life—not merely as an act of leniency but as a crucial mechanism for survival. This notion finds resonance in Lewis Smedes's work, "Forgive and Forget: Healing the Hurts, We Do not Deserve" (Smedes, 1984). Smedes astutely articulates that the journey of forgiveness does not obligate one to erase the memory of the transgression. It is essential to understand that granting forgiveness serves primarily as a conduit for your inner peace rather than an exoneration of others' misdeeds. In embracing forgiveness, we liberate ourselves, allowing for a healing process that transcends the need for forgetfulness.

In a crafty bid for sympathy, he donned the mantle of the aggrieved traditional African husband, weaving a tale of desertion where my professional commitments were cast as a dereliction of marital fidelity. Heavy with feigned martyrdom, his voice accused me of leaving him to fend for himself, alone and neglected. He pointed to my six-month academic sojourn to Canada and the USA—vital for my Ph.D. research—as the pinnacle of this alleged abandonment, claiming his tolerance of such absences was a testament to his virtue as a "good man." He proudly proclaimed that few African men would be as forbearing as he was, allowing their wives such freedoms.

This accusation was so steeped in irony that it bordered on satire. His attempt to solicit empathy through this narrative revealed a calculated manipulation of traditional expectations. It was a performance aimed at painting himself as a modern-day martyr who had graciously borne the weight of my ambitions on his supposedly solitary shoulders. The absurdity of his claims would have been laughable if not for the tense environment.

The accusation brought to light the cultural and societal expectations surrounding gender roles, particularly in African contexts. As Chimamanda Ngozi Adichie discusses in 'We Should All Be Feminists' (Adichie, 2014), the delineation between the roles of men and women is often starkly drawn, with societal norms dictating a rigid framework within which individuals must operate. Adichie's discourse highlights how these traditional expectations not only stifle the potential of women but also imprison men within a construct of masculinity that equates emotional resilience with silence and stoicism.

I countered, "Traveling for work is not abandonment. It is a responsibility, especially when I provide for the family."

With frustration and disbelief, I recalled the time I went on study leave for my Ph.D. program abroad. "I left you with fifteen signed blank checks to manage our expenses," I recounted. "By the time I returned, my account was drained, with no accountability from your end." His narrative of victimhood was unraveling, each word of mine stripping away the layers of his constructed reality.

As my husband sat there, his arguments crumbling like sandcastles under the relentless tide of truth, I came to accept the profound truth about my husband's unrepentant and narcissistic nature.

In retrospect, it is crucial to recognize the complexities of such situations for readers seeking understanding or grappling with similar challenges. The silence that often shrouds issues of sexual abuse and addiction within a marriage is a societal one that needs to be addressed openly. Marital counseling and psychology experts advocate for an environment where such complex topics can be broached with sensitivity and understanding.

Amidst this revelation, however, I confronted a painful irony. While I laid bare the deepest scars of our relationship, I found myself grappling with the hesitation to disclose one of its darkest facets – my husband's pornography addiction and the resulting sexual abuse I had endured. The embarrassment of articulating such a personal violation in the presence of our pastors was overwhelming. It felt like peeling back the layers of my dignity, exposing my vulnerabilities in the harsh light of scrutiny. My silence on this matter was a protective barrier for the little dignity I felt I had left. However, in doing so, I also realized I was perpetuating the cycle of silence that often surrounds such issues.

As the meeting progressed and emotions rose, I felt the pastor's gaze rest upon me. He seemed to sense my growing emotional turmoil and intervened with a perceptive nod. In his words, there was a blend of biblical wisdom and real-world pragmatism, a delicate balance to guide us toward reconciliation and mutual understanding. His approach was not just pastoral but deeply empathetic, recognizing the weight of our struggles.

The pastor, alongside his wife, began to unravel the spiritual implications and social consequences of my husband's actions. They highlighted the stark difference between the cultural context of our native Africa and the developed world where we now reside. For hours, they spoke words filled with counsel and admonition.

As the conversation unfolded, there was a noticeable shift in my husband's demeanor. The initial defiance etched on his face gradually gave way to a subdued calm. Once sharp and assertive, his arguments seemed to wane, losing their edge in the face of irrefutable truth. However, even as his tone softened, his words remained unyielding, devoid of genuine remorse or acknowledgment of wrongdoing. This subtle shift in demeanor did little to deceive me. I harbored no illusions about the man he was—a master in the arts of evasion and deflection.

I resolved to return home with our children the following day. However, this decision was not borne of a naive hope for a miraculous transformation. It was a strategic move, a calculated step in a larger plan. I needed to cover my tracks, gather evidence, and prepare for any eventualities that the future might hold. By this, I could safeguard myself and my children while laying the groundwork for whatever actions I might need to take.

Meanwhile, a faint sliver of hope lingered in the back of my mind. It was the hope that now, with his façade shattered and his true self exposed, my husband might finally recognize the gravity of his actions. Perhaps, just perhaps, this unveiling of his true nature would be the catalyst for him to embark on a journey of change and self-reflection.

So, with a heavy heart, I thanked the pastors for their intervention as we concluded the meeting. I returned with a sense of cautious hope, promising to return home with the children the following day. The path to healing and reconciliation seemed daunting, yet the pastor's guidance had sown seeds of hope and possibilities in the rocky soil of our relationship. Whether these seeds would take root and flourish remained to be seen, but the first steps toward potential change had been taken.

This dear reader, was an excruciating chapter of my life. It was a chapter where pleading, praying, and fasting seemed futile—where my husband's apathy was a roaring silence. However, amid the turmoil, I discovered the power of grace, the promise of hope, and the strength of resilience. I was pushed to my limits, yet God's grace held me. My prayer for you, dear reader, is that you will experience this same grace, mercy, and hope in your darkest moments. The storm may be fierce, but remember, it will pass. Hold onto your faith, lean into God's grace, and emerge stronger, brighter, and more resilient.

FORTY-TWO

A New Reality

It is not the strongest of the species that survive, nor the most intelligent, but the one most responsive to change.

Charles Darwin

That night, as I returned to the innocent faces of my children waiting at the hotel, the world's weight seemed to rest on my shoulders. My mind was prayerfully and strategically weaving through the monumental task ahead. While the full details of my tactics are beyond the scope of this book, it is sufficient to say they were carefully considered and deeply personal.

In the quiet of the night, as my children slept peacefully, oblivious to the storm raging within me, I embarked on a quest for understanding. The previous day's events had peeled back another layer of my husband's persona, revealing a depth of callousness that demanded a more profound comprehension. I delved into research on narcissism, seeking to understand the psychological underpinnings of his behavior.

My findings were enlightening yet disheartening. The traits and patterns I read about mirrored the behavior of my husband. The grandiosity, the lack of empathy, the need for admiration – all signs pointing toward narcissistic behavior. Dr. Ramani Durvasula, in her book 'Should I Stay, or Should I Go:

Surviving a Relationship with a Narcissist (Durvasula, 2015), describes such individuals as often charming yet profoundly self-absorbed and manipulative, leaving their partners feeling confused, inadequate, and unloved.

With this newfound knowledge, I realized the gravity of my situation. The idiom "sleep with one eye open" became a new, literal meaning for me. It symbolized a heightened state of awareness, a readiness to protect my children and myself from the unpredictability of living with someone who could not be trusted in any way.

As I walked back into our house with the children the following day, it no longer felt like the haven it was supposed to be. The revelations from the previous day's meeting had cast a new light on my husband's callousness, transforming our home into a battleground. It had become a place where vigilance, strategy, and unyielding resilience were not just necessary but vital for survival. Each room demanded a newfound strength from within me to navigate this complex terrain.

The first step was clear – I declared seven days of prayer and fasting for myself. This was a cry for divine guidance, a submission of my plight into the hands of a higher power to fortify my spirit, gain clarity, and prepare for the journey ahead. As Psalm 32:8 promises, "I will instruct you and teach you in the way you should go; I will counsel you with my loving eye on you." I sought this divine counsel, yearning for direction through my life's tangle.

> "I will instruct you and teach you in the way you should go; I will counsel you with my loving eye on you" (Psalm 32:8).

The Gospel of James clearly emphasizes the power of prayer in seeking wisdom and guidance (James 1:5). So, in the solitude of my prayers, I found strength and a sense of purpose. I knew the road ahead would be arduous and fraught with challenges. However, armed with faith, insight, and a strategic mindset, I was ready to navigate the unknown.

As I delved deeper into my days of prayer and fasting, a period I had hoped would usher in a wave of transformation and healing, I found myself engulfed in an ever-darkening storm as my husband's character transformed from bad to worse. That December, a month usually resplendent with festive lights and joyous carols, felt like a grim mockery of my predicament. The cheer and merriment of the season cast long, gloomy shadows over what I recognized as "dark December," in contrast to the warmth and light I so desperately sought.

Amidst this, my husband, the man who was supposed to be a pedestal of trust and love, became the architect of discord and pain within the walls of our home. Rather than change for the better, his behavior escalated alarmingly. His words transformed into weapons of verbal abuse flung with a precision that cut deep into the heart.

The impact of his harsh words was not confined to me alone. Our children, with their wide-eyed innocence, became unwilling spectators to these harrowing scenes. Witnessing their father transform into a source of hurt and intimidation was a heart-wrenching experience.

And then, my husband's actions began to betray a disturbing pattern, one that pointed toward adultery. He made strange, secretive phone calls, his voice hushed as he glanced furtively around. The doors of our home suddenly transformed into revolving gates for his unexplained and unaccountable comings and goings at odd hours. Each departure and arrival were shrouded in mystery, leaving a trail of suspicion and unease.

As these patterns became increasingly apparent, I realized that narcissism was not his only vice. The possibility of adultery loomed large, a sinister shadow darkening the already troubled waters of our marriage. Strangely, this revelation brought a twinge of relief amidst the turmoil. Adultery, a clear violation of marital vows, provided tangible evidence, a solid ground on which I could build my case if needed.

At the same time, this realization was also a source of bafflement and profound disappointment. How could a man who portrayed himself as a devout Christian engage in such betrayal without any apparent remorse? The hypocrisy was staggering. It compelled me to shift my approach from passive observation to active investigation. I began gathering facts and evidence, piecing together the fragments of his double life.

The time I had come to break the silence that had shrouded my struggles. I felt an urgent need to share the reality of my situation with my extended family, especially my siblings and mother. They had been blissfully unaware of the depth of my marital crisis, shielded from the truth by my attempts to preserve the façade of a happy marriage.

The day I revealed the truth about my marriage to my siblings was marked by a storm of emotions. It was a day of turning point, a moment of raw honesty I had avoided for far too long. I organized a WhatsApp conference call to facilitate this critical conversation, a virtual gathering that would soon become an emotional revelation.

As the call connected and the familiar faces of my siblings appeared on the screen, a knot tightened in my stomach. I took a deep breath, steadying myself for the confession that would shatter their image of my seemingly perfect life.

"Family," I began, my voice a tremulous whisper, "there is something I need to tell you." The words that followed poured out like a flood breaking through a dam. I narrated the actual reality of my marriage, a tale of emotional and financial manipulation, a daily struggle cloaked under the disguise of normalcy.

The silence on the other end was deafening. As I delved into the details—his financial schemes, his selfish nature, the abusive behavior that had become a shadow in my life—the expressions on their faces morphed from disbelief to horror. To them, these revelations were alien, incongruent with the image they had of my husband, a man they knew only through my carefully curated stories of our life together.

Tears began to stream down my sisters' faces. My brothers' expressions hardened, their features etched with a rage that simmered beneath the surface. The air was thick with a mix of sorrow and anger.

"But how?" My youngest sister managed to choke out between sobs. "We never suspected..."

"I know," I replied, my voice cracking. "I kept it all hidden under a smile and an 'everything is fine' mantra. However, it is not fine. It is far from fine."

As I unveiled the stark realities of my life, a life far removed from the happiness they presumed, I could see the dawning of a painful understanding in their eyes.

Throughout the years, my siblings have observed glimpses of my husband's true character. They recalled instances pointing to his gluttonous and self-centered nature. However, in their minds, these traits were overshadowed by what they perceived as his love for me. They had seen him indulge excessively, often putting his needs and desires before others. Still, they interpreted this behavior as merely a quirky aspect of his personality, not as a red flag indicating deeper, more troubling issues.

"We always thought he loved you deeply," my eldest brother confessed, his voice tinged with regret. "We saw his selfish ways but never imagined it went beyond that. We believed you were happy together."

One by one, my siblings voiced their thoughts, their words a chorus of support and indignation. The consensus was clear: I needed to escape this toxic environment, to remove myself and my children from the clutches of a man who was proving to be more harmful than any ailment.

As the call neared its end, a sense of unity and resolve enveloped us. Though miles apart, my siblings were my fortress, a bastion of strength and love. "We are with you every step of the way," my elder brother declared, his voice firm and resolute.

I hung up the call with tears streaming down my face, not just from the pain of the past but from the overwhelming sense of love and support my family had shown. It was as if a weight had been lifted off my shoulders, a burden I had been carrying alone for too long.

That call marked the beginning of a new chapter, one where I was no longer a silent sufferer but an empowered woman backed by the unwavering support of her family. It was the first step toward reclaiming my life, a journey fraught with challenges but one I would not have to face alone. My siblings, my pillars of strength, had given me the courage to face the storm ahead, armed with the knowledge that no matter how fierce the winds, I would not be swept away.

FORTY-THREE

Confronting the Storm

The gem cannot be polished without friction, nor man perfected without trials.

Confucius

In those moments of despair, I could not help but question my faith. "Is God listening?" I wondered as each day seemed to bring a new wave of challenges, seemingly unmitigated by my fervent prayers. The silence from the heavens was deafening, and doubts began to creep in, clouding my once unshakeable belief in the power of prayer.

To my dear readers who might resonate with my situation, I would like you to know that we often find the most profound lessons in the trials of faith. As renowned Christian author C.S. Lewis once wrote, "God whispers to us in our pleasures, speaks in our conscience, but shouts in our pains. It is His megaphone to rouse a deaf world" (Lewis, 'The Problem of Pain' 1940). This assures us that our ordeal is not a sign of divine neglect but a testament to God's complex and often mysterious ways.

The Bible is replete with instances where prayers seemed unanswered and faithful servants endured trials and tribulations. However, each story reminds us of a larger plan at work, a divine purpose that transcends our immediate understanding. Romans 8:28 assures, "And we know that in all things God works for the good of those who love him, who have been called according to his purpose." This scripture reminds us that even during turmoil, there is a purpose, a divine orchestration we may not yet comprehend.

During that long week of praying and fasting, as I wrestled with doubt and sorrow, I began to think that maybe the answers I sought were not in the form I expected. I realized that sometimes, the most excellent answer to our prayers is our transformation, the fortitude to face our trials, and the wisdom to navigate through them. This understanding became my guiding light, a beacon that illuminated my path through the shadows of despair and toward a dawn of renewed hope and strength.

Amidst my prayers, I adhered to the principle of 'watch and pray,' staying alert while seeking divine wisdom. My efforts to initiate dialogue with my husband were met with evasion, intensifying my concerns. However, I leaned into God's grace, understanding the importance of compiling evidence. This was not spurred by mistrust alone but as a necessary measure to shield me from potential financial devastation in the wake of a divorce—a scenario all too familiar in the narratives of American separations.

Aware of the potential consequences that a separation or divorce could have, especially in a foreign land like America, where tales of financial and emotional devastation abound, I recognized the necessity of being prepared. The thought that my husband, the man who was supposed to be my life partner, could lead me to ruin was a terrifying possibility. This was not the path I had envisioned, yet the person he had become was a stranger capable of unfathomable deeds.

The need to protect myself became a priority, compelling me to enter a realm I had never imagined. The act of investigating, of seeking evidence, was foreign to me. I valued privacy and trust, yet here I was, faced with a situation that demanded vigilance. My attempts to access his phone—a gateway to understanding his hidden world—were thwarted at every turn. He guarded his digital life with a zealousness that excluded even me and our children. His phone was barricaded with a solid wall of passwords and patterns, a digital fortress impervious to my attempts. On occasions, I approached him under the guise of needing to find some contacts in his phone, hoping he would unlock the device for me, but his refusal confirmed my fears, a testament to the secrets he held close.

This realization chilled me to the core. The man who was my life partner, the father of my children, had constructed walls so formidable that not even the innocent curiosity of our children could penetrate them. It was evident he harbored secrets dark enough to necessitate such vigilance. The irony of our life together was a bitter pill to swallow. It underscored a truth I could no longer ignore: The journey ahead would be as much about uncovering the reality of my marriage as it was about navigating my path to liberation and truth.

So, as I navigated this intricate web of suspicion and evidence-gathering, I clung to my faith more than ever. It was a source of strength and solace, a reminder that even in the darkest times, there is a guiding light. Moreover, in my heart, I knew that whatever the outcome, I was prepared to face it with dignity, strength, and an unwavering belief in justice and truth.

Then, an unexpected twist of fate occurred at the final dawn of my weeklong fasting. My husband's phone malfunctioned, and he sought my assistance in a rare moment of vulnerability. He had tried contacting the mobile service providers, but they required specific information only I could provide. The phone, registered under my name as part of a family pack, with the bills I paid, suddenly became a bridge between us.

As I took his phone in my hands, anticipation ran through me. This was the lifeline I had been praying for, an opportunity to glimpse into the digital veil he had meticulously drawn around his life. They deeded me to reset the phone, and I told him I could not do it unless he removed the password, and he obliged. With a mix of apprehension and the precision of the computer scientist I am, I navigated through the phone's contents and gathered enough evidence before he could realize what was happening.

The revelation that unfolded before my eyes was a tableau of betrayal. The details were too sensitive, too jarring to recount in this memoir. Each message, each photograph, each secretive rendezvous detailed on his phone sent chills down my spine. The evidence of multiple adulterous escapades was stark and undeniable, confronting me with the harsh reality of my 18 years of living with a stranger as my husband.

The pain was acute, yet there was a strange sense of clarity in this agony.

Even now, as I recall those moments, I am amazed at how I managed to maintain a semblance of calm when facing him. It was as if a veil had been lifted, revealing a strength within me I had not realized existed.

As I grappled with the enormity of this betrayal, I understood that the following day would mark a pivotal turn in our relationship. It was not just about confronting him with the evidence of his infidelity; it was about standing up to the years of deceit and emotional turmoil.

My recent spiritual journey fortified this resolve, which had imbued me with a newfound sense of purpose and strength. My faith, a source of solace during my fasting and prayer, now empowered me to face this difficult conversation. I was prepared to peel back the layers of lies and confront our relationship's raw, unvarnished truth.

The dawn of the following day was not just the end of my fasting; it was the beginning of a new chapter in my life, where I would no longer be a silent witness to my own life's erosion but an active participant in reshaping it. With a prayer on my lips and a conviction in my heart, I prepared myself for the confrontation that awaited, ready to face whatever lay ahead with grace and fortitude.

In the dim, early hours of the morning, while the world still slumbered, I approached the daunting task ahead. My heart was heavy, yet determined, as I gently rose from the living room couch that had become my refuge. I went to our bedroom to shake my husband awake. His initial reluctance to rise was palpable as he lay there, motionless. However, when I uttered the words about his adultery, a jolt of alertness seemed to pass through him.

I crafted my words carefully, a blend of strategy and desperation. "Tell me the truth," I implored, "and I promise, no one else will know. Not even the pastor." I concluded with a stern yet heartbroken ultimatum, "I will not utter a word to anyone, but I will leave you in the hands of God, for Him to expose you by Himself." It was a gamble, a play of emotional chess where I was both a player and a pawn, but I knew in my mind that my promise about not letting anyone know about it would not stand.

To my utter astonishment, he confessed. The words spilled out of him, a torrent of admissions that he seemed almost relieved to release. It was as if he had been silently yearning for this unburdening moment. My world, already in tatters, seemed to crumble further with each uttered word. I felt belittled and cheated, as if the years I had invested in this marriage were a farce.

His casual admission led to an even more shocking revelation. As a pastor, a man ordained to uphold the sanctity of marriage and the virtues of love and fidelity, his words struck a dissonant chord. He blatantly declared that I should accept the fact that I am incapable of satisfying his sexual urges. In its stead, he proposed a chilling compromise: a life together not bound by love but by a mutual agreement of emotional detachment. He was free to seek satisfaction outside our marriage in this mere coexistence.

His words cut through me, leaving me reeling in disbelief. At that moment, I wondered if I had married a madman and if this person before me was an unrecognizable entity, an alien cloaked in human guise.

Amid this surreal and painful discourse, I found the courage to remind him of his responsibilities, not just as my husband but as a pastor—a shepherd entrusted with leading his flock with integrity and example. I questioned whether he had forsaken his sacred role, betraying the principles he preached from the pulpit. His response was as shocking as it was dismissive. He coldly informed me that his spiritual journey and decisions were not my concern, asserting that I was in no position to judge him. "God understands," he proclaimed, suggesting that his actions were somehow justified in the eyes of God.

As he spoke, his words seemed to echo in the hollow chamber of my heart. This was no longer a conversation; it was a eulogy for the marriage we once had.

As the first light of dawn began to pierce the darkness in that early morning, I realized the journey ahead would be one of the most challenging I had ever faced. I was not just dealing with infidelity or emotional neglect; I was confronting a situation that defied logic and understanding. The path ahead was unclear, but one thing was sure: I was no longer bound to the illusions of the past. It was time to face the truth, no matter how harrowing, and forge a new path for myself and my children.

FORTY-FOUR

Breaking Bonds

We must accept finite disappointment, but we must never lose infinite hope.

Martin Luther King Jr

The revelation of my husband's infidelity, juxtaposed against his role as a pastor, was a grotesque paradox that could no longer be ignored. His nonchalant declaration that his adulterous actions were God's business, not mine, sent a cold shiver down my spine. I realized that the man I married was lost, perhaps irretrievably. This was a spiritual crisis of monumental proportions, one that demanded immediate action. I could not stand idly by while he desecrated the sanctity of our marriage and his spiritual responsibilities.

Burdened by the weight of reality, I went to our pastor's house to report the situation. The church had always been a citadel of support and guidance, and I clung to the hope that perhaps spiritual intervention could salvage the remnants of my husband's conscience.

Upon reaching, I unveiled the sordid details of my husband's betrayal. The pastor, a man of deep spiritual insight and wisdom, listened intently, expressing concern and disbelief. His response was immediate and unequivocal – he summoned my husband to hear his story.

The pastor suspended my husband from church ministrations until the issue was resolved. This was necessary to uphold the integrity of the church and its leadership, in line with the Bible's teachings in 1 Corinthians 5:11-13 about the importance of dealing with moral corruption within the church. This was a potential turning point where confession and repentance could pave the way for redemption.

Unfortunately, my husband refused to meet with the pastor in a move that was as predictable as disheartening. He chose to sever ties with the church, abandoning his ministerial duties and the community that had been our spiritual home. His refusal to confront the situation, to seek forgiveness and healing, was a telling sign of the depth of his moral and spiritual decline.

The spiritual insights from James 4:17 – "So whoever knows the right thing to do and fails to do it, for him it is a sin." My husband, fully aware of the righteous path, chose instead a road paved with deceit and dishonor, a betrayal of the trust and faith placed in him by our church family.

The moment my husband turned his back on the church, our lives took a harrowing turn into a realm where the unimaginable became our reality. His infidelity once shrouded in the shadows of deceit, erupted into a brazen display of disrespect and moral decay. The sanctity of our home was wholly desecrated as he audaciously engaged with his mistress through video chats in our shared bedroom, the very heart of our family's private world.

As the calendar pages fluttered toward the year's close, the night of December 31st approached - a night we had always revered as the 'crossover night.' This was the night when the faithful, and even those who strayed from the church's embrace throughout the year, would gather in a solemn assembly to usher in the New Year. It was a night of reflection and hope, casting off the old and welcoming the new under the watchful eyes of God.

That night, I approached my husband with a heavy yet determined heart, harboring a faint glimmer of hope that he might join us in this sacred tradition. However, his resolve was unyielding; he had detached himself from our congregation and seemingly from the essence of our shared spiritual life.

The weight of this realization bore down on me, yet it did not crush my spirit. Gathering our boys, I mustered the courage that had become my constant companion and drove us to church, leaving behind the shadow of the man who pretended to stand by my side in faith.

As we entered the church, I looked around at the congregation, a mosaic of souls united in their yearning for a blessed new year. In that moment, I felt a kinship with each person there, a shared understanding of life's trials and tribulations.

As the clock ticked closer to midnight, the crossover moment, I poured out my heart to God. My prayers were a tapestry of sorrow, hope, and unwavering faith. I prayed for strength, wisdom, and the ability to navigate the uncertain waters of the coming year. I prayed for my children that they would be shielded from the pain and confusion of our family's turmoil. Despite the odds, I also prayed for my husband that he might find his way back to the path of righteousness.

When the clock struck midnight, marking the birth of a new year, a collective cheer erupted from the congregation. However, it was not just a change of date but a moment of profound spiritual renewal. I poured out my heart to God, laying bare the agony, the betrayal, and the uncertainty that had plagued me. In that moment of surrender, I felt a burden lift from my shoulders, replaced by a divine assurance that my anchor in God would hold me no matter the storm.

Driving home, the stars shone brighter, the night air less oppressive. I retired to the sofa that had become my place of comfort as I watched our children go into their bedroom.

The night's events replayed in my mind as I lay to sleep. A newfound clarity emerged, a resolve fortified by my trials. I knew the road ahead would be fraught with challenges, but one thing was clear: nothing, not even the crumbling of my marriage, could separate me from the love of God.

In the silence of that night, I reflected on Romans 8:38-39: "For I am convinced that neither death nor life, neither angels nor demons, neither the present nor the future, nor any powers, neither height nor depth nor anything else in all creation, will be able to separate us from the love of God that is in Christ Jesus our Lord." With these words echoing in my heart, I closed my eyes, not to escape reality, but to rest assured of God's unfailing grace and the hope of a new beginning.

FORTY-FIVE

A Path to Rebirth

The darkest hour has only sixty minutes.

Morris Mandel

The dawn of the New Year is often greeted with joy and celebration, a time when families gather to welcome a fresh start. However, that dark shadow of betrayal clouded New Year's morning for me. As my husband sat, engrossed in intimate conversations with his mistress, his laughter and sweet whispers piercing the stillness of the morning, I felt an overwhelming sense of desolation. His blatant disregard for my presence, as he delighted in his affair, was unimaginable.

I could no longer bear the situation on the second day of the new year. The insidious nature of my husband's addiction once shrouded in secrecy, gradually seeped into the open, threatening not just my sanity but the innocence of our children. It became painfully clear that this was also a battle to safeguard my children from the harmful influences of their father's actions.

The situation necessitated immediate action. The thought of my children, young and impressionable, being exposed to such depravity was unbearable. Their well-being and mental health were my utmost priorities. A mother's instinct to protect her young and the divine wisdom that guided my steps propelled me into action.

With a voice firm yet laden with the weight of a broken heart, I confronted him instantly, making it clear that our home could no longer be a place for his presence. Despite his claim that I was taking things too far, I stood my ground, intending to involve the social welfare department if necessary. This threat unveiled his true nature as he resorted to emotional blackmail, uttering unspeakable things. The most devastating blow came when he disrespected my beloved parents, pushing me to the brink. My resolve hardened; I demanded his immediate departure, offering a compromise of one week to find alternative accommodation. My demand was met with a plea for a month's grace to find alternative accommodation. However, the peace and well-being of my children and myself could not endure another day of turmoil. Thus, I stood resolute, offering him a week to make arrangements.

Seeking solace and guidance, I hastily arranged a video conference with my siblings, who had become my support pillars. Their faces on the screen were a mosaic of concern, empathy, and resolve. I recounted the morning's events, each word testifying to my crumbling world.

My elder brother voiced his fears for our safety. He urged that it was no longer safe for me and the children to continue living under the same roof as my husband. His words resonated with a truth I had been reluctant to accept. The danger was emotional and now a tangible threat to our physical well-being.

Explaining the situation to my children was one of the most challenging conversations I have ever initiated. How does one paint the grim reality of their father's actions without tainting their innocent perspectives? However, as difficult as it was, the conversation unfolded unexpectedly. My children, who had always seen me as their rock, their unwavering provider, seemed to understand the gravity of the situation instinctively. They trusted my judgment implicitly, ready to follow my lead into this uncertain chapter of our lives. They packed their essentials - computers, schoolbags, and cherished games - with a resilience contrasting their young years.

The hours that followed were a flurry of activity. Securing a hotel room nearby was straightforward, but the emotional weight of leaving our home was anything but easy. I had a new car, a recent purchase driven by foresight, which now served as our escape vessel. Time was of the essence. We could not afford to linger, for every moment was a step closer to my husband's return from work. So, with only the essentials in hand, we prepared to depart.

As we were about to leave, a sudden realization struck me. I rushed back into the apartment to retrieve the bond of our property document in our home country. Readers who have followed along with me in this story would recall that I had acquired this land before we left Nigeria, and I had poured my heart and soul into building it, with minimal contribution from my husband.

Though a simple act, holding on to the property document was laden with significance - it was a testament to the wisdom of securing one's assets in the face of discord. It was a decision that would prove to be a lifesaver in the times to come, a foresight that underscored the importance of financial independence and security, particularly for women in challenging marriages.

The journey to the hotel was a mix of silent contemplation and unspoken resolve. My children, seated quietly, entrusted their fate into my hands, their innocent faces a constant reminder of my responsibility.

I found peace in that hotel room surrounded by unfamiliar yet comforting walls. It was a space where we could breathe, away from the oppressive atmosphere of our home. As I watched my children sleep that night, I whispered a prayer of gratitude. I am forever grateful for the strength to make this decision and the divine guidance that led me to this point.

That night, as I lay awake, pondering the path ahead, I clung to Psalm 46:1, "God is our refuge and strength, an ever-present help in trouble." In the quiet of that room, I knew we were not walking it alone while the road ahead was uncertain. With faith as our compass and love as our guide, we would navigate this storm, emerging more robust and resilient on the other side.

As the night enveloped our temporary sanctuary, my phone buzzed incessantly with calls from my husband, but I chose not to answer. Instead, I sent a text, a firm yet necessary message, informing him that we had left the house and granted him a week to make alternative living arrangements. I also made him realize I would prefer text only as our means of communication going forward. His response, a simple thanks, was almost comical in its nonchalance, an irony that did not escape me.

From that point on, I consciously decided not to answer his calls. This was a strategic move, a protective measure in a rapidly evolving battle of wills and wisdom. By restricting our communication to text messages, I inadvertently created a paper trail, a documented account of our interactions that could prove invaluable in case of future legal proceedings. It was a precaution rooted in the recognition that trust, once shattered, transforms every interaction into a potential minefield.

The imposed separation became an asylum for introspection, a precious interval for realigning my inner compass, and a period to bolster my resolve and that of my children, equipping us to face the uncertain future with preparedness and fortitude.

As the semblance of routine life beckoned with the close of the holiday season, we found ourselves navigating the unfamiliar cadence of daily life from our transient abode in the hotel. The transition was marked by a seamless adaptation, particularly by my children, whose remarkable resilience unfolded before my eyes. Their capacity to embrace this new normal, to unearth continuity amidst the disarray, was nothing short of inspiring. It spoke volumes of their inherent strength and adaptability, which filled me with pride and hope.

Meanwhile, the children's father, my husband, remained ensconced in the comfort of our home, seemingly under the impression that by refusing to vacate, he could wield his familiar manipulation tactics to compel me to return. This belief, however, was predicated on a version of me that no longer existed. The trials and tribulations had forged me into a being of greater resolve, strength, and wisdom. His tactics, once effective, now fell on stony ground. I stood firm in my decision, undeterred by the prospect of his continued occupancy in our home. It was an explicit declaration of my emancipation from the cycles of manipulation that had characterized our relationship.

In the following weeks, my interactions with my husband evolved into a stretched strategic contest reminiscent of a chess game, where each move was meticulously calculated. He persistently sought to delay his departure from our shared apartment under the guise of not finding suitable alternative housing. However, I have arrived at a stage where I can no longer be deceived by his carefully orchestrated attempts to manipulate the passage of time to his advantage.

As time passed, his appeals shifted; he implored me to return to our matrimonial home. Despite the fervor of his pleas, my resolve remained unshaken. I was acutely aware that to return prematurely would be voluntarily re-entering an environment rife with unpredictability and emotional discord.

For readers facing similar trials, let this serve as encouragement to stand firm in your convictions, to seek wisdom in your decisions, and to lean on your faith for strength. Remember, the journey to reclaiming your peace may require walking through valleys of shadow, but you do not walk alone. As Isaiah 41:10 reassures, "So do not fear, for I am with you; do not be dismayed, for I am your God. I will strengthen and help you and uphold you with my righteous right hand."

In every chess game that life presents, especially those fraught with personal conflicts, the strategy lies not only in the moves we make but in the patience, wisdom, and courage we exhibit throughout the game. Let this chapter of life remind you that resilience, guided by divine wisdom, is your most potent strategy against the manipulations and trials of this world.

FORTY-SIX

A New Dawn

Strength does not come from winning. Your struggles develop your strengths.

Arnold Schwarzenegger

That night, amidst the dim glow of the hotel room, I sat with my laptop open, my fingers hovering over the keyboard, preparing for the following day's lectures. As I reflected on the past, a collage of memories unfurled before me – moments of joy overshadowed by the deep scars of betrayal and disappointment. Three weeks passed, and my husband had yet to vacate the apartment for us to return home. I pondered the unknown future, each thought tinged with fear and hope.

As I pondered, my phone buzzed with messages from my husband. His texts seemed almost humorous, explaining his expenses and struggles to find a new place or the need for more time. It dawned on me that his nature, one I had come to understand all too well, was not inclined toward swift action or change. The realization hit me like a cold wave: My husband, entrenched in his ways, was unlikely to leave our apartment willingly.

Another thought followed this perception, a more personal one. Even if he did vacate the apartment, could I ever return there? Could those walls ever feel like home again, or would they forever echo the memories of my agony? The thought of returning to that space, laden with the residue of our shared life and its eventual breakdown, filled me with a deep unease.

Meanwhile, the hotel bills were piling up. Each day spent in that temporary abode was a drain on resources that would be crucial for the journey ahead. It was time for decisive action, time to steer my life away from the shadows of the past and toward the light of a new beginning.

In that moment of introspection, with a renewed sense of purpose, I made a decisive move. I grabbed my phone and began scouring apartment listings. It was a quest for a fresh start, a space untainted by the shadows of the past, a place where we could heal, rebuild, and, most importantly, feel safe. The search for a new home was imbued with a sense of urgency. Our children deserved a space where they could grow, laugh, and learn, free from the specter of a toxic relationship.

Within forty-eight hours of meticulous searching, I found a modest two-bedroom apartment not too far from my children's school and workplace, and I signed the contract with a mixture of trepidation and relief. This was a bold declaration of independence, a break from the chains that had bound us to a situation that was no longer tenable. In those quiet moments, I felt empowered as I finalized the contract for our new home. I was shedding old skin, emerging stronger, wiser, and more resilient.

With a sense of resolve, I sent a message to my husband, informing him of my decision. I told him I had secured a new place for the children and me, and he could keep our former apartment if he chose. He responded by thanking me for this gesture. This confirmed my suspicions of his stalling, a tactical maneuver to prolong his stay in the comfort of the home we once shared. I subsequently took proactive action to officially inform the landlord of the situation, and he was kind enough to continue accommodating my husband in the apartment.

I offer my readers this advice: Trust your instincts and dare to make difficult decisions, especially when they lead to healthier and more fulfilling lives. Change, though daunting, often brings about growth and new opportunities. Remember, you are the author of your story, and sometimes, the most challenging chapters lead to the most rewarding endings. In making this move, I was rewriting my destiny. I was embracing a future where my children and I could thrive, away from the shadows of a relationship that had lost its way.

Settling into our new apartment began a profound journey that required courage and resilience. Purchasing essential items for our fresh start was symbolic; it was a declaration of independence and a commitment to forging a new path. As I carefully selected each item and decorated our new abode, the biblical principle in Isaiah 43:18-19 became my guiding light, "Forget the former things; do not dwell on the past. See, I am doing a new thing!"

After establishing myself in the new apartment, I made a calculated decision to return to our previous residence to collect my belongings at a time when I was sure my husband would be away at work. This tactic was chosen to circumvent any potential confrontation with him. My actions were fueled by an understanding of resilience and rebuilding, as elucidated by Wagnild and Young (1993). They define resilience as the capacity to recover from setbacks, adapt to change, and keep going in the face of adversity while preserving personal integrity. With this framework in mind, I carefully selected items of significant personal and professional value — my academic certificates, computers, and the Bible. These were tangible representations of my resilience, symbolizing my capacity to overcome obstacles, reconstruct my existence with honor, and persist with determination.

As I gathered these items, I stumbled upon an unexpected sight. My clothes, once neatly arranged in our shared closet, were now unceremoniously packed into trash bags. This indicated my husband's readiness to expunge my presence. Under normal circumstances, this could have been a source of pain, but it only solidified my resolve. I saw it as an affirmation of my decision to move on.

Leaving behind a Toyota Highlander, the car we had acquired together—a purchase in which my financial contribution had been substantial—was a decision that transcended material loss. However, it symbolized my commitment to prioritizing what truly mattered: the safety, emotional health, and future of myself and my children. It was nothing compared to the priceless value of our peace and happiness. In our new apartment, I endeavored to create a nurturing environment where healing and growth could occur within this new sanctuary.

Thus, echoing the melodrama of a telenovela, my life took a sharp turn, plunging me into the unfamiliar role of a single mother. The following years were akin to navigating through a tempestuous sea, each day a struggle against waves of emotional upheaval and turmoil. These years, a span of three years and four months, were marked by trials and tribulations that would fill volumes with their intensity and complexity. The journey was one of pain, resilience, revelation, and victory.

The path that eventually led to our official divorce after 21 years and 10 days of marriage was a path paved with a multitude of experiences - some heart-wrenching, others enlightening. The journey taught me profound lessons about love, forgiveness, and the strength of the human spirit. It reminded me of the biblical story of Job, a man who endured unimaginable losses yet remained steadfast in his faith. Like Job, I learned that enduring hardship could lead to profound personal growth and a deeper understanding of God's grace.

As my journey unfolded through the tempest of life's challenges, the guiding light in my darkest moments was the unwavering golden grace of God. This grace, a divine thread woven through the fabric of my trials, became my anchor amidst life's storms. This golden grace illuminated my path, transforming the most harrowing experiences into lessons of resilience and blessings.

'Golden grace' embodies the precious, unmerited favor and mercy God bestows upon us, especially in times of hardship. Like gold, this grace is rare, valuable, and enduring. It is beautifully encapsulated in 2 Corinthians 12:9, where Paul recounts the Lord's words, "My grace is sufficient for you, for my power is made perfect in weakness." In my weakness, in my moments of despair, it was His grace that empowered me, turning my vulnerabilities into strengths.

This journey was a pilgrimage toward more profound understanding and spiritual awakening. Though laden with pain, each step was also closer to recognizing the golden grace that enveloped my life. It was this grace that allowed me to endure emotional turmoil, rise from the ashes of a broken marriage, and protect my children from the scars of conflict.

As I navigated through the complexities of single parenthood, with full custody of two sons, the golden grace of God was my compass. It was a reminder that even amid legal battles, emotional upheavals, and societal judgments, there is a higher purpose at work. This grace did not exempt me from suffering but transformed my suffering into a source of strength and wisdom.

Now, as I reflect on those turbulent years, I see them not just as a time of loss but as a period rich with the golden grace of God. In the golden grace of God, there is healing, restoration, and peace that surpasses all understanding. May this grace be your guide, comfort, and strength as you journey toward a future filled with hope and renewed purpose.

To those who may find themselves in similar valleys of shadow and despair, I offer this insight: the golden grace of God is ever-present, even when it seems most distant. It is in our weakest moments that His strength shines brightest. May you recognize this grace in your journey, allowing it to guide, uplift, and transform you.

As I close this chapter of my life and look toward the future, I pray that you may find the strength to navigate through your storms, the courage to make tough decisions, and the wisdom to learn from each trial. Remember, as stated in Romans 8:28, "And we know that in all things God works for the good of those who love him, who have been called according to his purpose."

May you discover, as I did, that our trials are obstacles and opportunities for divine grace to manifest in our lives. Remember, as stated in 1 Peter 5:10, "And the God of all grace, who called you to his eternal glory in Christ, after you have suffered a little while, will himself restore you and make you strong, firm, and steadfast."

FORTY-SEVEN

The Enigma Unraveled

Forgiveness does not change the past, but it does enlarge the future.

Paul Boese

After walking away from my husband, I navigated a labyrinth of confusion and revelation. The man I once thought I knew, the one I believed depended on my presence, had transformed into an enigma. The period of separation, which I had hoped would be a healing balm, became a battleground of relentless harassment.

His calls and messages, once the chords of connection, turned into relentless whips of intimidation. It was as if he was determined to maintain a hold over me, to assert a control that no longer had any legal or moral standing.

I insisted on not answering his calls but used text-only communication. Despite that, the barrage of text messages I received was chaotic – from embarrassing charges to intimidating threats and attempts at manipulation to the extent that his relentless onslaught began to interfere with my responsibilities as a single mother and a professional.

Balancing my duties at work with raising two teenage sons was challenging enough. Adding his constant harassment to this mix was like juggling balls while standing on a crumbling platform. It was during this time that I stumbled upon the powerful words of Joyce Meyer in 'Battlefield of the Mind: Winning the Battle in Your Mind' (Meyer, 1995): "Patience is not the ability to wait, but how you act while you are waiting."

The harassment reached its zenith when he demanded the transfer of our jointly-owned Toyota Highlander, which I had left in his custody title to him. In a moment that tested the very limits of my endurance, I consented. This decision, though seemingly a defeat, was a strategic retreat. It was a sacrifice I was willing to make for peace, a sentiment echoed in Romans 12:18, "If it is possible, as far as it depends on you, live at peace with everyone." The relinquishment of the car was a small price to pay for the tranquility and safety of my family.

This chapter of my life, fraught with trials and tribulations, taught me that sometimes, the most brutal battles are fought not on physical grounds but within the realms of our minds and hearts.

Navigating this complex and emotionally draining scenario required not just strength but also a profound understanding of narcissistic behavior. It demanded recognition that my husband's actions were rooted in a personality disorder characterized by a lack of empathy, a need for admiration, and an inability to accept responsibility for one's actions. Understanding this was crucial in framing my response to his behavior and guiding my decisions.

After our separation, my husband continued to cling to the notion that marriage is an unbreakable bond with a stubbornness that defied reality. In his eyes, the sanctity of our union was immutable, a covenant that transcended even the most grievous transgressions. This perspective, while rooted in the noble ideals of marital commitment, just the way God orchestrated it, failed to acknowledge the fundamental principles of love, care, respect, and partnership that form the bedrock of marriage.

While the Christian faith upholds marriage's sanctity, it also recognizes the importance of individual dignity and safety. As noted in Ephesians 5:25-33, marriage is described as a relationship of mutual love and respect, mirroring the love of Christ for the Church.

As I navigated these challenges, I was reminded of the words of Mandy Hale, "You can love them, forgive them, want good things for them... but still move on without them." So, I continued to pray for him from a distance.

For individuals navigating the complex dynamics of a relationship with a narcissistic partner, I present a refined guide drawn from my own experiences and those shared by many in similar situations. This guide aims not only to offer practical advice but also to foster resilience and hope.

For those navigating the complex dynamics of a relationship with a narcissistic partner, this guide offers a beacon of hope and practical strategies, drawing from a blend of personal experiences, psychological insights, and universal wisdom. The journey through such trials is deeply personal yet universally challenging, requiring a nuanced approach to foster resilience and empowerment.

1. Understanding Narcissism: Recognize that narcissism is more than just self-absorption; it is a complex personality disorder characterized by a lack of empathy and an inflated sense of self-importance. Understanding this can help you set realistic expectations and protect your emotional health.
2. Setting Boundaries: Establishing and maintaining clear boundaries is crucial. This might mean limiting interactions to necessary communication and opting for written forms to keep a record. Boundaries are not hostile; they are vital for your emotional safety.
3. Building a Support System: You are not alone. Seek friends, family, or professionals who understand and validate your feelings. Support groups offer a community of shared experiences, providing both solace and practical advice.
4. Documenting Interactions: Document all interactions involving legal proceedings or custody disputes. Keep records of conversations, incidents, and decisions. This documentation can be invaluable in legal contexts and personal reflection.
5. Prioritizing Self-Care: Your well-being is paramount. Engage in activities that nourish your spirit, such as exercise, meditation, or hobbies. Self-care is your right, especially when facing the stress of a tumultuous relationship.
6. Educating Yourself: Knowledge is power. Familiarize yourself with your legal and financial rights, especially if separation or divorce is a consideration. Understanding your financial situation, including assets,

debts, and entitlements, is crucial for empowerment.

7. Seeking Emotional Independence: Find strength and fulfillment within yourself. Cultivating emotional independence means not relying on your partner for validation or happiness, which is empowering amidst the unpredictability of the relationship.
8. Creating Personal Space: Establish a physical and emotional sanctuary where you can find peace and recharge. This space is your refuge from your partner's influence, where you can cultivate your inner strength and clarity.
9. Assessing Your Well-being: Regularly evaluate your mental and emotional health. Be honest about the impact of the relationship on your well-being and consider whether staying is in your best interest.
10. Leaning on Faith: If you are a person of faith, lean into it. My faith in Christ has taught me that prayer, meditation, and spiritual support can provide comfort and resilience in trying times. Remember, your worth is not defined by how others treat you but by your inherent value as a cherished child of God. For those without religious beliefs, finding strength in personal values and the support of a compassionate community can offer solace and resilience.
11. Anticipating Resistance: Know that establishing boundaries or ending the relationship may provoke adverse reactions from a narcissistic partner. Prepare for this and remain firm while prioritizing your safety and well-being.
12. Planning for Safety: If there is any risk of harm, have an exit strategy. This includes financial preparation, legal consultation, and a support network to ensure your safe departure. Your safety is the top priority.
13. Embracing Forgiveness: Forgiveness is about freeing yourself from resentment. It does not excuse the behavior but allows you to move forward without carrying the weight of anger. This step is personal and contributes significantly to healing.
14. Protecting your offspring: It is essential to safeguard your children's emotional and psychological well-being, especially if they are minors. Open, age-appropriate communication ensures they feel seen and heard while maintaining stability and routine, which offers them a

sense of security. Professional support, such as therapy, can be invaluable in helping them process their experiences and emotions. Above all, prioritize their safety, ensuring they are shielded from any direct harm and are provided with a nurturing environment to grow and thrive.

15. Focusing on the Future: Visualize a life beyond the current challenges. Planning and taking small steps toward a future of respect and genuine love can help shift your focus from present difficulties to hopeful possibilities. Remember, the path may be fraught with challenges, but it also offers opportunities for growth and empowerment. Embrace the journey with hope, drawing strength from the knowledge that you can navigate this through grace and resilience.

Finally, I want you to know you are not alone. Remember, many have walked this path and found peace and fulfillment on the other side. Your current situation is not the end of your story; it is a chapter that will lead to greater strength and understanding.

In closing this chapter, I leave you with a thought from the book of Psalms, "The Lord is close to the brokenhearted and saves those who are crushed in spirit" (Psalm 34:18). In your times of struggle, may you find solace in the knowledge that there is hope, healing, and a new beginning awaiting you.

FORTY-EIGHT

The Path to Forgiveness

To forgive is to set a prisoner free and discover that the prisoner was you.

Lewis B. Smedes

As I navigated the tumultuous aftermath of our separation, my husband's relentless harassment and stalking intensified to an alarming degree. Despite my numerous appeals for him to cease this hostile behavior, my pleas fell on deaf ears. His actions, steeped in a disturbing persistence, left me grappling with a deep-seated fear for my safety and well-being. It was a harrowing period, where each day brought a sense of dread and uncertainty.

Left with no other recourse, I found myself propelled toward seeking legal protection. The courts, recognizing the severity of the situation, not only granted but extended a restraining order to a permanent one due to my husband's steadfast refusal to amend his ways. The details of these proceedings are too intricate and painful to delve into entirely in this memoir. However, it is essential to convey that the restraining orders were extended twice over two years before becoming permanent.

Amid this chaos, a profound transformation occurred within me. Despite the trials and tribulations, I could forgive him within my heart. This forgiveness is not born from a place of reconciliation or a desire to rekindle our relationship but rather from a deeper spiritual understanding. It is a form of love that transcends the personal – a love for his soul, a wish for redemption and healing. After all, he remains the father of my children, and for their sake and his own, I continue to harbor hope for his transformation.

This journey has taught me the profound power of forgiveness, not as an erasure of past hurts but as a release from their hold over my life. It is forgiveness that seeks no retribution but yearns for healing – for both the wrongdoer and the wronged. It is a reminder of Christ's teachings on love and forgiveness, encapsulated in Matthew 5:44, "But I say unto you, love your enemies, bless them that curse you, do good to them that hate you, and pray for them which despitefully use you, and persecute you."

In forgiving my husband, I am not condoning his actions but freeing myself from resentment and bitterness. It is an act of self-liberation, a step toward healing and wholeness. This act of forgiveness is underpinned by a divine love that sincerely wishes for the redemption of even those who have wronged us.

Though fraught with pain and adversity, this chapter of my life has been essential to my spiritual journey. It has reinforced the belief that even in the darkest times, there is an opportunity for growth and deepening our understanding of love, compassion, and forgiveness. It is a testament to the resilience of the human spirit, guided by the unwavering light of faith and the boundless grace of God.

To my husband, should these words find their way to you, understand that my prayers for you are borne out of genuine concern. The scriptures affirm that "God is not mocked: for whatsoever a man soweth, that shall he also reap" (Galatians 6:7). This universal law of cause and effect, often referred to as 'karma,' operates irrespective of our desires or denials. I hope you will see the true reflection of your actions and find a path toward reconciliation with God before karma beckons.

To my esteemed reader, I extend an invitation to pause and deeply reflect on this pivotal moment in our journey together. This chapter encapsulates themes of resilience, forgiveness, and profound spiritual awakening. As you proceed, I encourage you to ponder these reflections and pieces of advice carefully curated to guide you:

1. **Embracing Forgiveness:** View forgiveness as a pillar of hope

amidst adversity. It represents not weakness but remarkable strength, offering liberation from anger and resentment. As you face life's challenges, embrace forgiveness as a key to unlocking inner peace.

2. **Distinguishing Forgiveness from Reconciliation**: Understand that forgiving someone does not obligate you to reconcile with them, especially if they are unrepentant. Forgiveness is a personal journey toward healing, independent of the actions or decisions of others.
3. **Drawing Strength from Faith**: Allow your faith to be your fortress. Whether your beliefs are grounded in Christianity or another spiritual path, let this faith serve as a beacon, guiding you through uncertain times. My faith has been a cornerstone through my trials, and I hope you find similar solace and guidance.
4. **Acknowledging Emotional Complexity**: Recognize and accept the multifaceted nature of human emotions. It is expected to experience a range of feelings toward those who have hurt us. Forgiveness allows us to confront these emotions without allowing them to dictate our lives.
5. **Learning from Love and Compassion**: Reflect on the profound teachings of love and compassion found in sacred texts like Matthew 5:44. These lessons hold invaluable wisdom for facing adversity with grace and empathy.
6. **Utilizing Legal Protections**: In situations of ongoing harassment or danger, seeking legal protection is both a right and a necessity. Trust in the mechanisms designed to safeguard your well-being and provide the security you deserve.
7. **Believing in the Power of Growth**: Every trial presents an opportunity for personal growth, enhancing our resilience, faith, and empathy. Embrace these challenges as avenues for development, even in the darkest moments.
8. **Extending Compassion:** On your journey, practice compassion toward yourself and others navigating similar storms. Your empathy can serve as a healing balm to those around you,

fostering a community of support and understanding.

9. **Clinging to Hope**: Maintain hope for the future, as I do for my husband's transformation. Hope shines through the darkest times, guiding us toward healing and a deeper understanding of our trials.
10. **Trusting in Prayer**: The narrative shared in these pages bears witness to the transformative power of prayer. It offers refuge, strength, and connection to higher guidance amidst life's tumult. Embrace prayer as a source of hope, healing, and divine grace.

In closing this chapter, I offer a prayer for all in tumultuous seas. May you navigate your challenges with dignity, make courageous choices, and gain insight into the redemptive qualities of prayer and forgiveness. May your journey bring you to tranquil shores, where peace and understanding flourish, nurtured by God's everlasting love and mercy. Amen.

FORTY-NINE

Beyond the Storm

You never know how strong you are, until being strong is your only choice.

Bob Marley

As the chasm of time widened, marking three years and four months of separation, the faintest glimmer of hope that once flickered in the depths of my heart for redemption with my husband had extinguished. What began as a slow disintegration of our bond had accelerated into a plummet, descending into an abyss of despair and unrepentance. The intricate and tortuous journey of these years is a saga too complex, too laden with the intricacies of pain and conflict, to be confined within the pages of this memoir.

However, in the eyes of this relentless storm, a moment of clarity has emerged, stark and unyielding in its truth. The man I once shared my life with had wandered too far from reconciliation and understanding. Hence, I took a heart-wrenching decision to file for divorce. This decision came after countless tears, prayers, and the precise conviction that this was God's chosen path for me.

This decision, however, was not met with quiet resignation. Instead, it triggered a torrent of challenges, a relentless series of confrontations and evasions from my husband. Each maelstrom of his reactions was more jarring and unpredictable than the last. He blatantly refused the responsibility to provide child support, claiming that I was the one who decided to separate. It was as though he had donned a cloak of apathy, shielding himself from the reality of his obligations as a father and the emotional needs of our children.

As the final act of our divorce proceedings unfolded, a facet of my husband's character, hitherto veiled in ambiguity, was unveiled in a jarring light. Witnessing this transformation was both shocking and profoundly disheartening. In a maneuver marked by both audacity and desperation, he attempted to distort the truth of his financial situation, presenting a falsified income statement to the court to gain more benefit from the ruins of the marriage.

This deliberate act of deception, designed to manipulate the legal outcome to his favor, teetered on the edge of the comical due to its sheer defiance. It stripped away any remnants of the man I thought I knew, revealing his true motivations in complete relief. His actions transcended mere evasion of the court's decree; they were a calculated attempt to shirk his financial responsibilities, not only to sidestep child support but also to circumvent his contribution to our children's looming college costs.

Moreover, it became apparent that his strategy was not solely about avoidance. He was also maneuvering to see what he could extract from me regarding a settlement, hoping to leverage the situation to his financial advantage. This added layer of opportunism, aiming to profit from the dissolution of our marriage, underscored a distressing willingness to prioritize his interests at the expense of not just me but our children's future.

This maneuver, however, did not go unnoticed by the vigilant eyes of justice. The court, as if guided by a divine sense of fairness and truth, saw through the smokescreen of his deceit. His financial statements were so riddled with inconsistencies and irregularities that they were dismissed outright. This dismissal felt like a moral victory, a vindication of the truth I had long known but struggled to prove.

When the final gavel echoed through the courtroom, it signified more than the legal dissolution of our 21 years plus approximately 10 days of marriage. It was heralding a new chapter, a turning point where the shackles of a burdensome past were finally broken. Going forward, the judge decided to garnish the child support dues from his paycheck every two weeks. Although this was a modest victory in the grand scheme, it was a moment of beautiful triumph in a prolonged and weary battle.

The monetary support awarded was meager, particularly considering the phase our children, now young men embarking on their college journey, were navigating. Despite the clear court mandate, my ex-husband has persistently avoided paying his portion of our children's college expenses (up to the point of penning this memoir). However, through this, a profound realization dawned upon me. The financial struggles, the battles over child support, and the entire legal entanglement paled compared to the freedom we had gained. The price paid was steep in emotional currency and years of struggle. Moreover, it was worth every moment of the fight, every tear shed, every prayer whispered into the stillness of the night. The freedom to start anew, unburdened by the chains of a toxic marriage, was a breath of fresh air, a release into a world of possibilities and hope.

As I stepped out of the courtroom, I felt closure. I was not just leaving behind a broken marriage but also shedding the skin of my former self. I emerged more robust, more resilient, and with a renewed sense of purpose. The journey ahead was uncharted, but I was ready to navigate it with grace, strength, and unwavering faith in the future.

In this new chapter of my life, I embraced the role of mother and father to my children, guiding them with love, strength, and the wisdom of God. Their well-being and happiness became my primary focus, and I dedicated myself to ensuring they had the support and opportunities they needed to thrive. Despite the financial hardships, we found joy in simple pleasures and learned to appreciate the value of unity and resilience.

Thus, a remarkable transformation unfolded in the heart of the storm that once threatened to consume us. My sons, the innocent bystanders in this tumultuous chapter of our lives, emerged not as victims of circumstance but as victors of resilience. Under my care, they have blossomed into exceptional young men, their characters sculpted by the trials we endured together. Their growth is a living testament to the unyielding power of love and the relentless spirit of perseverance.

These two young men now stand tall with a maturity and wisdom far beyond their years. They have learned to harness the adversities of their youth into a drive for excellence and empathy. In their eyes, I see not the shadow of past pain but the bright spark of future potential. Their journey speaks to my efforts as a mother and the remarkable resilience inherent in the human spirit.

As for me, the scars of the past have healed into lessons of the present. My health, once a casualty of relentless stress and emotional turmoil, has been gloriously restored. This restoration is nothing short of a miracle, a tangible manifestation of the redemptive power of God working in my life. It is as if each day brings with it a renewal of strength, a reaffirmation of my faith, and a deepening of my gratitude for life's second chances.

Looking back at the path we have traversed, marked by loss and heartache, I now stand at a vantage point where I can see the silver lining in every dark cloud. The arduous journey has imbued in me an undeniable strength, a resilience that resonates louder than the echoes of my past struggles. It is as though each challenge we faced was a fire that tempered our spirits, forging us into more robust, more resilient beings.

I can declare, with unwavering conviction, that the losses endured in those 21 years of marriage, though profound, are dwarfed by the promises that lie ahead. The future beckons with a kaleidoscope of hope and possibilities, illuminated by the unceasing grace of God. I know that the chapters of my life yet to be written are waiting to be filled with stories of triumph, lessons of faith, and endless possibilities.

To you, dear readers, if you find yourself in any battle, know this: There is a power within you more significant than any challenge you face. The trials that seem to threaten your very being are but stepping stones to a higher place. Embrace the journey, however daunting it may seem, for it is in the crucible of adversity that the most precious aspects of our character are refined and revealed.

As I stand today, with the wisdom gleaned from the past and the optimism for what lies ahead, I am reminded of the words in Romans 8:28, "And we know that in all things God works for the good of those who love him, who have been called according to his purpose." May this assurance guide you as it has guided me, leading you from the shadows of past struggles to the dawn of a new, hopeful, and grace-filled tomorrow.

FIFTY

An Interlude of Gratitude

In the depth of winter, I finally learned that within me there lay an invincible summer.

Albert Camus

In the serene embrace of pre-dawn tranquility, surrounded by the comforting whispers of my bedroom, I sit nestled among a sheath of pillows. With my laptop as my companion and the soft glow of my bedside lamp casting a gentle light, I begin writing this closing chapter. This book has been a therapeutic release, a deeply felt mission, where my heart's musings transform into words that reach out to the world. These honest reflections, born from the depths of my experiences, were woven from the trials and triumphs of my life, underscored by unwavering faith and a divine purpose that often transcends my understanding.

The journey chronicled in this memoir traces the arc from my innocent childhood and a youth lacking a mature emotional compass to an adult life fraught with the complexities of a marriage woven with heartache and learning. The narrative transcends beyond individual grievances to illuminate the often-unseen struggles many people face and serve as a guiding light for those navigating similar turbulent waters.

A divine mandate had compelled every word of this memoir, a story guided by the hand of God Himself. Throughout the narrative, I have endeavored to weave a tapestry of resilience, illustrating how faith can transform despair into hope and adversity into strength. This book is an offering, a service to those who may find themselves lost in the labyrinth of life's challenges. It is a story that speaks to the power of forgiveness, the importance of self-discovery, and the unbreakable bond between human frailty and divine strength.

In writing these pages, I have often conversed deeply with God, seeking His guidance and wisdom. Through these dialogues, I have understood the true purpose of my experiences. Each trial, each tear, and each moment of uncertainty were not just random threads of fate; they were part of a divine tapestry intricately woven to serve a greater purpose.

To my former husband, if these words reach your eyes by chance, understand that they are penned from a place of hope rather than malice. Within these passages, there is no bitterness or any quest for vengeance. My genuine aspiration is that through these words, you may discern the contours of our shared past and recognize an opportunity for profound personal evolution and betterment.

As I devote myself to the upbringing of the children we have brought into this world together, I earnestly pray that you will discover the fortitude to accept the grace and serenity that life, in its generosity, extends to us all. May this grace guide you toward harnessing the strength and insight needed to constructively impact their lives in the future. My most important prayer is that your path leads you to inner peace and true reconciliation with God before our inevitable meeting with our Maker.

In penning this concluding chapter of "Golden Grace," nestled in the quietude of my study, a profound certainty strikes me: Among the myriad readers of these words, some have witnessed and actively participated in my journey. Though silent in the public eye, their presence was a beacon of hope on my darkest nights. These individuals, friends, family members, students, colleagues, church members, pastors, and confidants, whom I affectionately think of as my "Silent Guardians," played a pivotal role in my journey toward healing and resilience at my most desperate times. Their names, carefully anonymized in these pages for privacy, are etched in my heart, their kindness a melody that will forever resonate in the corridors of my memory.

As these guardians read these words, I imagine a knowing smile lighting up their faces—a smile of recognition, not of their names, but of their acts of compassion and wisdom that were lifelines thrown to a drowning soul. They, who walked with me through the valley of shadows, bear witness to the silent tears, the whispered prayers, and the shared moments of despair and hope.

They stood as pillars of strength, their advice and guidance like a lighthouse guiding a lost ship through a stormy sea. In a world where recognition often takes center stage, these guardians chose the path of quiet service. Their anonymity in this book is not a veil of invisibility but a cloak of humility, a powerful reminder that true heroism does not always seek the spotlight. They are the unsung heroes whose impact transcends the need for public acclaim. This chapter is a tribute to their unseen sacrifices and willingness to walk beside me on a journey fraught with pain and uncertainty. They were the embodiment of Christian love and empathy, their actions a testament to the teachings of Christ about bearing one another's burdens.

As they read these lines, I hope they see a reflection of their selfless service and the profound impact of their actions. They have sown seeds of hope and resilience in a heart once shrouded in despair. I may not have the opportunity to engrave their names in public records, but their legacy is forever inscribed in this book as the silent support that helped me rise from the ashes of a broken spirit. To each of you, my "Silent Guardians," I extend my deepest gratitude. Your unheralded support and unwavering presence have been the greatest gifts of my journey. Thank you for being the light in my darkest times and the melody of hope in my heart.

I extend my heartfelt gratitude to my esteemed readers who have accompanied me through these pages. Through my words, you have seen my arduous path from matrimony to separation. The path was fraught with challenges that tested my spirit, faith, and essence. I have navigated through emotional turbulence, battled against shadows of despair, and found strength in places I never knew existed within me. However, the lessons learned and the growth experienced in "Golden Grace" are merely the tip of the iceberg compared to the story ahead, which is being released in my next volume,

"From Separation to Salvation."

In "From Separation to Salvation," my narrative transitions from detailing the complexities of leaving a narcissistic relationship to embracing life as a single mother of two teenagers. This sequel delves into the transformative journey of redefining my identity, rediscovering joy, and navigating the challenges of single parenthood and a contentious divorce with resilience and grace. It is a testament to the unwavering hope and the discovery of inner strength amidst adversity, offering insights and encouragement to those on similar paths. It celebrates the journey toward healing, self-discovery, and the relentless pursuit of peace and joy.

May my story remind us that we are never alone, even when the path seems insurmountable. We can emerge stronger and wiser with faith as our guide, resilience as our companion, and grace as our sustenance.

Until we meet again in the pages of my next volume, I leave you with my prayers and blessings.

Bibliography

Adichie, C. N. (2014). *We should all be feminists.* Anchor Books.

Amato, P. R., & DeBoer, D. D. (2001). The transmission of marital instability across generations: Relationship skills or commitment to marriage? *Journal of Marriage and Family, 63*(4), 1038-1051.

American Psychological Association. (2020). Understanding and treating sexual addiction. Retrieved from https://www.apa.org/topics/sexual-addiction

Angelou, M. (1969). *I know why the caged bird sings.* Random House.

Atwood, J. D., & Schwartz, L. (2002). The new reality of money: Understanding the dynamics of financial infidelity. *Journal of Financial Planning, 15*(12), 50–59.

Bancroft, L. (2002). *Why does he do that? Inside the minds of angry and controlling men.* Berkley Books.

Bonhoeffer, D. (1959). *The cost of discipleship.* Macmillan.

Dostoevsky, F. (1866). *Crime and punishment.* The Russian Messenger.

Durvasula, R. S. (2015). *Should I stay or should I go: Surviving a relationship with a narcissist.* Post Hill Press.

Fiorenza, E. S. (1984). *In memory of her: A feminist theological reconstruction of Christian origins.* Crossroad.

Elkayam, U. (2011). Clinical characteristics of peripartum cardiomyopathy in the United States: Diagnosis, prognosis, and management. *Journal of the American College of Cardiology, 58*(7), 659–670.

Emerson, R. W. (1841). Self-reliance. In *Essays: First series.* James Munroe and Company.

Evans, P. (2009). *The verbally abusive relationship: How to recognize it and how to respond.* Adams Media.

Fink, L. D. (2012). *Creating significant learning experiences: An integrated approach to designing college courses.* Jossey-Bass.

Fiorenza, E. S. (2001). *Wisdom ways: Introducing feminist biblical interpretation.* Orbis Books.

García-Moreno, C., Jansen, H. A. F. M., Ellsberg, M., Heise, L., & Watts, C. H. (2006). Prevalence of intimate partner violence: findings from the WHO multi-country study on women's health and domestic violence. *Lancet, 368*(9543), 1260-1269.

Geronimus, A. T. (2003). Damned if you do: Culture, identity, privilege, and teenage childbearing in the United States. *Social Science & Medicine, 57*(5), 881-893. https://doi.org/10.1016/S0277-9536(02)00456-2

Gladwell, M. (2008). *Outliers: The story of success.* Little, Brown and Company.

Gotell, L. (2001). The discourse of domestic violence and rape. *Canadian Journal of Women and the Law, pp. 13*, 171–197.

Gottman, J. M., & Silver, N. (1999). *The seven principles for making marriage work.* Crown Publishing Group.

Gottman, J. M., & Levenson, R. W. (2000). The timing of divorce: Predicting when a couple will divorce over 14 years. *Journal of Marriage and Family, 62*(3), 737–745.

Greer, J. (2010). *What about me?: Stop selfishness from ruining your relationship.* McGraw-Hill.

Haghikia, A., Röntgen, P., Vogel-Claussen, J., Schwab, J., Westenfeld, R., Ehlermann, P., Berliner, D., Podewski, E., Hilfiker-Kleiner, D., & Bauersachs, J. (2015). Prognostic implication of right ventricular involvement in peripartum cardiomyopathy: A cardiovascular magnetic resonance study. *ESC Heart Failure, 2*(4), 139-149.

Hawkins, D. (2017). *When loving him is hurting you: Hope and help for women dealing with narcissism and emotional abuse.* Harvest House Publishers.

Hochschild, A. R. (1983). *The managed heart: Commercialization of human feeling.* University of California Press.

Adams, J. (2021). Understanding sexual addiction and marital dynamics. *Journal of Marital Therapy.*

Gottman, J. (1994). *Why marriages succeed or fail: And how you can make yours last.* Simon & Schuster.

Johnson, M., & Sacco, V. F. (1995). Researching financial abuse as a form of intimate violence. *Family Relations, 44*(4), 400-403.

Johnson, M. (2019). Ethics at the crossroads: Decision making in complex environments. *Professional Integrity, 22*(1), 17–29.

Johnson, M. P., Amato, P. R., Rogers, S. J., & Booth, A. (2002). Continuity and change in marital quality between 1980 and 2000. *Journal of Marriage and Family, 64*(1), 1–22.

Journal of the American College of Cardiology. (2019). Peripartum cardiomyopathy: JACC State-of-the-Art Review. Retrieved from https://www.jacc.org/doi/full/10.1016/j.jacc.2019.08.1019

Jung, C. G. (1953). Two essays on analytical psychology. In *Collected Works of C.G. Jung, Volume 7*. Princeton University Press.

Keller, H. (1903). *The story of my life.* Doubleday, Page & Company.

Lorde, A. (1988). *A burst of light: and other essays.* Firebrand Books.

MacArthur Foundation. (2009). The MacArthur Foundation in Nigeria: Report on activities. Retrieved from https://www.macfound.org/press/grantee-publications/the-macarthur-foundation-in-nigeria-report-on-activities

Mandela, N. (1994). *Long walk to freedom*—little, Brown and Company.

McEwen, B. S. (1998). Protective and damaging effects of stress mediators. *New England Journal of Medicine, 338*(3), 171-179.

Mezirow, J. (1991). *Transformative dimensions of adult learning.* Jossey-Bass.

Obama, M. (2018). *Becoming.* Crown Publishing Group.

Ogbu, J. U. (1981). Origins of human competence: A cultural-ecological perspective. *Child Development, 52*(2), 413–429.

OpenAI. (2024). ChatGPT Large language model. /g/g-lN1gKFnvL-creative-writing-coach

Papp, L. M., Cummings, E. M., & Goeke-Morey, M. C. (2009). For richer, for poorer: Money as a topic of marital conflict in the home. *Family Relations, 58*(1), 91–103. https://doi.org/10.1111/j.1741-3729.2008.00537.x

Phyllis Trible. (1984). *Texts of terror: Literary-feminist readings of biblical narratives.* Fortress Press.

Schneider, J. P., & Weiss, R. (2001). *Cybersex Exposed: Simple fantasy or obsession?* Hazelden.

Schulte, B. (2015). *Overwhelmed: How to work, love, and play when no one has the time.* HarperCollins.

Segerstrom, S. C., & Miller, G. E. (2004). Psychological stress and the human immune system: A meta-analytic study of 30 years of inquiry. *Psychological Bulletin, 130*(4), 601-630.

Smith, J. (2020). Community and faith: The role of lay leadership in churches. *Religious Studies Journal, 45*(2), 120–134.

Søren Kierkegaard. (1849). The sickness unto death. (Original work published 1849)

Susan Johnson, Dr. (2021). *Emotionally focused therapy for couples.* Guilford Press.

Thomas, G. (2015). *Sacred marriage: What if God designed marriage to make us holy more than to make us happy?* Zondervan.

Trible, P. (1984). *Texts of terror: Literary-feminist readings of biblical narratives.* Fortress Press.

Twenge, J. M., & Campbell, W. K. (2009). *The narcissism epidemic: Living in the age of entitlement.* Free Press.

Van Epp, J. (2007). *How to avoid falling in love with a jerk.* McGraw-Hill Education.

Wagnild, G., & Young, H. (1993). Development and psychometric evaluation of the Resilience Scale. *Journal of Nursing Measurement, 1*(2), 165–178.

Wilde, O. (1890). *The picture of Dorian Gray.* Ward, Lock and Company.

Williams, K. (2018). The hidden struggle: Pornography in modern marriage. *Family Dynamics Review, 33*(4), 45–59.

World Health Organization. (2021). Malaria. Retrieved from https://www.who.int/news-room/fact-sheets/detail/malaria

Made in the USA
Middletown, DE
24 March 2024